DATE DUE			

European University Studies

Europäische Hochschulschriften
Publications Universitaires Européennes

Series I
German Language and Literature

Reihe I   Série I

Deutsche Sprache und Literatur
Langue et littérature allemandes

Vol./Bd. 961

PETER LANG

Frankfurt am Main · Bern · New York

Philip Payne

Robert Musil's Works, 1906-1924

A critical introduction

PETER LANG
Frankfurt am Main · Bern · New York

CIP-Kurztitelaufnahme der Deutschen Bibliothek

Payne, Philip:

Robert Musil's works, 1906 - 1924 : a crit.
introd. / Philip Payne. – Frankfurt am Main ;
Bern ; New York : Lang, 1987.
    (European university studies : Ser. 1,
    German language and literature ; Vol. 961)
    ISBN 3-8204-8642-9
NE: Europäische Hochschulschriften / 01

Library of Congress Cataloging-in-Publication Data

Payne, Philip.
    Robert Musil's works, 1806-1924.

    (European university studies. Series I, German
language and literature, 0721-3301 ; vol. 961 =
Europäische Hochschulschriften. Reihe I, Deutsche
Sprache und Literatur ; Bd. 961)
    Bibliography: p.
    1. Musil, Robert, 1880-1942–Criticism and
interpretation. I. Title. II. Series: Europäische
Hochschulschriften. Reihe I, Deutsche Sprache und
Literatur ; Bd. 961.
PT2625.U8Z843 1987   833'.912   86-31264
ISBN 3-8204-8642-9

ISSN 0721-3301
ISBN 3-8204-8642-9

© Verlag Peter Lang GmbH, Frankfurt am Main 1987

printed in Germany

TO MY MOTHER AND FATHER

PREFACE

This study of Musil's works from 1906-1924 was conceived
originally as a platform for an examination of Der Mann ohne
Eigenschaften (The Man without Qualities).   But the earlier works,
Die Verwirrungen des Zöglings Törleß, Vereinigungen, Die Schwärmer and
Drei Frauen, deserve consideration in their own right.   In contrast
to Der Mann ohne Eigenschaften, they were finished so we are not left
to guess how they might have looked when complete - we can measure
Musil's intentions against the published text.

In this study I have not taken the paths pointed by recent
developments in 'Literaturwissenschaft' because I believe that, for
all the wealth of material on Musil's works, there are still important
areas which merit investigation by a more traditional
literary-critical approach.   My primary concerns are, first, the
placing of the text in the context of Musil's personal life, his views
about the individual work and his Weltanschauung, second, close study
and evaluation of each text as a literary entity.

I wish to thank all those who have helped with this study:
Adolf Frisé whose fine editions of Musil's Tagebücher (Diaries) and
Briefe (Letters) helped to make it possible, and who has been more
than generous with hospitality, advice and support;   Martin Swales who

first suggested the project and offered continuing criticism and
guidance; Graham Bartram, a Lancaster colleague, who has read and
commented on many drafts; Peter Stern who supervised my earlier
research into Musil's work.

I should like to express my gratitude to the Austrian Cultural
Institute who made funds available for a research visit to Vienna and
the University of Lancaster who provided financial support for my work
on Musil from the Humanities Research Fund.

Lancaster,

August, 1986.

CONTENTS

Editions to which reference is made

Quotations from Musil's earlier works in the text below are taken from Robert Musil, Gesammelte Werke ('Collected Works'), edited by Adolf Frisé, 2 vols (Reinbek bei Hamburg) 1978 - page references are to Volume Two of this hardback edition. These correspond to Volume Six of the nine-volume paperback edition of the Gesammelte Werke, since the pagination is identical. In end-notes, I refer to the hardback edition as GWI and GWII.

In the text below Musil's Tagebücher ('Diaries'), edited by Adolf Frisé, 2 vols (Reinbek bei Hamburg, 1976) are referred to as TbI and TbII, respectively.

Reference is also made to Robert Musil, Briefe ('Letters'), edited by Adolf Frisé, 2 vols (Reinbek bei Hamburg, 1981).

A note on the translations

In the translations, which are my own, I have attempted to give some impression of the vitality, precision and style of Musil's prose. Readers will realise, wherever the English version is found conspicuously wanting, that this is my fault and not Musil's. Where all else fails, I have at least tried to render Musil's words as accurately as possible.

Chapter 1   INTRODUCTION

In this study, I address all Musil's readers, whether experts or
not.   The main chapters concentrate on individual works, presented in
broadly chronological order.   Each work poses considerable
difficulties but, as I shall show, some of these can be overcome
through examination of the genesis of the work and close textual
analysis.   In each chapter, I proceed by establishing connections
between Musil's personal life and events in the given work, between
what he wanted to achieve and what he actually achieved, between his
general views on the role of the creative author and detailed
statements on the purpose of the particular work, between his
Weltanschauung as a whole and the specific contribution of an
individual work to that total statement.   In addition, I examine the
connections which are internal to the text in question and which form
its structure of significance.

It is well-known that Musil built his works from material that
lay to hand in personal experience.   This can be amply demonstrated
by reference to Musil's diaries and letters, and, below, I shall
attempt to do so.   But such investigations are not an enterprise of

literary hagiography; I intend these to be seen rather as evidence of the quality of the material from which Musil built each work. In <u>Der Mann ohne Eigenschaften</u> ('The Man without Qualities') he was frequently forced by the scope of the project to work at second hand, from imagination and observation of other people, borrowing the thoughts, experiences and words of strangers (and, of course, he did so brilliantly). But in the earlier works he scarcely needed to do this - almost all he required was directly available in his own emotional and intellectual experience, either present or past. It may be objected that many of the characters who are central to particular works are women, and that Musil, with his obsession with physical exercise and strength, was anything but effeminate. But it is vital to realise that his wife's inner life had become part of Musil's store of material for his creative work. He expressed this with characteristic forthrightness: 'Martha (...) ist etwas, das ich geworden bin und das ich geworden ist' (TbI,226) ('Martha is something that I have become and that has become "I"'). Thus, even Musil's psychic portraits of women are drawn directly from life; here, too, Musil had no need to suppress his scientific scruples about evidence, to have any mental reservations about the authenticity of the private emotional data on which his literary experiments [1] were based. Following as he did in the tradition of Cartesian scientific scepticism, Musil might have said of the works from 1906-1924: 'If I can vouch for nothing else, I can confirm, at least, that the material from which I shape my works is utterly authentic.'

In view of the importance of autobiographical detail in Musil's work, it is helpful to consider briefly his life, above all in the period spanned by the works in question. Musil was born in 1880 in Klagenfurt, Austria, moved with his family several times as a child but, in 1891, settled with them in Brünn, Moravia, which was then part of the Austro-Hungarian Empire. His father was an engineering professor at the local 'Technische Hochschule' ('Technical University') and, accordingly, young Musil was brought up in a materially comfortable household. It was, however, by no means entirely conventional. His father, a rational but anxious and retiring figure, tolerated in his home as permanent house-guest, another male, Heinrich Reiter, who appears to have been the lover of Hermine Musil. [2] Musil's mother was a beautiful, passionate woman, both neurotic and domineering. As a twelve-year-old Musil persuaded his parents to send him to board at a 'Militär-Unterrealschule' ('Lower-level Military Technical School') at Eisenstadt in Austria - a couple of years later he passed on to the 'Militär-Oberrealschule' ('Upper-level Military Technical School') at Mährisch-Weißkirchen, near his home in Brünn. These two institutions seem to have offered a sound basic training in scientific and technical subjects combined with strict discipline; Musil was unhappy at both, particularly the latter. In 1897, after graduating from Mährisch-Weißkirchen, he spent a few months at an officers' academy in Vienna which confirmed his dislike for the Army and he returned to Brünn to study engineering in his father's department, from which he graduated in 1902.

While at Brünn, he came into contact with contemporaries who had
been educated at humanistic grammar schools and who therefore knew far
more than he did about literature and culture. He even did some
creative writing but his earliest work gives an impression of a
dilettante lack of direction and absence of stamina. This changed,
however, when Musil's father arranged a post for him as a research
assistant at the 'Technische Hochschule' in Stuttgart; here, with
time hanging heavy on his hands after the day's work, Musil found a
literary theme which did keep his attention: some of his experiences
at military boarding school. This became Die Verwirrungen des
Zöglings Törleß ('The Confusions of Young Törleß'), published in 1906.

But to write a novel was not immediately to discover a vocation as
an author. Musil had felt impelled to give up his assistantship at
Stuttgart in 1903, not in order to devote himself to literature, but
to study at the University of Berlin. This may appear to be a detour
from Musil's essential path but, as a student of the mind, he believed
that he was going to the source of the most subtle and advanced
information available in the contemporary world on philosophy and
psychology. However, by the time he had gained his doctorate in
1908 it was clear to him that purely academic study of the mind would
not offer him the opportunity for the kind of work that he found most
rewarding and it was only then that he turned to full-time creative
writing.

Musil had little to show for the time he spent in Berlin after
finishing his studies in 1908 - though he worked on a play, Die

Schwärmer ('The Enthusiasts') (based largely on the relationship with
Martha), he only actually published one work, Vereinigungen (this has
the meaning of 'Unions' in a sexual and psychological sense).   The
two short stories that made up this book represent virtually
two-and-a-half years of intellectual hard labour.   Just as he had
been unwilling to reconcile himself to the demands of careers in
soldiering, engineering or academic life - to adapt, in other words,
to the matrix of duties and other obligations which each occupation
placed upon him - so he brought to the writing of short stories and
plays a stubborn unwillingness to respond to conventional expectations
and demands.   He wrote about himself, and it must sometimes have
seemed to the few who read his work that he wrote for himself as well
(though it was characteristic that, when the book failed to achieve
the success of his far more accessible, though by no means
unproblematical, earlier novel, Die Verwirrungen des Zöglings Törleß,
he was deeply disappointed).

 In 1911, after having been supported by his parents for thirty
years, Musil could no longer resist their pressure on him to take a
permanent job;   reluctantly he accepted a position as a librarian at
the 'Technische Hochschule' in Vienna.   Though his scientific
training made him eminently qualified for the post and his duties only
exacted four hours work per day, he found the interruption to his
literary and intellectual pursuits intolerable and took extended
periods of sick leave.   He was, however, not so unwell as to deny
himself another visit to Berlin where he negotiated with the

publisher, Samuel Fischer, for a post on his cultural periodical, Die
Neue Rundschau.   In late 1913 he went back to Berlin yet again to
become editor of the journal.   World War I, in which he saw active
service on the Italian Front as an officer in the Austro-Hungarian
Army, brought all sustained literary activity to a standstill once
more.   After the war he worked in various government departments,
finding time to finish his drama, Die Schwärmer, which was published
in 1921.   Eventually, in 1922, he gave up all security to devote
himself to literary work again.   He wrote short stories, reviews and
essays, but his major concern quickly became the novel which was later
to be entitled Der Mann ohne Eigenschaften.   In 1924 a collection of
stories, Drei Frauen ('Three Women'), appeared; two of these were
based on experiences during the war, the other on his relationship
with Herma Dietz, a working-class girl from Brünn which had ended with
her death in Berlin in 1907.

        Since Musil's energies were largely engaged elsewhere, up to
his mid-forties his only works of lasting significance were the novel,
stories and play mentioned above.   They are all relatively short,
filling only one volume in the nine volume paperback edition of
Musil's works, published in 1978.   (By comparison, the edition of Der
Mann ohne Eigenschaften takes up five of these volumes.)   In one
striking way these works - with the possible exception of the play -
appear to belong in a different phase of Musil's career as a creative
author.   Any reader who first reads Part I and Part II of Der Mann
ohne Eigenschaften - which are illuminated by moments of brilliant,

satirical wit - will be surprised by the early novel and the short
stories, with their mood of utter seriousness and their almost total
absence of any humour.   (Of course, Der Mann ohne Eigenschaften is
also, essentially, a deeply serious work; the surface irony and
satire are a pose which Musil adopts to serve specific ends in the
novel.) [3]   Seriousness is the mark of Musil's sense of mission as a
writer.

We have seen that Musil attaches a great deal of weight to
personal experiences.   This is true, of course, of many creative
writers.   But the distinguishing features of Musil's work, in this
context, are the almost exaggerated single-mindedness of the
self-scrutiny and the unshakeable resolve to find the right words with
which to express the given experience.   The result is often passages
in which profound insights are expressed in prose of breath-taking
precision and harmony. [4]

The works which we shall examine below express two major
concerns.   First, Musil's desire to see what happens when close
analysis reduces human problems to the separate segments from which
they are composed.   He tries to set the elements of human existence
into the best kind of order that the human mind can achieve in the
modern age.   Even in this commitment there is detachment.   One
cannot desire the new while accepting the old without reservation.
A conviction of the need for a new social and moral order distances
Musil from the things, and the people, that surround him.   Even in

private Musil remains an observer, watching his own mind and body at
work and making a record of what he perceives, transforming immediate
life into the medium of words.   Perhaps the strength of Musil's
rational drive, the analytical compulsion within him, gives rise to
his fascination with non-rational experiences.   This second concern is
given less prominence by literary critics but is of crucial importance
to Musil.   He returns time and again to experiences which, though
they can be trawled up in the reflective net of the mind, resist
attempts to analyse them.   Since they tend to be overlooked or
discounted as unimportant by contemporaries, Musil believes that he
must give them special attention so that they can take a proper place
in the balance-sheet of twentieth-century experience.   In the
following studies of Die Verwirrungen des Zöglings Törleß,
Vereinigungen, Die Schwärmer and Drei Frauen I have tried to give them
the prominence they deserve.

Chapter 2   'DIE VERWIRRUNGEN DES ZÖGLINGS TÖRLEß'

In 1903, as a young research engineer in Stuttgart, Musil
started work on his first novel.   He had had, it is true, tried to
make up for the the philistine environment of the military
institutions where he had received his secondary education by taking
advantage of the opportunities available in Brünn - the library with
its stock of works for spare-time reading, including Goethe, Novalis,
Dostoievsky, Nietzsche, Baudelaire, Verlaine, Wilde, Poe, Rilke, the
theatre with its productions of plays by Ibsen, Hofmannsthal,
Hauptmann, Bahr and Schnitzler;   these authors, a few exhibitions of
contemporary painters at the local art gallery and some
undistinguished dabbling in creative writing represented the outer
limits of Musil's cultural experience in this phase of his life. [1]

The subject for his new work was an account of his own
experiences as a schoolboy at Mährisch-Weißkirchen.   In a letter to a
former fellow-pupil at the time when Die Verwirrungen des Zöglings
Törleß was published Musil asked for discretion about the identity of
several of the characters who were readily recognisable from their
fictional counterparts. [2]   Musil insisted here that he had made up
many of the important elements of the plot but one suspects that more
was true than he was prepared to admit.   The essential features of
the plot are rather unpleasant: Törleß, a boarder at a military
college, probably about sixteen years of age, has made friends with

two older boys, Reiting and Beineberg; Reiting discovers that one of
their classmates, Basini, is a thief; deciding not to expose Basini
but to take punishment into their own hands, Reiting and Beineberg
bully, beat, humiliate and sexually abuse Basini.   Törleß, after
being a more or less passive observer at some of these 'punishment'
sessions, has homosexual relations with Basini but refuses to do
anything to help him escape Reiting's and Beineberg's attentions.
Matters came to a head when Reiting and Beineberg tell the class that
Basini is a thief; Basini, having been forced to 'run the gauntlet'
of the class, confesses to the school authorities (apparently on
Törleß's secret prompting); Törleß, frightened by the prospect of the
enquiry that will follow and the questions he will have to answer,
runs away from school.   When he is found, Törleß is treated
leniently since his involvement with Basini has not been betrayed but
the headmaster, in view of Törleß's state of mind, advises his parents
to withdraw him from the school.   The novel ends as he leaves for
good.

It would have been astonishing had Musil, as a young
inexperienced writer with a far better grounding in science than the
humanities, had been able to write a flawless novel - he certainly did
not do so.   Before considering what he did achieve, we ought to
review briefly some of the weaknesses of the work.

A flawed work?

In March 1905 he wrote in a letter to a woman friend: 'mein
Roman ... Sie gähnen? Ja, also, er ist fertig. Schon seit Wochen.
Natürlich ist er schlecht (....). Sechzehnjährige Knaben reden
darinnen wie Bücher (....), wie schlechtgeschriebene Bücher' (Briefe
I, 12) ('my novel ...you're yawning? Well, then, it's finished.
Finished it weeks ago. Of course it's bad (...) Sixteen-year-old
boys in it talk like books (...), like badly-written books'). Most
readers will agree with this last observation. The sixteen-year-old
Törleß does often sound unnaturally precocious, more a mature
philosopher than a teenage neurotic; Beineberg, his friend, behaves
like an adolescent - a disagreeable adolescent - but speaks like a
cultured adult. For Der Mann ohne Eigenschaften Musil was to develop
a sophisticated technique for reproducing authentic speech and thought
'signatures' for many of his characters by borrowing from the
published work of the real people on whom they were based. The words
of the fictional character were then a collage of statements taken
from the writings of the real-life counterpart fused with sentences of
Musil's own invention. [3]   But in Die Verwirrungen des Zöglings
Törleß Musil shows his inexperience. His prose lacks the subtlety
and accuracy that he was to develop later; [4] the images he uses are
sometimes more obtrusive than revealing; [5] and Musil has difficulty
in handling with the necessary subtlety the necessary distinction

between the relatively naive perspective of the hero and that of the
more sophisticated narrator.

Despite the faults and subject-matter of the work, Musil's
original judgement in the 1905 letter was positive: 'Einen Roman
nicht ganz gewöhnlicher Art - Mit Fehlern behaftet, aber einer neuen
Weise zu schreiben zustrebend' (Briefe I, 14) (my emphasis) ('a novel
of a rather unusual kind - flawed but struggling towards a new way of
writing'); he maintained this view throughout his life. [6]

The narrative

Musil approaches the writing of the novel with the efficiency
one would expect from a trained engineer: we can imagine him
organising the undertaking into manageable sub-problems - how to
present the central consciousness, how to distinguish between the
perspective of the hero and that of the narrator, how to arrange the
events in the best order, how to handle the images, how to tackle the
central moral issue.   He does this with the enthusiasm of someone who
is not overwhelmed by tradition, by the burden of other writers'
achievements.   Since the primary problem is emotional he does not
focus on the central character from without - he does not concentrate
on external description, events and dialogue which might gradually
have revealed aspects of the hero's personality and views as he would
have done if he had been guided by realist techniques.   Instead he

looks at Törleß from the inner perspective of personal experience,
examining the tensions and stresses that affect the internal structure
of the youthful personality as it develops through adolescence, and
takes the strain of a more dynamic and individually responsible
interacting with the environment.   This choice of focus has important
implications for the shape of the narrative itself.

Törleß's arrival at boarding-school marks a break with the
security of life at home where he was in close contact with his
parents; he starts to think independently and finds that ideas and
attitudes which he has hitherto adopted without question do not match
his experiences.   For example, he has always felt that his family
and friends are quite different from peasants and working people;
the latter he consigns to another category of humanity because they
are both dirty and subject to wild passions; [7] soon after his arrival
he begins to doubt that this distinction is right.   Earlier he
looked upon men like Goethe, Schiller and Kant as intellectual and
spiritual map-makers who had drawn up the boundaries of possible
experience; [8] now, as his developing consciousness encounters strange
and unexpected contours, he starts to chart the world for himself.
His 'Verwirrungen' ('confusions') arise as he leaves behind the false
'certainties' that protected his childhood and takes hesitant steps
towards the attitudes which - so the narrator assures us - he develops
in adult life.

If the text were literally a projection of the 'confusions of

Törleß at boarding-school' and nothing besides, it would be a
virtually unintelligible episodic account of perceptions, feelings and
images which swirl through Törleß's consciousness.   But this is not
so.   Things are put in their place by a narrator who presents a
background that is recognisably 'real' (so real in fact that Karl
Corino was able to visit the place where the school used to be, to
find the actual building where Bozena, the prostitute, lived and even
to trace some of the original names of characters whom Musil includes
in the novel). [9]   This narrator is, Martin Swales argues, someone
rather like the mature Törleß: '(Törleß) develops to the point where
he can be the narrator of his own experience, to the point where his
voice, his perceptions, his formulations, merge with the voice, the
perceptions, the formulations of that narrative voice which sustains
the novel.' [10]

    But this does not mean that Törleß is wrong about the nature of
things and the narrator is right; it is rather a case of the narrator
acting as an intermediary between Törleß's preoccupations and a world
recognisable to the readers in the first decade of this century and
indeed to all readers since.   For Musil tries to capture not only
the confusions, but also the passions, of an adolescent youth of
unusual sensitivity before they are lost in a process of maturing
which involves the acceptance of adult reality - a reality which, as
Musil shows us not only here but in subsequent works - is made not
only of fact but of fiction, of mutually sustaining illusions and
shared misconceptions.

Musil does not tell the story by beginning at the beginning and proceeding straight on through to the end.   The narrative is not governed by a chronological sequence, but rather by a complex formula, as one might expect from an engineer.   His narrative technique is indeed, as Elisabeth Stopp puts it: 'the logical organising principle (...) of a mathematician applying himself to the solution of a (...) problem.' [11]   It takes us back in time to a fictional scene at a railway station - which we shall call point Ai - then moves forward in time to a scene in a railway carriage shortly after a train has left the same station - which, in view of the short span of real time which this narrative portrays ('real', of course, only within the context of a fictional narrative which we therefore place between round brackets), we shall call point B.   We shall indicate the passing of real time by placing episodes in chronological order thus: Ai, Aii, Aiii and so on through to B.   But within this chronological sequence we have to insert a number of angular brackets to represent sections of narrative where the chronological sequence, Ai, Aii, Aiii through to B, is interrupted - single angle brackets for past time, double for future time.   Our formula for Musil's narrative would then look like this:

(Ai...⟨x...y⟩ Aii...Aiii/a ⟨p⟩ ⟨⟨F⟩⟩ Aiii/b...etc. ...B)

How does the formula correlate with the text?   First we find (pp.8-12) an account of Törleß's relationship with a young prince from

the period he spends at school before point Ai - we shall call this
episode 'x'. Then we have (pp.12-14) another pre-Ai episode but one
which follows 'x', so we shall call this 'y'. We are then taken back
into the Ai - B chronology at point Aii (p.15) and see Törleß taking
leave of his parents at the station which was described in the opening
scene of the novel. We move on within this chronology for a few
pages until a point - let us call this Aiii/a - at which Törleß, in a
conversation with Beineberg in a cafe, takes us back to the earliest
point touched on in the narrative so far, point 'p' (pp.23-24) - of
course, since it is the adolescent Törleß who is relating this
incident it does fit within the Ai - B chronology. Within the same
scene the narrator points forward to a time, 'F', well into the future
beyond 'B', when Törleß has reached maturity. We then return to the
Ai - B chronological progression at point Aiii/b; thus, with
intermittent regressions into the past and insights into the future,
Musil's narrative proceeds. (From the point of view presented in
this formula the only problematical part of the rest of the narrative
is the scene in which Basini is whipped by his fellow-pupils,
Beineberg and Reiting, for having stolen some money. Here Törleß
falls into a kind of trance as he thinks back over what has happened
to him over the past few days. These events are recounted first in
the pluperfect tense which indicates that the narrative has moved
backwards; then, after several pages, the narrative reverts to the
simple past - and therewith into 'Ai - B' time again - at a point
after the whipping scene has finished, even though there has been no
sign of when the reverie came to an end. The narrative hiatus in the

text starts at the top of page 73 in Volume II of Adolf Frisé's
edition of the Gesammelte Werke; by page 84 the narrative has
returned to Ai - B time with Törleß back in bed, deep in thought.)

The formula we have examined illustrates the relative complexity
of the narrative structure of Die Verwirrungen des Zöglings Törleß.
Was such an elaborate design really necessary? Certainly the hiatus
we examined in the passage in brackets in the paragraph immediately
above seems unnecessary - indeed it is perhaps quite simply an
oversight. The excursions into the future, such as that at 'F' may
be necessary, for reasons we shall examine below, but they are often
awkward interruptions which break the reader's involvement in a
particular scene. However, certain scenes are so crucial to an
appreciation of the work as a whole - and the one where Basini is
whipped while Törleß, who is within a few feet of him, falls into a
trance, is clearly such a scene - that Musil felt it necessary to
provide an internal commentary on them with selected moments from the
past or reassurances from the future.

The chronological section Ai - B represents a period of crisis
in Törleß's life associated with puberty; Musil attempts to catch in
words something of the change that is taking place here. To start
the narrative earlier would be to widen the scope of the novel and to
divert some attention away from this change. What is happening in
the span of real time that starts with the opening scene of the novel
is that a psychic development within Törleß is being confirmed and

consolidated in the main events within the novel - this development involves, broadly speaking, an emphasising of the more active rational faculty at the expense of the emotional.   The direction in which Törleß develops is not the direction in which he might have developed given different circumstances.   A few months earlier it seemed possible that he might develop quite differently.   This lost potential is symbolised by the interlude with the prince with whom Törleß formed a deep but short-lived friendship.   Törleß comes from a 'bürgerlich-freidenkenden Hause' (11) ('bourgeois and free-thinking home'), the prince from an aristocratic one;   the prince has been brought up a Catholic and is filled with the mystery of the divine, Törleß, we assume, is an agnostic who puts his trust in scepticism and rationality.   In view of the difference in origin, Törleß and the prince can be expected to differ on religious questions.   However, despite his aggressive analysing which dissects and dismisses the prince's religious faith, Törleß is aware that there might be something of value here: 'Törleß war sich wohl dunkel bewußt, daß er etwas Sinnloses getan hatte, und eine unklare, gefühlsmäßige Einsicht sagte ihm, daß da dieser hölzerne Zollstab des Verstandes zu ganz unrechter Zeit etwas Feines und Genußreiches zerschlagen habe' (12) ('Törleß was probably dimly aware that he had done something senseless, and an unclear feeling, a kind of insight, told him that this wooden yardstick of the intellect (Verstand), at precisely the wrong time, had smashed something fine and pleasurable').

Törleß is not simply attacking the beliefs of the other but

rooting out a tentative religious awareness in himself.   In his
attack on the prince, Törleß is shaping his own self in the image of
the sceptic who insists on direct critical examination of things,
because he has been brought up to believe that it is appropriate to
approach all important matters from an intellectual angle.   Törleß
appears to be convinced that the reward for dogged and wilful
questioning will be a breakthrough to a reality beyond all illusion.
This stance of uncompromising and unrelenting positivism first makes
Törleß experiment on himself and on Basini, and later brings him to
the point of mental breakdown.   But its first victim - and here we
see the intention behind the narrative flash-back towards the
beginning of the work - was the young prince.

Musil employs a similar technique in the scene where Törleß does
nothing while Basini is tortured.   Tom Brown in his schooldays would
never have paused to reflect - he would have leapt to the defence of
Basini even if it meant a beating at the hands of older, stronger
(but, in moral terms, inferior) boys.   Musil has the narrative move
back on itself at this point in order to provide a perspective which
helps to explain Törleß's inactivity, scanning the previous days'
events as evidence of growing confusions.   Thus the narrative is
designed to throw light on a process taking place within Törleß, on
the inner psychic structure which grows quickly at this phase in
Törleß's adolescent development.   Otto Wagner, the Viennese
architect, overturned traditional nineteenth-century practice by
opening to public view the inner structure of what he built, showing

the network of inner supports that take the strains which the edifice must withstand.   Musil, in this novel, designs his narrative to uncover the tensions which outer events exert in the psychic substructure of the central consciousness, the adolescent hero, making these tensions public.

Here, of course, Musil was not dealing with a building but a human being - and not any human being, but the one he knew most intimately, literally 'inside-out', from within, looking out at the outside world.   The reader senses that, in reexamining as a man in his early twenties, his own psychic growth as an adolescent, he could sense the development of the perceptive apparatus as bundled nerves connecting inner and outer worlds.   By expressing it in words, he wanted to make public this private world.

At an exhibition on human biology entitled 'Ourselves' at the Natural History Museum in London in 1977, a model homunculus was on display whose limbs and features were shaped to express the degree to which different areas of the body are represented in the nervous tissue of the brain.   Eyes, lips, nose and ears of the homunculus were grotesquely distended to indicate the extensive brain areas to which the dense network of nerves in these parts were joined;   huge hands with great fingers like bananas issued from emaciated arms, identifying homo habilis, man the tool-maker and manipulator.   If we let a standard linear narrative in which events are presented in

chronological order be equivalent to the image of a man sculpted by
Michelangelo where every limb is a lesson in anatomy and is
proportioned to harmonise with the whole frame, then Musil's narrative
is the homunculus expressing an inner interpretation whose
proportions, though they appear grotesque to any observer who expects
a classical form, correspond nonetheless to the preoccupations, the
frenetic nervous activity of this strange subject, Törleß.

Musil is so preoccupied with Törleß that he neglects other
characters.   Beineberg's odd metaphysics are offered as a
counterweight to Törleß's concern with sense impressions and thought
fragments, but otherwise the narrator seems to have no interest in
other characters except where they impinge on Törleß's horizon.   Some
critics detect expressionist elements in the novel and, certainly in
its concentration on the inner world of one person and its
articulation of a protest at the restrictions that outer reality
places on the sensitive consciousness of a young person, the novel can
be seen as a precursor of this movement.   A reader might expect each
character in the novel to be drawn according to the same criteria, if
not necessarily in the same detail, as the next.   This would have
been the case if Musil had carried on the realist tradition in his
novel.   But his narrator is guilty of 'favouritism': he spends page
after page analysing Törleß's changes of perception in the course of a
single night, but then has only four brief paragraphs for a finished
portrait of Basini, despite the evident importance of this character

for the work as a whole. The narrator's antipathy for Basini is
undisguised: 'Er war etwas größer als Törleß, jedoch sehr schwächlich
gebaut, hatte weiche, träge Bewegungen und weibische Gesichtszüge.
Sein Verstand war gering (...)'(50) ('He was a little taller than
Törleß but very frail in build, his movements were gentle and
lethargic and his features effeminate. His intellect was feeble
(...)'). This character sketch becomes almost hostile: 'Zu Bozena
war er seinerzeit nur gekommen, um den Mann zu spielen. Eine
wirkliche Begierde dürfte ihm bei seiner zurückgebliebenen Entwicklung
durchaus noch fremd gewesen sein (...) Mitunter log er auch aus
Eitelkeit (...) Die moralische Minderwertigkeit, die sich an ihm
herausstellte, und seine Dummheit wuchsen auf einem Stamm' (50/51)
('He had come to Bozena when he did only in order to play the man.
Genuine desire, in view of his retarded development must still have
been quite out of the question (...) Occasionally vanity made him
tell lies (...) The moral inferiority which he developed and his
stupidity were off-shoots of the same growth'). This kind of writing
has its focus not in the external world but in the inner perspective
of Törleß's mind. It has its own in-built immature bias - it exposes
part of the substructure of the adolescent psyche at the centre of the
novel, explaining (though, of course, not excusing) Törleß's disregard
for Basini's feelings.

This central character, from a moral point of view, is trapped
in subjectivity; lost in private confusions, he is in danger of

developing into a callous monster. Are we to see the text as a whole
as similarly lacking in any semblance of moral concern? Certainly
this was a danger which Musil was aware of, and he made attempts to
forestall the kind of criticism which the external world would
inevitably make of his novel.

Moral Dimensions

In 1907 Musil drafted two letters to 'Onkel Mattia', a friend of
his father, who according to Adolf Frisé, was a representative of the
cultured 'Bürgertum' and who, without being stuffy, found it difficult
to come to terms with Musil's new view of human behaviour. [12] In
these drafts Musil explained that art was concerned, among other
things, with the moral evolution of culture. [13] To conform was to
remain fixed in the grip of the past; art, in so far as it forced men
to see what needed changing, was about the future. 'Kunst schafft
(...) Werte' (Briefe, I,46) ('Art creates values'), Musil wrote. To
alter society's perception of what it is to be a human being – and
certainly this was what Musil was attempting in Die Verwirrungen des
Zöglings Törleß – was to change the shape of contemporary morals. It
is interesting to note that the means which he employed to express
this idea were that of the bond of sympathy between an audience and
the heroes of classical tragedy. This was evidently a legacy of his
visits to the theatre in Brünn and his attempts to emulate his
grammar-school contemporaries who knew the classics far better than he

did.   He wrote that he had to evoke in his readers the same sympathy
for Törleß as they had for the tragic hero: '(wichtig) sind die
Sympathiegefühle, die Tatsache, daß ein Mensch, mit dem uns vieles
sympathisch verbindet, kurz daß ein Teil von uns (...) sündigt u
zugrundegeht' (Briefe, I,43) ('(important) are the feelings of
sympathy, the fact that a being for whom we feel a bond of sympathy,
in short a part of us, commits sins and is destroyed').   He felt that
he had done enough to persuade readers that Törleß, at least from the
inner perspective put forward in the narrative, could be excused for
having abused Basini - he still retained the sympathy of the reader.
Contemporaries were divided on this issue: some praised the work as
an important contribution to the understanding of young people;
others were offended by what they saw as its immorality.

Today, readers of the work may may find it even more difficult
than Musil's contemporaries to be sympathetic in the face of Törleß's
mistreating of Basini.   Törleß sees a fellow-pupil bullied,
humiliated and reviled yet feels no stirring of pity whatsoever, no
urge to plead Basini's cause.   Why not, the modern reader asks?   It
is important to remember that he or she brings to bear on the issue a
different kind of peripheral awareness from the one for which this
text was written.   He or she may judge partly in the light of what
was later to happen in the German-speaking world, seeing Beineberg and
Reiting as prototypes for the beasts who surfaced in the Third
Reich [14] and Törleß as one of those who would go into 'inner
emigration' when violent men held others in their power.   The reader

at the time of the novel's publication in 1906, of course, would have
had no such perspective; on the other hand, he or she would have had
a much deeper immediate awareness of the world that had fostered
Törleß's confusions. In those days adolescent boys were not thought
to be on the threshold of manhood. A sixteen-year-old would have had
to wait a further couple of decades to 'enter his prime'. In
Austrian society at that time, youth was not encouraged as it is
today; energy and a spirit of initiative were not at a premium in the
Habsburg state for which change represented a threat. In Die Welt
von Gestern, Stefan Zweig, who was born only one year later than Musil
and who had the grammar-school education (in Vienna) which Musil
missed, looks back on his experiences as a boy at his school where the
masters sat at high desks, looking down at beings who had not yet
reached their level of culture and humanity. To achieve this level
their pupils had to undergo a long initiation through boredom,
rote-learning and harsh discipline. In the upper forms of secondary
school Zweig and his fellow-pupils turned to literature as an escape
from monotony; in the martial atmosphere of Törleß's military
academy, literature is not encouraged. The boarders there are cut
off from the restraining and civilising influence of home and have
little contact with the masters outside the classroom. The boys
appear to wander about the academy and its environs with no adult
supervision. Despite the constant nocturnal wanderings of four
members of the same dormitory, no master ever discovers an empty bed.
At night, at least, conditions for the boarders are like those on the
remote island in William Golding's Lord of the Flies where children,

deprived of any adult guidance, set upon each other under the pressure
of inner compulsions and fears.

The reader in the late twentieth century may also tend to forget
- partly because the mood of the novel is so modern - that the society
which Musil depicts still maintained strong ties with the feudal age.
Törleß and his fellow-pupils are under pressure to conform not to a
prevailing climate of support for democracy and the attitudes which
this entails - they are expected to resist such attitudes.
Academies, such as the one which Törleß attends, were set up to
educate an élite for leadership.   Democracy - at least in its
association with social democracy - was anathema to the members of the
upper classes whose minds were set against egalitarianism.   Thomas
Mann, who in the time of the Third Reich was to become perhaps the
leading representative of German culture in exile was, until after
World War I, an opponent of democracy which he saw as something
distinctively French and therefore foreign to the spirit of
Germany.[15]   In Die Verwirrungen des Zöglings Törleß Musil shows
clearly that his central character is obsessed with a sense that
people differ in their very nature according to the class to which
they belong; for the original readers there were undoubtedly many
class code signals within the text - Törleß, for example, disapproves
of his maths teacher's carelessness with his appearance (he notices
stains of boot polish on the legs of his long underpants!).[16]
Törleß identifies others by their manners, speech, clothing, state of
cleanliness and habits; he assumes that they are also committed by

their social status to certain patterns of thought and feeling.   The
moral virtues which his class proclaims - he has not yet realised that
so many make secret concessions to human frailty - are absolute for
Törleß.   He asks himself whether he has the strength to live up to
these and fears that the feelings which he is now experiencing will
prevent him from doing so.   If he is not able to prevent 'despicable'
inner compulsions from coming to light, his parents will thrust him
away 'wie ein kleines unsauberes Tier' (32) ('like a dirty little
animal').   Then he will sink to the unhygienic and brutish level of
the peasants he sees in the local village.[17]   He is convinced that
Basini, by his thieving, has disqualified himself from entry into
higher society, that he has fallen;   from Törleß's point of view the
treatment which Basini receives at the hands of his fellow-pupils may
seem simply an initiation into a new state of debasement.   When his
parents write advising Törleß to be charitable to Basini he is
outraged by their request;   in rejecting their advice he sees
himself, paradoxically, as the advocate of their way of life, the
champion of their morality.   (His 'confusion' stems in part from
scattered evidence that turns up which seems to indicate that his
criteria are wrong - this is the case, for example, when he begins to
glimpse his parents' sexuality: 'Sie tuen es auch!   Sie verraten
dich!' (35) ('They do it, too!   They betray you!').   But
intellectuality, dangerously allied to inexperience, drives all before
it.)

Instead of looking on Basini as a fellow human-being, he acts as

if Basini and he did not belong to the same species. Basini has
fallen; if Törleß were to sympathise, or offer support, this would be
to risk falling himself. [18] This sense of self-preservation may be
misguided but Musil is successful in making the reader feel how
powerful it is. Apart from the letter from Törleß's parents, there
is nothing in Törleß's surroundings to help him to recognise why what
he is doing is wrong.

The onset of puberty and the feelings it engenders are analysed
subtly but pervasively; in this novel Musil's frankness on sexual
matters contrasts with the hypocrisy of contemporary attitudes. [19]
Since it was not possible to repress sexuality completely, society
banished it from consciousness wherever possible. While young men
sowed their wild oats in secret, young women were kept in an unhealthy
state of ignorance of sex. The price that some paid for the tyranny
of social convention was venereal disease or hysteria. In 1909, when
Sigmund Freud introduced North America to his theories on
psychoanalysis in a series of lectures in Massachusetts, he offered
his audience images of the working of their own minds and emotions. [20]
But fearing that his ideas would be swept aside by a tidal wave of
moral outrage Freud was careful to conceal such controversial matters
as the phenomenon of infantile sexuality and the Oedipus complex until
the later lectures. Since they were such dangerous medicines, he
administered sexual insights in discreet doses. Musil is similarly
cautious in his handling of the sensibilities of his readers. He,
too, prepares the ground for an understanding of the confusions of his

central character by presenting sexual insights in instalments. The
night when Törleß has sex with Basini is the climax of a sequence of
experiences - the unspecific yearnings of puberty, the breaking-off of
visits to Bozena when Törleß discovers that his feelings for her are
somehow linked to his feelings for his mother,[21] Basini's moral fall
which leads Törleß to an unwonted intimacy with this somewhat girlish
figure, the opportunities offered by a vacation where Törleß is in
almost constant contact with Basini in the near-deserted school,
Basini's advances to him, the natural desire to embrace warm flesh in
this cold building - that have collectively built up an intolerable
head of pressure in Törleß's psyche. The reader, sharing Törleß's
anguish and confusion, is disposed to say 'there, but for the grace of
God, go I'.

Thus, for the most part, Musil is successful in establishing a
bond of sympathy between Törleß and the reader. As Martin Swales
puts it 'the reader is buttonholed into conceding the cognitive
importance of the protagonist's (....) confusions'.[22] Indeed, so
anxious is Musil to persuade the reader to take Törleß's side that he
has his narrator interrupt the narrative at what for the contemporary
reader must have been the nadir of depravity - when Törleß's
relationship with Basini has established itself as overtly homosexual
- and assure the reader that 'Törleß wurde später, nachdem er die
Ereignisse seiner Jugend überwunden hatte, ein junger Mann von sehr
feinem und empfindsamem Geiste' (111) ('Later when he had got over the
events of his youth Törleß became a young man of very fine and

sensitive intellect (Geist)'). Musil's intentions, here, are almost
embarrassingly transparent – the assurance that the hero, on maturity,
is fit to take his place in society is scarcely a sufficiently
substantial counterweight to all the dire events which affect the
adolescent – and Uwe Baur is probably right to call this the
'kompositorisch wohl schwächste Stelle des Romans' ('probably the
weakest point in the composition of the novel'). [23]

In this novel, then, Musil draws a self-portrait, his own
adolescence seen primarily from an inner perspective; he also
attempts to make the feelings and actions of the hero, which from a
traditional moral standpoint are utterly perverse, comprehensible to
the majority of readers.   The book is, in one sense, a Trojan horse.
To persuade readers that Törleß's confusions have some legitimacy is
to challenge the legitimacy of notions such as 'character' and 'moral
conduct' as well as current attitudes to sexuality, all of which are
essential parts of the fabric of contemporary society.

The 'Idee' of the novel

In another draft of the letter to Onkel Mattia Musil writes that
Die Verwirrungen des Zöglings Törleß 'illustriert eine Idee.   Um
nicht mißverstanden zu werden, habe ich ein Wort von Maeterlinck, das
ihr am nächsten kommt, vorangesetzt' (Briefe I, 47) ('illustrates an
idea.   In order to forestall any misunderstanding I have prefaced it

with an epigram of Maeterlinck's which comes closest to expressing the
idea'). The 'Wort von Maeterlinck' to which Musil refers is the
epigraph to the novel which reads: 'Sobald wir etwas aussprechen,
entwerten wir es seltsam. Wir glauben in die Tiefe der Abgründe
hinabgetaucht zu sein, und wenn wir wieder an die Oberfläche kommen,
gleicht der Wassertropfen an unseren Fingerspitzen nicht mehr dem
Meere, dem er entstammt' ('As soon as we express something we devalue
it strangely. We believe we have dived down into unfathomed depths
and when we return to the surface the droplet of water on our pale
finger-tips no longer resembles the sea which it came from'). There
can be no doubt that this epigraph points to the difficulties which
Musil had in finding words adequate to express the experiences of
adolescence. But this literary devaluation of the power of words is
a contemporary commonplace. At the turn of the century in Austria,
creative writers frequently complained about the gulf between words
and things. [24] What appears to be a self-critical response is also,
in fact, a criticism of contemporary culture. Törleß, himself,
though he scarcely qualifies as a 'creative writer' has made precisely
this discovery; in the crisis which follows his arrival at the
academy he lives for the moments when he will pour out his feelings in
wonderful letters to his parents; but as he matures and faces the
main crisis with which the novel is concerned he discovers that words
fail him; he can no longer describe his experiences. [25] Die
Verwirrungen des Zöglings Törleß deals, then, with a youth who makes a
discovery characteristic of authors and intellectuals in the culture
into which he is now emerging, namely that their awareness of reality

has outstripped the potential of the idiom in which reality is commonly expressed. This does not, however, lead many to lay down the pen in favour of less frustrating tasks. It prompted them rather to break with traditional forms of literary expression. To represent Törleß's dilemma Musil had to help in the fashioning of a new idiom, which bore within it the germ of a new Weltanschauung based not on objective norms but on the priority of subjectivity. His narrator,the man who Törleß might become, looks back at adolescence and sets out to express what his younger self could not. What literary means does Musil make available to his narrator?

Within the narrative are two levels of narrative, one closer to realism, the other to expressionism. The former is concerned broadly with the depiction of the world through which Törleß moves, the physical background, the village and its inhabitants, the school and the people Törleß has contact with there; the latter embraces Törleß's thoughts and feelings. [26] Törleß's confusions stem from his attempts to reconcile what he feels within with how he believes he ought to feel, and what he does with what he believes he ought to do; or, to express this in another way, he finds difficulty in mediating between inner and outer reality. J.P.Stern examines the friction which occurs when a central character applies the principles to which he is committed in the social world which the novelist creates around him;[27] someone seeks to act, for example, in accordance with specific beliefs and then, in the social situations created within the fictional world which represents the world of historical reality, 'lives through' the consequences of his actions, by experiencing what that world makes of them.

The first scene in which Törleß tests things out in this way helps us to identify his inner design - in fact Musil singles the scene out for special attention: 'Eine Episode dieser Zeit war für das charakteristisch, was sich damals in Törleß zu späterer Entwicklung vorbereitete' (10) ('An episode from this period was characteristic of what was then taking shape in Törleß in readiness for later development'). This is his short-lived friendship with the young prince who has come to the school:

> In der Gesellschaft dieses Prinzen fühlte (....) sich (Törleß) etwa wie in einer abseits des Weges liegenden Kapelle, so daß der Gedanke, daß er eigentlich nicht dorthin gehöre, ganz gegen den Genuß verschwand, das Tageslicht einmal durch Kirchenfenster anzusehen und das Auge so lange über den nutzlosen, vergoldeten Zierat gleiten zu lassen, der in der Seele dieses Menschen aufgehäuft war, bis er von dieser selbst ein undeutliches Bild empfing (11).

> (In the company of this prince (....) Törleß felt rather as if he were in a remote chapel so that the thought that he really did not belong there gave way completely to the pleasure of watching, for once, the daylight passing through church windows and of letting the eye glide over the useless, gilded decorations that were heaped up in the soul (Seele) of this person until, however indistinctly, he caught an image of the soul itself.)

But then Törleß and the prince quarrel over religion: 'wie von Törleß unabhängig, schlug nun der Verstand in ihm unaufhaltsam auf den zarten Prinzen los. Er überschüttete ihn mit dem Spotte des Vernünftigen, zerstörte barbarisch das filigrane Gebäude, in dem dessen Seele heimisch war, und sie gingen im Zorne auseinander' (12) ('as if

independent of Törleß, the intellect (Verstand) struck out repeatedly
at the delicate prince.   It heaped on him the scorn of rationality,
wreaked barbaric destruction on the filagree-work of the structure in
which the prince's soul was at home, and they parted in anger).

The reader is probably justified in assuming that Törleß's
reponse to the prince's religious views is an extension of the
atmosphere in which he has been brought up – his parents probably see
religion as an irrational throw-back to non-enlightened times; his
schooling at the military college has probably confirmed him in his
scepticism.   The response which can be seen as the child reproducing
the outlook of parents and teachers – as predictable in this
Bürger-son as his concern with appearances or his alienation from the
poorer members of society – develops as Törleß matures into
distinctive elements in his psychic make-up: a love of inner order, a
sense that feelings or thoughts which disturb this order are foreign
to him, a wilful intellectuality. [28]   He develops what we might call,
in deference to Descartes who was one of its forebears, Törleß's
'method'. [29]   But such a method is far from easy: like a collector
handling some precious object, he tries to turn each new experience
over in his mind; but it is difficult to develop the mental skills
needed for such manipulation.   Thoughts, and the things they try to
hold, constantly slip through his fingers.

This happens even with something as apparently universal as
'character'.   At home and at school 'character' is on the lips of

those he meets - since everyone has a 'character' he must have one
too.   The realist strand of the narrative seems to confirm this by
using the term 'character' as it is commonly used in the contemporary
world; [30] but Törleß can find no evidence of any pattern to the way
he feels: 'Es schien damals, daß er überhaupt keinen Charakter habe'
(13) ('In those days it seemed that he had no character at all').
According to Frederick Peters, Musil demonstrates in the novel that
'"character" can be defined as a (....) formula for that mechanism of
simplification that limits man to a single perspective of seeing'. [31]
In other words, in this novel Musil attempts to show that the term
'character' is only social shorthand for something whose subtlety
merits much more sophisticated expression.   Musil, through Törleß,
examines the way that a word in common use implies a substantiality
which on closer scrutiny turns out to be an illusion: Törleß,
searching for his character, finds only fleeting moods.   Other boys
accept the 'character' that is assigned to them, Törleß does not; even
ham-fisted attempts at applying the 'method' to this concept are
enough to show that it is a sham.   But to apply the 'method' is only
a stage in Törleß's development - in fact a stage when he is most
deeply confused.

Törleß fights against the sexual attraction that makes him
flirt with Bozena, the village prostitute; he recognises here a force
that undermines the order in his mind - an order which he associates
with home and its civilised pleasures.   When fused with his own
distinctive rationality this order helps to shape his life and guides

48

his decisions. But it is utterly subverted when, as we have seen, he
is not able to suppress the sense that his feelings for Bozena are
somehow connected with those for his mother – a notion which seems to
him so perverse that he dare not expose himself to it again. He
stops visiting Bozena. [32]

Even after his sexuality has been sacrificed to the 'method',
it still comes to the surface again after Basini has been unmasked as
a thief. In Törleß's view, by stealing, Basini has not simply
committed a criminal offence, but has shown that he is not fit to
share the life of civilised people. He has flouted the code and
fallen. The image used to convey Törleß's horror at what has
happened to Basini is theatrical: 'eine Falltüre hatte sich geöffnet,
und Basini war gestürzt' (46) ('a trap-door had opened and Basini had
fallen'). All the (civilised) world's a stage; but, as far as young
Törleß is concerned, the actors in the play have not only to convince
their fellow-actors that they can play their parts – they must also
order their private emotions in such a way that these, too, conform to
the character they portray. At the outset of the novel, Törleß seems
unaware that concealment and hypocrisy are recurrent strategies of
civilised existence. Through his 'fall' Basini becomes an object of
fascination for Törleß. One of the reasons for Basini's stealing has
been the expenses incurred in attempts to impress Bozena; this
liaison, which Basini in fact cultivates more for show than for any
other reason, ensures that Basini is tainted with sensuality in
Törleß's eyes. Having not yet learnt that different people

experience the world differently – though he will soon discover this –
Törleß sees in Basini the image of a self that has already fallen. [33]

Törleß is desperate to grasp what it would be like to 'fall' – such
knowledge might help either to keep him 'on the stage' of polite
society or, at worst, to prepare him for his own fall.   His
fascination with Basini is connected with the desire to see into the
mind of the being who has, so to speak, broken the taboo; [34] Törleß
wants to grasp what it is to suffer guilt, but experimentally, at
second hand.   The immature extravagance of Törleß's feelings is
represented in the narrative by fulsome images: he now sees for the
first time:

(....) daß von der hellen, täglichen Welt, die er bisher allein
gekannt hatte, ein Tor zu einer anderen, dumpfen, brandenden,
leidenschaftlichen, nackten, vernichtenden führe.   Daß zwischen
jenen Menschen, deren Leben sich wie in einem durchsichtigen und
festen Bau von Glas und Eisen geregelt zwischen Bureau und Familie
bewegt, und anderen, Herabgestoßenen, Blutigen, ausschweifend
Schmutzigen, in verwirrten Gängen voll brüllender Stimmen
Irrenden, nicht nur ein Übergang besteht, sondern ihre Grenzen
heimlich und nahe und jeden Augenblick überschreitbar
aneinanderstoßen (46-47).

((...) that from the bright everyday world, which was the only one
he had known so far, a gate led into another one where all was
gloomy, foaming, passionate, naked, destructive.   He saw that
between those people whose lives, as if ordered within a
transparent and stable structure of glass and iron, move between
office and family, and others, outcast, bloody, wallowing in filth
and excess, wandering lost in confused passages full of bellowing
voices, there is not only a connecting passage but that their
borders are secretly contiguous and can be crossed at any moment.)

Törleß's response to this new insight is to ask questions: '(....) wie
ist es möglich?   Was geschieht in solchem Augenblicke?   Was schießt
da schreiend in die Höhe und was verlischt plötzlich?' (47)

('(...) how is it possible? What happens at such a moment? What is it that then shoots into the air with a scream and what is it that is suddenly extinguished?'). It is evident that such questions have an urgency which is more than mere intellectual curiosity: 'Das waren die Fragen, die für Törleß mit diesem Ereignisse heraufstiegen. Sie stiegen undeutlich herauf, mit verschlossenen Lippen, von einem dumpfen, unbestimmten Gefühl ... einer Schwäche, einer Angst verhüllt' (47) ('These were the questions that for Törleß rose up with this event; they rose up vaguely, with sealed lips, veiled in a heavy, indistinct feeling (...) in a weakness, a fear'). His anxiety clearly stems from the threat from inner feelings of which he was scarcely aware in the world of his parents and for which he can accordingly find no proper place now that he must shift for himself.

His sense of discomfort increases as he becomes more aware of the gulf between his world and the world his teachers accept. For his maths teacher, infinity is a notion tamed by familiarity; for Törleß, too, the concept has been unproblematical until the day when, lying on the grass, he gazes up at a patch of blue sky which has appeared between the clouds – without warning, infinity suddenly jumps right out of its frame. Törleß tries to reach out and plumb the depths of the sky in an act of intense intellectual concentration:

Aber je weiter er hineindrang (...), desto tiefer zog sich der blaue leuchtende Grund zurück (...) Darüber dachte nun Törleß nach; er bemühte sich möglichst ruhig und vernünftig zu bleiben. 'Freilich gibt es kein Ende', sagte er sich, 'es geht immer weiter, fortwährend weiter, ins Unendliche.' Er hielt die Augen auf den Himmel gerichtet und sagte sich dies vor, als gälte es die

51

Kraft einer Beschwörungsformel zu erproben. Aber erfolglos; die
Worte sagten nichts, oder vielmehr sie sagten etwas ganz anderes,
so als ob sie zwar von dem gleichen Gegenstande, aber von einer
anderen, fremden, gleichgültigen Seite desselben redeten.
    'Das Unendliche!' (62/63).

(But the further he penetrated (...), the further the blue
brilliant depths receded (...) Törleß now thought deeply about
this; he tried to stay as calm and rational as possible.   'Of
course, it never comes to an end', he said to himself, 'it goes on
and on, continuously, into eternity.' He directed his gaze
towards the sky and recited this to himself as if he were trying
out the power of an evocation. But without success; the words
said nothing, or rather they said something quite different, as if
they were speaking of the same object but from another,
unfamiliar, indifferent aspect of it.
    'The Eternal!')

Törleß tries to repair this tear in the fabric of his world-order; he

visits the maths teacher but finds that this young man is never

troubled by the wider implications of such a concept.[35] This is

only the first of several encounters with representatives of outer

order, each of which increases Törleß's sense of the inadequacy of

contemporary culture. His maths teacher inadvertently stimulates in

Törleß an interest in Kant as the philosopher who was supposed to have

traced the limits of human understanding, but Törleß finds Kant's work

impenetrable and inhumanly dry.[36] By the time that Törleß is

interviewed by senior members of the school staff after running away

from the academy, he is fully aware that they do not share his

concerns because they are part of an older, redundant view of the

world. He no longer thinks that they hold the answers to things even

within the narrow fields of their individual subjects. When he is

brought before them it seems to Törleß that it is not he who is being

judged but they; he feels 'eine (...) hochmütige (...) Überlegenheit über diese älteren Leute, die von den Zuständen des menschlichen Inneren so wenig zu wissen schienen' (136) ('an (...) arrogant (...) superiority over these older people who seemed to know so little of the conditions in the interior of the human being'). He straightens his shoulders and confronts them proudly and with scorn 'als sei er hier Richter' (136) ('as if he were the judge here'). At a symbolic level, Musil here confronts external reality and shows its limitations. At a more immediate level, the reader recognises that a change has taken place in Törleß - he taken a decisive step towards maturity. But the development, the narrator explains, is not a purely intellectual one - the 'method' is becoming only one facet, rather than the dominant feature, of his attitude to things; intellectual activity has to be 'bedded down' in deeper recesses of the psyche: 'Ein Gedanke (....) wird erst in dem Momente lebendig, da etwas, das nicht mehr Denken ist, zu ihm hinzutritt, so daß wir seine Wahrheit fühlen, jenseits von aller Rechtfertigung, wie einen Anker, der von ihm aus ins durchblutete, lebendige Fleisch riß' (136/7) ('A thought (...) only comes alive at the moment when something that is no longer thinking is added to it, so that we feel its truth beyond all justification like an anchor which, reaching out from it, bites into living flesh and blood').

There can be little doubt that Musil, in explaining this painful but necessary process, was borrowing from Nietzsche. At about the time that he was working on Die Verwirrungen des Zöglings Törleß he had noted down in a diary extracts from Der Fall Wagner where

Nietzsche had written: 'Die Krankheit selbst kann ein Stimulans des
Lebens sein, nur muß man gesund genug für dieses Stimulans sein!'
(TbI,28) ('Sickness itself can be a stimulus for life, but one has to
be healthy enough for this stimulus!'). [37] Maturity has been
reached only through the anguish of confusion and the breakdown which
followed.   Where Törleß's maths teacher acknowledges the authority
of Kant, Törleß, himself, - though at this stage in his life he will
almost certainly not have realised it - is under the aegis of
Nietzsche.   The philosopher of 'Vernunft' ('reason') has given way to
the philosopher of 'freier Geist' ('the free spirit').   The 'method'
is rejected in favour of individualistic creativity.   So, towards the
end of the novel, Törleß has taken the decisive step towards becoming
his mature self.   In other words, at the end of the novel the hero's
perspective merges with the narrator's point of view, since, as we saw
above, the narrator of the novel may well be Törleß in his maturity.

We examined briefly above the relevance of the quotation from
Maeterlinck which serves as epigraph to the novel, showing the way
this expresses Musil's sense of the shortcomings of the language that
was available to him.   His answer to this problem was, in the absence
of any alternative vocabulary, to set words in new kinds of structures
in which not all were linked directly to things in the external world
- some, in evident deference to Nietzsche's sense of the loss of an
objective frame of reference, created their own 'gravity field' by
mutual definition.   In a way, Musil anticipates here the computer
age: some of the words and expressions he uses appear to be in a sort

of simple binary code (just as such simple opposites as 'on-off',
'in-out', 'up-down' might be seen to be in such a code) and take their
significance 'internally', by reference to each other. The coding is
attached to notions expressing the tensions of adolescence:
agorophobic freedom and the rigidity of authority, endless space and
the claustrophobia of closure, the humility of being shown the way and
the fear that there is no way, the inadequacy of conventional morality
and the confusions of self-determining.

A new way with words?

We should remember the problems that face the narrator. He has
to write at two levels: a realist level at which Törleß is seen
moving through a world made substantial by Newtonian time and space,
and where objects and characters obey the law of causality, and
another level which is innocent of all Newtonian order. The narrator
has also to reach below the level of adult consciousness to the
experiences of adolescence and bring these experiences up to the
surface of consciousness again; the epigraph from Maeterlinck points
to a narrative problem as well as an existential one. [38] To what
extent is the narrator successful?

In a scene located at the centre of the novel, Reiting,
Beineberg and Törleß wait in the attic for Basini to arrive. The
narrator leaves no doubt in the reader's mind that this attic exists:
he invites the reader to take up position in the dark, oppressed by

the stuffy air, next to the three youths: 'Überhaupt war die ganze
Umgebung äußerst beklemmend: Die Hitze unter dem Dach, die schlechte
Luft and das Gewirre der mächtigen Balken, die teils nach oben zu sich
im Dunkel verloren, teils in einem gespenstigen Netzwerk am Boden
hinkrochen (..) Beineberg blendete die Laterne ab, and sie saßen,
ohne ein Wort zu reden, regungslos in der Finsternis - durch lange
Minuten' (68) ('Indeed the whole environment was extremely oppressive:
the heat under the roof, the bad air and the maze of mighty beams,
some receding into darkness above, others creeping along the floor in
a ghostly network (..) Beineberg dimmed the lantern and, without
saying a word, they sat motionless in the darkness - for several long
minutes'). But the narrator is concerned not only with the external
setting of the scene, he is tuning in the reader's awareness to
Törleß's frequency: the narrative picks up the slightest sounds and
so reproduces something of the tension which Törleß feels: 'Da
knarrte am entgegengesetzten Ende im Dunkeln die Tür. Leise und
zögernd (...) Es folgten einige unsichere Schritte, das Anschlagen
eines Fußes gegen erdröhnendes Holz; ein mattes Geräusch, wie von dem
Aufschlagen eines Körpers... Stille... Dann wieder zaghafte Schritte
...Warten... Ein leiser menschlicher Laut...<<Reiting?>>' (68-69)
('Then in the darkness at the far end of the attic a door creaked.
Quietly and hesitatingly (...) There followed a few uncertain
footsteps, the echoing sound of a foot striking wood; a muffled thud
as if from a body colliding with something .... Silence ....Then again
hesitant footsteps ...waiting .... a soft human sound ...
<<Reiting?>>').

Up to this point, one sense has not been fully exercised - that of sight which we associate with the light of reason and which, in this text, is closely identified with Törleß's searching for certainty. Then, suddenly, the scene is illuminated: 'Beineberg (zog) die Kappe von der Blendlaterne und warf einen breiten Strahl gegen den Ort, woher die Stimme kam' (69) ('Beineberg (drew back) the blind from the lantern and directed a broad beam of light towards the place where the voice came from'). In this instant of natural theatre the reader is made to see with the almost unbearable anticipation which Törleß experiences as he waits for Basini, the 'Doppelgänger' of his own sensuality; the reader's attention could scarcely be focussed more intensely on the object about to enter the glare of the light: 'im nächsten Augenblicke tauchte in der breiten Basis des Lichtkegels das (....) Gesicht Basinis auf' (69) ('the next moment at the broad base of the cone of light Basini's face emerged').

Then things happen quickly: Beineberg recites all Basini's misdeeds, Reiting smashes his fist into Basini's face and he and Beineberg tear Basini's clothes off and start whipping him. The lamp has been knocked over 'und ihr Licht floß verständnislos und träge zu Törleß' Füßen über den Boden hin...' (69) (my emphasis) ('and its light flowed uncomprehendingly and sluggishly over the floor towards Törleß's feet...' (my emphasis)). Törleß can no longer see what is going on and seems paralysed: 'Gleich anfangs hatte ihn wohl eine viehische Lust mit hinzuspringen und zuzuschlagen gepackt, aber das

Gefühl, daß er zu spät kommen und überflüssig sein würde, hielt ihn

zurück. Über seinen Gliedern lag mit schwerer Hand eine Lähmung'

(69-70) ('Right at the beginning he had been seized by what felt like

a brutish urge to leap up, too, and join in the beating but the

feeling that he would be too late and would not be needed held him

back. Over his limbs lay the heavy hand of paralysis').

The narrator intimates that it is partly because this intense

activity is taking place in darkness that Törleß behaves as if he were

not present, half-shutting his ears to the sounds and, in a typical

movement of the mind, following the beam of light from the upturned

lamp:

Scheinbar gleichgültig sah er vor sich hin zu Boden. Er spannte
sein Gehör nicht an, um den Geräuschen zu folgen, und er fühlte
sein Herz nicht rascher schlagen als sonst. Mit den Augen folgte
er dem Lichte, das sich zu seinen Füßen in einer Lache ergoß.
Staubflocken leuchteten auf und ein kleines häßliches
Spinnengewebe. Weiterhin sickerte der Schein in die Fugen
zwischen den Balken und erstickte in einem staubigen, schmutzigen
Dämmern (70).

(With seeming indifference he looked at the floor in front of him.
He did not strain his ears to hear the sounds and he did not feel
his pulse beating faster than usual. His eyes followed the light
which spilled into a pool at his feet. Specks of dust glinted,
as did an ugly little spider's web. Further off the light
trickled into the beam joints and was stifled in a dusty dirty
twilight.)

What makes this passage so powerful is that it describes a moment of

dynamic deadlock between intellectuality and sensuality, between the

urge to know and the urge for violent release of tension; close

reading reveals that several of the elements which are described

objectively in this paragraph have a special weight in Törleß's
subjectivity.   Since he associates sex with the dirt of the peasants'
houses, the dirt and dust of his present surroundings are, for him, a
sexual allusion. [39]   Within the same scene the narrator follows up
two more allusions.   Törleß is not unmoved by the sounds of the
beating which he appeared to ignore - in fact he is sensually aroused
by Basini's whimpering: 'Törleß fühlte sich durch diese klagenden
Laute angenehm berührt.   Wie mit Spinnenfüßen lief ihm ein Schauer
den Rücken hinauf und hinunter;   dann saß es zwischen den
Schulterblättern fest und zog mit feinen Krallen seine Kopfhaut nach
hinten' (70) (my emphasis) ('Törleß was pleasantly affected by these
sounds of complaint.   A shiver like the touch of spider feet ran up
and down his back; then it halted, sat between his shoulder blades
and, with delicate claws, drew the skin of his scalp back' (my
emphasis).)

    Sensual excitement is experienced through the image of spiders
whose webs he has seen in the light of the lamp.   The lamplight
itself is worked into the mesh of Törleß's perception - indeed it is
an image of that struggling perceptive power itself.   A few lines
later we read: 'Beineberg bückte sich und wollte die Lampe aufheben.
Törleß hielt seinen Arm zurück.   <<Ist das nicht wie ein Auge?>>
sagte er und wies auf den über den Boden fließenden Lichtschein (...)
<<(...)Aus (Augen) wirkt (...) mitunter eine Kraft, die in keinem
Physikunterricht ihren Platz hat (...)   Mir ist dieses Licht wie ein
Auge.   Zu einer fremden Welt (...)>>' (71) ('Beineberg bent down and

was about to pick up the lamp. Törleß held his arm back <<Isn't that like an eye?>> he said and pointed to the light flowing over the floor. (...) <<(...) There are times when, through (the eyes) comes a force that isn't found in any physics lesson (...) To me this light seems like an eye. An eye looking into a strange world (...)>>').

A quotation from Plotinus which Musil copied into his diary for 1904-1905 clearly provided the inspiration for this notion:

Wenn (der Intellekt) die Objekte vergißt, welche (er) betrachtet, u. nur die Klarheit anschaut, die diese sichtbar macht, sieht er das Licht selbst u. das Prinzip des Lichts. Aber nicht außer sich betrachtet der Intellekt das intelligible Licht. Er gleicht darin dem Auge, das ohne äußeres ... Licht ...wahrzunehmen, plötzlich von einer Klarheit getroffen wird, die ihm selbst eignet (...) (TbI,135).[40]

(When (the intellect) forgets the objects which it is observing, and only examines the brightness which makes them visible, it sees the light itself and the principle of the light. But it is not outside itself that the intellect observes the intelligible light. In this it is like the eye which, without perceiving ... external .... light, is suddenly struck by a brightness which is of itself.)

Here then, in this crucial scene, Törleß experiences the tug-of-war between the strong forces within his psyche, namely Dionysian abandon and a visionary quality which reaches out towards the realm of the mystical.

Thus the narrator makes the reader sensitive to the charge of significance which particular things have for Törleß. But there is another way in which Musil avoids the difficulties of words and their meanings which obsess Törleß. He builds into the narrative a representation of the way words function, to show how they create meanings. Geoffrey Leech explains in his work, Semantics, that one of the ways in which words represent objects and characteristics of objects is by antithesis: 'small' is meaningful in its relationship with 'big', 'hot' in its link with 'cold'. Words can thus be arranged on a linguistic scale representing some aspect of reality. [41] Musil makes use of a similar principle in his creation of a structure of significance to help the reader to make sense of Törleß's confusions. The novel starts with the antithesis between that which can be perceived and that which cannot, between the 'here' of the railway station and the rails which, in geometric perfection, disappear into eternity: 'Eine kleine Station an der Strecke, welche nach Rußland führt (...) Endlos gerade liefen vier parallele Eisenstränge nach beiden Seiten zwischen dem gelben Kies des breiten Fahrdammes' (7) ('A small stop on the line which goes to Russia (...) Endlessly straight, four parallel iron rails run in both directions between the yellow gravel of the broad track').

The message here is that man is a maker. He marks out his designs on the open spaces of eternity. The vast purity of snow is crossed by the symbol of nineteenth-century man: [42] the parallel iron tracks with their dirt and noise and busy human activity. Musil impresses the image of the railway on the reader: it marks the beginning and the end of the narrative. The train becomes a symbol

of certainty: of all points of the compass a train can travel at a
given moment only towards one; thus it can represent the act of going
in one direction rather than any other. In other words, the train
here stands for the finite set against a vision of the infinite.

Musil does not let us lose sight of this, it is one axis of the
work. [43] When Törleß , with all his options before him, submits to
the 'direction' of an older youth and follows in his footsteps (it
is, in fact, Beineberg - in view of what later happens, Törleß could
scarcely have chosen a worse 'leader') the wording 'ohne miteinander
zu sprechen, schlugen sie einen bestimmten Weg ein' (26) ('without
saying anything to each other they took a specific path') reinforces
the sense of the antithesis of the definite with the indefinite, the
finite with the infinite.   Similarly, after the scene where masters
interrogate Törleß and attempt to fit his sentences into their frames
of reference, Törleß's gaze goes out through the window to a crow
sitting on a branch surrounded by snow-covered space.   Inside we have
the school with its rigorous shaping of the minds of the young to the
interests of the existing social order; we have teachers who
represent disciplines involving long training within the confines of
abstruse theories; we have the building itself with its boxed-in,
man-made, architectural geometry; [44] outside, there is the crow with
nowhere and everywhere to go across a blank landscape where the
evidence of man has been obliterated: 'Draußen vor dem Fenster saß
eine Krähe auf einem Ast, sonst war nichts als die weiße, riesige
Fläche' (136) ('Outside, in front of the window, a crow sat on a

branch, otherwise there was nothing but the huge white plane').

Thus, through antithesis (definite/indefinite, finite/infinite, open/closed, freedom/bondage) the narrator traces the way in which Törleß drafts the contours of experiences that cause him anxiety; the narrator takes the measure of things that trouble Törleß precisely by measuring them with words . As Törleß leaves the station to return to the village with some fellow-pupils, it is as if all that he does is governed by that force which lies in wait for all who relax their effort of will. A single page of narrative - page sixteen - bristles with references to the influence of some kind of necessity on Törleß:

> Törleß sah nicht rechts noch links, aber er fühlte es. Schritt für Schritt trat er in die Spuren, die soeben erst vom Fuße des Vordermanns in dem Staube aufklafften, - und so fühlte er es: als ob es so sein müßte: als einen steinernen Zwang, der sein ganzes Leben in diese Bewegung - Schritt für Schritt - auf dieser einen Linie, auf diesem einen schmalen Streifen, der sich durch den Staub zog, einfing und zusammenpreßte.
> (....)
> (....) bei jedem Schritte, der ihn der Enge des Institutes nähertrug, schnürte sich etwas immer fester in ihm zusammen.
> Jetzt schon klang ihm das Glockenzeichen in den Ohren. Nichts fürchtete er nämlich so sehr wie dieses Glockenzeichen, das unwiderruflich das Ende des Tages bestimmte - wie ein brutaler Messerschnitt.
> (....)
> Nun kannst du gar nichts mehr erleben, während zwölf Stunden kannst du nichts mehr erleben, für zwölf Stunden bist du tot ...
> (16) (my emphases).

> (Törleß did not look to right or left but he felt it. Step by step he trod in the prints which had just been opened up in the dust by the feet of the boy in front of him, - and this was how he felt: as if it had to be so: as a petrified compulsion which caught his whole life up in this movement and pressed it together into this movement - step by step - on this line, on this narrow strip which was drawn through the dust.
> (....)
> (....) With every step which brought him closer to the

confinement of the institute, something within him contracted,
drawing tighter and tighter.
     The school bell was already ringing in his ear.   For he
feared nothing as much as this bell, which set an irrevocable end
to the day - like a brutal knife stroke.
     (....)
     Now you can experience nothing more, for twelve hours you
can experience nothing more, for twelve hours you are dead...' (my
emphases).)

Necessity is one end of an axis; at the other is a freedom so

total that it sometimes verges on existential Angst.[45]   What is

Törleß to make of time that moves in ways that no watch can record

when he has been released from school?   What is he to make of the

inner world of sensations, feelings and thoughts which seems as

disorganised and chaotic as the outer world is regimented and fixed?[46]

So labile are young people, the narrator argues, that they have to

borrow feelings from the characters they read about in books;   this

helps them 'über den gefährlich weichen seelischen Boden dieser Jahre

hinweg. (....)   Wenn man da solch einem jungen Menschen das

Lächerliche seiner Person zur Einsicht bringen könnte, so würde der

Boden unter ihm einbrechen, oder er würde wie ein erwachter

Nachtwandler herabstürzen, der plötzlich nichts als Leere sieht' (13)

('to cross the dangerously soft psychic ground of these years (....).

If one were able to make a young person like that aware of how

ridiculous he appeared, the ground under him would collapse or he

would fall headlong like a somnambulist, roused from sleep, who

suddenly sees only the void').   What principles, what rules can be

found within Törleß's psyche, what 'closure' has taken place within

Törleß that might help him to detect some habitual shape to his

thoughts and feelings?   He cannot find any.   He is troubled as we
have seen, by the idea of 'character', and perceives that the boys who
most impress him, Beineberg and Reiting, can be identified by the
definite shape to their personalities - he can find nothing in himself
that corresponds to that.

       As Törleß's mind stretches it makes even more ambitious efforts
to encompass the unknowns that fill it with anxiety, driven by the
hope that, ultimately, all will be explained, his anxiety will be
banished, the 'method' will ultimately triumph.   His expectations are
born of the optimism of the nineteenth century that will not last long
into the twentieth.   Törleß hopes he will find certainty;   the
narrator knows he will not.   Törleß's focussing on the idea of
infinity as he gazes into the depths of the sky are part of an
energetic quest to grasp the ultimate, to make the world into
somewhere with final frontiers, to be 'at home' within it.   Nowhere
does he find that limit and, despite his youth, he sees through those
who appear to be at home in their worlds. [47]   The narrator makes
plain that such order is artificial, a construction which William
Blake describes in his poem, Jerusalem:

    'The Spectre is the Reasoning Power in Man, when separated
    From Imagination and closing itself as in steel (....)
    (....)   It thence frames Laws and Moralities
    To destroy Imagination (....)'. [48]

65

Blake's words provide the appropriate perspective from which to view

the first scene of Die Verwirrungen des Zöglings Törleß when Törleß's

parents are about to leave from the railway station:

> Gegenstände und Menschen hatten etwas Gleichgültiges, Lebloses,
> Mechanisches an sich, als seien sie aus der Szene eines
> Puppentheaters genommen. Von Zeit zu Zeit, in gleichen
> Intervallen, trat der Bahnhofsvorstand aus seinem Amtszimmer
> heraus, sah mit der gleichen Wendung des Kopfes die weite Strecke
> hinauf nach den Signalen der Wächterhäuschen, die immer noch nicht
> das Nahen des Eilzuges anzeigen wollten, der an der Grenze große
> Verspätung erlitten hatte; mit ein und derselben Bewegung des
> Armes zog er sodann seine Taschenuhr hervor, schüttelte den Kopf
> und verschwand wieder; so wie die Figuren kommen und gehen, die
> aus alten Turmuhren treten, wenn die Stunde voll ist (7).

> (Objects and people had something indifferent, lifeless and
> mechanical about them as if they had been taken from the stage of
> a puppet theatre. From time to time, in equal intervals, the
> station master left his office and, with the same motion of his
> head, looked up the long stretch of track towards the signals at
> the watchman's hut, which still did not want to indicate the
> approach of the express which had been seriously delayed at the
> border; with one and the same motion of the arm he then drew out
> his pocket watch, shook his head and disappeared again; coming
> and going just like the figures which step out of old tower clocks
> when the hour comes round.)

This description captures, as Uwe Baur expresses it, 'den starren

Gleichlauf normierten Daseins' ('the rigid equilibrium of life run

according to norms'); [49] the norms are artefacts that tyrannise the

people who made them.

In Die fröhliche Wissenschaft, a work which we know Musil read

as an adolescent, Nietzsche describes a scene in a market place. A

madman enters carrying a lantern and cries out that he is looking for

God. [50] Since it is broad daylight and most of the by-standers are

untroubled non-believers - those who, as Blake said, are governed by
the 'Spectre of the Reasoning Power in Man' but who find nothing wrong
in that - they find this search for God by the light of a lantern
rather diverting and break out in loud laughter.   This rouses the
madman to a furious outburst against them: 'Gott ist tot! Gott bleibt
tot! Und wir haben ihn getötet' ('God is dead!   God stays dead!
And we have killed Him!'). [51]   In this image Nietzsche presents the
contrast between those who see in the spread of atheism nothing more
than a cultural development which does not really concern them, and
those who, like this 'madman', grasp the wider cultural and historical
implications of the passing of belief - the void of unmeaning that
belief leaves behind it.   Where are we now, the madman rants,
'Stürzen wir nicht fortwährend?   Und rückwärts, seitwärts, vorwärts,
nach allen Seiten?   Gibt es noch ein Oben und Unten?   Irren wir
nicht wie durch ein unendliches Nichts' ('Are we not falling
continuously?   Backwards, sidewards, forwards, to all sides?   Do
Above and Below exist any longer?   Are we not wandering hopelessly as
if through an unending nothingness?') [52]   Behind the account of the
effect of Basini's disgrace on Törleß we can distinguish a sensibility
that is alive to what Nietzsche's madman was saying.   We remember
that, when Törleß heard that Basini was a thief, he was seized by a
sensation which is described in the following image: 'eine Falltüre
hatte sich geöffnet, und Basini war gestürzt' (46) ('a trap-door had
opened and Basini had fallen').   Basini has not simply fallen through
some stage trap-door to crumple in a heap somewhere out of sight; he

has fallen completely through the universe of Törleß's social
categories. He has gone out into the void. In body he remains at
the academy; in spirit he now falls through the infinity of the
madman's space. It is partly this that makes him an object of such
strange fascination for Törleß. For surely he must know, Törleß
thinks - since even now Basini is falling - what it is like to be
utterly lost, to lose one's grip on the certainties of contemporary
life, on the morality of one's class, on the sense of belonging to a
community embracing family, friends, schoolmates, the members of one's
social estate. (It does not affect the argument here that Basini has
experienced nothing of the sort - that, intellectually and
emotionally, he is not made for such experiences. [53] The point is
that Törleß for a while thinks that Basini has experienced this.)

Törleß is on the verge of a breakdown. We have to read closely
to recognise the signs. He cannot suppress his sexuality even though
this seems to lead to the loss of the love of his family and his
self-respect. Even sleep does not bring relief, for in sleep lurks
the fear of death. [54] In his fear Törleß cuts himself off from
others and retreats into himself - as he does in the scene when Basini
is whipped; in this terrible isolation, where others shrink to mere
objects, Törleß loses contact with the human world. The path of
intellectuality, the 'method', leads out into the icy depths of
Pascal's space.

In 'Das Unanständige und Kranke in der Kunst' ('The Obscene and
the Sick as Subject-Matter of Creative Work') which was published a
few years after Die Verwirrungen des Zöglings Törleß , Musil wrote:
'Kunst zeigt, wo sie Wert hat, Dinge, die noch wenige gesehen haben
(...).   Sie sieht also auch an Geschehnissen, vor denen anderen
graut, Wertseiten, Zusammenhänge' (GWII,981) ('All art of value makes
manifest things which only a few have yet glimpsed (...)   Thus it
sees, even in events which fill others with horror, valuable aspects
and contexts').   I believe that Die Verwirrungen des Zöglings
Törleß, despite the flaws which we have noted, did indeed have the
effect which Musil describes here.   From the distasteful experiences
of an unfortunate youth Musil fashioned a work which challenged
conventional attitudes.   Through the medium of a bewildered and
deviant adolescent he made his readers face aspects of their own
repressed emotional experience: 'In Wahrheit gibt es keine
Perversität oder Unmoral, die nicht eine sozusagen korrelate
Gesundheit und Moral hätte.   Das setzt voraus, daß zu allen
Bestandteilen, aus denen sie sich aufbaut, analoge auch in der
gesunden (....) Seele sich finden' (GWII,982) ('In truth, there is no
perversity or immortality which does not have a, so-to-speak,
correlative state of health and morality.   This presupposes that, for
all the elements of which it is composed, analagous ones can be found
even in the healthy (....) psyche (Seele)').

Contemporary readers were presented in Die Verwirrungen des
Zöglings Törleß with a new vision of human subjectivity and a critical

view of the external world around them. To what extent the novel itself contributed to the new climate of awareness which we now associate largely with the influence of Freud and his followers is impossible to determine. However, it is perhaps a measure of this contribution, and of Musil's extraordinary modernity, that many present-day readers find little in this portrait of youth, drawn in the first few years of the twentieth century, which they would consider 'dated' or unconvincing.

Chapter 3   'VEREINIGUNGEN'

Background and Theory

In his diary on 8 September, 1910, Musil looked back with
disappointment on what he had achieved in the past five years: '(Die
Periode) 1905-1910 schließt mit einem Defizit an erreichten Zielen ab.
1905 noch der Törless, 1910 nichts' (TBI, 226). ('(The period)
1905-1910 finishes with a deficit in goals achieved. 1905 (there was)
still Törleß, 1910 nothing.') Perhaps his mood was influenced by his
failure, that same day, to persuade a director of a Berlin newspaper
to take him on as a literary critic - certainly he left out of account
in this 'balance sheet' his doctorate at the University of Berlin and
Alexius Meinong's offer of an assistantship at Graz. What he really
wanted, however, was a sense of making progress as a creative writer,
and his work on Vereinigungen (which means 'Unions' in both a sexual
and spiritual sense), two short stories, was going very slowly.

Other things besides writing were competing for his attention.
He was reading very widely - Meister Eckehart, Novalis, Schopenhauer,
Nietzsche, Rilke, Goethe, Kleist, Baudelaire and Schnitzler - and
studying Hermeticism, Gnosticism and Manichaeism. [1] He was carrying
out, with himself as 'guinea-pig', informal but nonetheless intensive
research into human consciousness; as he wrote in a letter draft in
1907: 'mein Leben besteht in nichts anderem als auf die feinsten

Bewegungen in meinem Inneren zu achten' (<u>Briefe</u> I,39) ('my life is
made up of nothing but attention to the finest movements in my inner
self'). He regularly attended the art salon run by Paul Cassirer
(brother of the philosopher, Ernst Cassirer) who organised the first
showings of works by Van Gogh and Cezanne. It was here that he met
Martha Marcovaldi (nee Heimann), a painter, whom he later married.
Martha's influence on his creative work is crucial. Musil left her
out of his 'balance-sheet' for a special reason: 'Martha gehört nicht
in diese Rechnung, sie ist nichts, das ich gewonnen, erreicht habe,
sie ist etwas das ich geworden bin und das ich geworden ist' (TbI,226)
('Martha does not belong in this calculation, but she is not something
that I have won, (or) attained, she is something that I have become
and that has become "I"'). Their relationship was, from the
beginning, a source of inspiration and, indeed, of material for his
work. The two stories in <u>Vereinigungen</u> grew directly from this
relationship: 'Die Versuchung der stillen Veronika' from Martha's
life as an adolescent in an unusual household which included two male
cousins of about her age, [2] each of whom she was in love with at
different times; 'Die Vollendung der Liebe' from the trauma of Martha
and Robert adjusting to the experience of their mutual love given the
complexity of the love affairs that each had had before - indeed it
has been suggested that, like the woman in 'Die Vollendung der Liebe'
Martha was unfaithful to Musil shortly after they had met. [3]

In 1938 Musil wrote a brief commentary on <u>Vereinigungen</u>; making
no attempt to disguise the difficulties posed by the work he says:

Erschienen 1911. Musil verläßt in diesem Buch mit einem
entscheidenden Schritt die realistische Erzählungstechnik, die ihm
seinen Erfolg eingebracht hat, und stellt zwei Geschichten nicht
in der üblichen Schein-Kausalität dar, sondern so, daß die
Personen im Spiel höherer Notwendigkeiten erscheinen. Tief,
luzid, aber infolge mancher Eigenheiten schwer lesbar, leitete
dieses Buch, vielleicht durch Irrtum, den literarischen
Expressionismus in Deutschland ein, mit dem Musil aber weiterhin
nichts zu schaffen haben wollte' (GWII,950). [4]

(Appeared in 1911. In this book, Musil takes a decisive step away
from the realist narrative technique which brought him success and
offers two stories which function not, as is usual, on the level
of a pseudo-causality but in which the characters appear subject
to a higher necessity. Deep, lucid, but as a result of some
eccentricities, difficult to read, this book introduced, perhaps
by mistake, literary Expressionism to Germany - but Musil wanted
to have nothing further to do with the movement.)

Musil thought of his own work as unique; he did not like to be

considered a member of any literary school or movement - to this

extent his reference to Expressionism is typical. But leading

Expressionists saw in Vereinigungen a work which was very much akin to

their own. [5] It is, if only implicitly, a work of protest - Musil

challenges literary and social conventions: he seeks to alter both

the way men and women conceive of their lives and the linguistic means

through which such lives are rendered in a prose narrative. Like

Expressionists Musil searches for a new mode of living, for the 'Neuer

Mensch' ('New Human Being'). However, Musil goes his own way. He

felt that, although the Expressionists insisted that their work

exposed the irrationality of contemporary society, they themselves

tended to sacrifice rationality in favour of an excess of feeling.

They saw their writing as explosive, and indeed their works were

imposing displays of pyrotechnics, but ultimately the effects were disappointing. Musil, by contrast, laid small but deadly charges where they would do the most damage: he tried to dynamite the structure of personality itself, or, to be precise, the conventional fabric of assumptions from which men and women fashioned their attitudes to themselves and others. In this he is less Expressionist than literary anarchist.

If every contemporary author of like mind had expended as much effort on his or her writing as Musil, the collective effect on society as a whole would have been, no doubt, considerable. The difficulties which the reader faces pale beside those which the author faced in composition. Although the two stories amount to less than seventy pages of text in the edition of the Gesammelte Werke, Musil worked on them almost night and day for two and a half years. [6] If effort were a guarantee of literary quality then these stories would be masterpieces.

Musil seeks to capture feelings and thoughts which are so transitory, or so profound, that they barely touch the fringes of the consciousness of his characters. [7] It is clear that, in this phase of his life, artistic creation for Musil had taken on a quasi-religious significance; the act of writing is expressed in the image of worship. In a suppressed preface to the stories he writes: 'Der Kopf eines so Arbeitenden ist wie eine kahle Zelle, nackte Wände, die immer in den gleichen engen Raum hineinstarren, ein Fenster durch das man nichts als den leeren Himmel sieht. Aus solcher verbissenen

Wut und In-brunst mögen mittelalterlich-scholastische Gedankensysteme
entstanden sein, die sich selbst mit der Zahl der Haare der Engel
befaßten' (GWII,1313) ('The head of someone who works in this way is
like a bare cell, naked walls which always stare in on the same narrow
space, a window through which one sees nothing but the empty sky.   It
may have been through such dogged rage and fervour that
medieval-scholastic systems of ideas, concerned with how many hairs
there are on the heads of angels, took shape').

        It is difficult to overestimate the importance which Musil
attached to his work.   For those who approach him through Der Mann
ohne Eigenschaften he may seem at times to be supercilious and
ironical.   Certainly he is often scathing about his fellow-men and
their ways.   Yet throughout his work, and in Vereinigungen
particularly, he gives expression to a profound reverence for creation
which is akin to religious awe. [8]   Musil stands in the Lutheran
tradition; he brooks no intermediary between himself and the divine.
He tries repeatedly to lift to one side the attitudes, illusions, and
preconceptions of his fellows in order to make them confront the world
beyond.   To express this in the terms of a structuralist like Roland
Barthes, we might say that Musil was convinced that each culture
develops its own system of signs, its own ways of perceiving things
which the individual learns as he or she grows up within that culture;
Der Mann ohne Eigenschaften is, at one level, a study of such signs
in Austrian society.   But Musil believed that it was the duty of the
creative writer to help to guide readers through the signs and help

them to grasp the realities beyond them – to put the reader in closer
touch with the world.   In other words, far from confirming the
typical learning process of the integrated member of society, he
demands a process of unlearning: he seeks to alienate the reader from
cultural signs that have become too familiar, an obstacle to
understanding.   Works like Vereinigungen are conceived as part of the
'unlearning process'.   To express this another way: the 'facts'
which make up the cultural baggage of an age are largely fictions;   in
his fiction Musil wants to teach readers to distrust these 'facts'.
To confront the prevailing orthodoxy was no light enterprise;   Musil
could not expect a large audience.   Indeed, as Jürgen Schröder put
it, this was art with a sign 'No entry for unauthorised readers'! [9]

     To qualify, in this respect, for 'authorisation' readers need to
satisfy three conditions: they should be willing to accept that
Vereinigungen is a work in which the narrative plot is partly
suppressed, and almost peripheral to the author's concerns; they
should repress the urge to interpret the psychology of the characters
and concentrate on the substance of the experiences depicted rather
than search for some meaning hidden behind them (they should develop,
in other words, that immanent approach to life that the Zen master
tries to cultivate in his pupils by leading them away from
preoccupation with what lies beyond them towards attention to what
lies before them);   they must be willing to experience an intense
empathy with the characters concerned, suspending any moral judgement
based on convention, even where this leads them into a degradation

which they find abhorrent.

I have drawn up these principles on the basis of Musil's own
specifications which we will now consider in turn. On the question
of the plot he writes:

Man überschätzt die Schwierigkeit des 'Fabulierens' Keinem
Begabten darf sie groß sein. Steht das ideelle Gerüst fest, ist
es mit Szenen zu verkleiden, die entsprechend getönt sind. Jeder
Leitsatz könnte der Tenor einer Szene sein (....)
    Hier (in Vereinigungen) ist nur Konzentration fast
mathematischer Strenge, engstes Gedankenmosaik. Interessant die
Technik als Konsequenz der Grundeinstellung: Alles Erzählende ins
Beiwerk, Bild, Satz genommen' (GWII,1313-4).

(People tend to overestimate the difficulty of literary invention.
    No gifted person has much difficulty here. Once the framework
of ideas has been set up it has to be covered with scenes that
have the corresponding tone. Each lead-sentence could set the
tenor of a scene.
    Here (in Vereinigungen) there is only concentration of
almost mathematical rigour, the most precise thought mosaic. Of
interest is technique as a consequence of the basic attitude: all
narrative absorbed in peripherals, image, sentence.)

This stress on the structure at the expense of the content is rather
like the emphasis in a symbolist poem on words which negate the
substantial and divorce themselves from the material world, thereby
creating a purely linguistic structure of significance. [10] Musil,
however, 'rubs out' external action not in order to escape from the
world but to focus on aspects of it that are commonly neglected,
namely feelings and thoughts.

In his discussion of the reader's urge to probe beneath thoughts
and feelings 'to get at the truth beneath', Musil draws a distinction

between what he sees as the narrative of 'causation', where the author
not only portrays the actions and thoughts of his or her characters
but speculates on the motives behind their actions, and his own
emphasis in Vereinigungen on a 'purer' narrative.   In his narrative
we find 'Das Zurückdrängen des Causalen (... und) das Vortreten des
Bildlichen' (GWII,1322) ('The repression of the causal (...) (and) the
emphasising of the image'). He makes it clear that what interests him
in Vereinigungen is not theories about human life but as accurate a
representation as possible of the experiences of particularly
sensitive and introverted characters who concentrate not so much on
external life but on consciousness itself. [11]   So attempts to
theorise on the motivations of the characters in Vereinigungen, like
attempts to construct a clear line of external plot, run counter to
Musil's intentions in the composition of the works.   Perhaps this
notion can be expressed most clearly by contrasting Musil's approach
to dreams with that of Freud.   Musil, in his diary, attempts to
reconstruct the dream itself as the dreamer originally dreamt it; [12]
for Freud, the reconstruction of the dream (the 'Trauminhalt' ('dream
content')) is only a stage in the process of discovering the impulses
at work behind the dream (the 'Traumgedanke' ('dream idea')). [13]
There is a further important difference: Musil writes of
Vereinigungen: 'Ich hatte den Weg zu beschreiben, der von einer
innigsten Zuneigung beinahe bloß binnen 24 Stunden zur Untreue führt.
Es sind psychologisch hundert und tausend Wege.' (GWII,972). ('I had to
describe the path which leads, within virtually only 24 hours, from
the most intimate feeling for someone to infidelity.   In

psychological terms there are a hundred, a thousand paths'). Where
Freud presented the particular actions that a patient has performed as
determined by psychological mechanisms set in motion by earlier
traumatic experiences, Musil believed that the functioning of the mind
was far more complex. It could not be grasped in terms of any
mechanism however intricate; no psychologist, however skilled, would
ever be able to trace the exact causation of an action. This, in any
case, was not what Musil wanted to do; he wanted to describe the
process itself, the emotional steps from one inner point to another:
'Da bildete sich in mir die Entscheidung, den <<maximal belasteten
Weg>> zu wählen / den Weg der kleinsten Schritte / den Weg des
allmählichsten, unmerklichsten Übergangs' (GWII,972) ('Then I slowly
came to the decision to take the <<path of maximum difficulty>> / the
path of the shortest steps / the path of the most gradual, the most
imperceptible transition'). The way to do this was through
self-observation and close and intimate observation of, and discussion
with, his collaborator in this literary enterprise, Martha Musil.
But even when Musil had identified and examined the emotions
themselves there remained the problem of how to transmit them to the
reader. Musil had a theory of how this could be brought about
through empathy.

Empathy Musil divides into separate components: first what he
calls the 'suggestive Wirkungen' (GWII,1321) ('suggestive effects'),
in other words, the narrator's implicit imperative to the reader to
experience the events of the text as if they were real; second, the

act of understanding in which 'sich die im Hörer das Gelesene
begleitenden Gefühlsketten oft aus ganz anderen eigenen Erlebnissen
zusammen(setzten)' (GWII,1321) ('chains of feelings with which the
audience accompanies the reading that are often made up from quite
different experiences of their own') whereby the reader 'cannibalises'
his or her own emotions and grafts feelings onto the narrative (but,
all the time, the reader remains aware that what is put together in
this way is 'ein Fremdes ' (GWII,1321) '(something outside oneself');
finally the third component which may seem to be part of the act of
understanding is 'Billigung, das Erschüttertwerden udgl. (welches)
gerade darauf beruht, daß man das Erzählte wie etwas neues Eigenes
fühlt' (GWII,1321) ('approval, the sense of being deeply moved etc.
(which) relies precisely on the feeling that what is related is a new
experience of one's own') - where the experience of the other is
integrated fully into the field of the reader's own experience. [14]
In other words, Musil argues, 'Das Verstehen eines Menschen heißt, ihn
aus Elementen der eigenen Erfahrung aufbauen' (GWII,1322) (my
emphasis) ('Understanding a human being means building him or her up
out of elements of one's own experiences' (my emphasis)). This
principle is one to which Musil holds in all his works.

These demands on the reader's powers of empathy have moral
implications. As we have seen above, Musil's narrative demands a
suspension of conventional moral judgment on the part of the reader.
For Musil, such contemporary morality was part of the system of
social signs which he considered outmoded and illusory. He

considered the prevailing moral system to be deductive, relying on
precepts which were themselves ambiguous and which were often
interpreted with self-indulgent latitude by pillars of the
establishment.   His own feeling - and it was scarcely more than that
- was that true morality involved not deduction from precepts but a
kind of ethical guess-work; not action by admonition but by intuition.
In the absence of guide-lines, however, even abhorrent actions - and
in the case of Vereinigungen this includes sodomy - may, in given
circumstances, be sanctioned by intuition.   No doubt the majority of
readers will feel that this is to stretch moral innovation too -
though the legislators of the Federal Republic of Germany seem to have
followed Musil's lead and removed this offence from the statute books.

Whatever our view of his attitude to morality, we must respect
his will to reach down to the most fundamental levels of human
consciousness.   In Musil's 'archaeology' of perception, he finds at
the surface 'Temperamente, Charaktere' (GWII,1314) ('temperaments,
characters'); when he digs further down to a deeper level at which
great dramas and novels function 'haben die Ehrlichen Flecken von
Schuftigkeit, die Schufte Flecken von Ehrlichkeit' (GWII,1314) ('the
upright have touches of blackguardry, the blackguards touches of
uprightness'), in other words, that reservoir of feeling is reached on
which all humans draw, there are no distinctions of personality or
temperament, there is no conventional morality or taboo. [15]   It was
this level - accessible to those with a profound faculty of empathy -
that Musil hoped some readers of Vereinigungen would reach.

Analysis of a sample of 'Vereinigungen' text

Before examining the two 'Novellen' which form Vereinigungen it
is instructive to submit a passage from the work to close scrutiny;
in this way we gain insight into the detail of the work, and can
better understand why Musil took so long to complete it.   The passage
in question was originally selected by Jacqueline Magnou to illustrate
aspects of the structure of 'Die Vollendung der Liebe'; [16] as we shall
see below, it does indeed provide excellent insight into the creative
process behind Vereinigungen.   Instead of presenting the passage in
the form in which it appears in the 'Novelle' - namely as a normal
piece of prose narrative - Jacqueline Magnou sets it out in such a
way that the linguistic patterns appear in sharp relief. Mme Magnou
identifies the dominant principle of linguistic organisation in this
passage: feelings roll in upon the subject like a series of waves -
an effect which Musil achieved by employing parataxis and
juxtaposition of words and expressions.   I have made only minor
changes below in her graphic presentation of the passage; I have
concentrated, however, less on structure 'per se' and more on the
substance, the meaning of the passage.   Thus my findings complement
hers.   (The alphabetic sequence of letters in the text refers to my
footnotes.)   In this passage I have adopted Mme Magnou's practice and
underlined the words and particles which signify negation, thus
emphasising the extent to which Musil is creating a structure of
meaning through words which, though having a clear logical function,

do not refer to things in the external world. It may be that we are
reminded here of the techniques of the symbolists who wanted to escape
into a purely formal world of words; however, here Musil is, in
contrast to them, attempting to focus attention on actual experiences.
What he wishes to avoid, in my view, is words which conceal rather
than reveal aspects of experience; here any injudicious choice of
words - purporting to identify directly the experience at the centre
of this passage - would be a distortion of that experience, which is
inherently intangible. What Musil does is entirely fitting here: he
conveys that familiar sense of being on the very threshold of
identifying a particular feeling or thought, without however quite
managing to catch hold of it. He does so by means of words which
somehow both blur and delineate the contours of the world - which
affirm, in the act of denying. Or, to express it in the words of
Jacqueline Magnou, 'Musil (...) löst (das Paradoxon) durch die Sprache
etwas zum Ausdruck zu bringen, was im Text selbst als "unsagbar"
charakterisiert wird' [17] ('Musil solves (the problem) of expressing in
the text something that is characterised in the text itself as
'unsayable'). The passage in question is as follows:
(The English translation with corresponding footnotes will be found a
few pages below in my text.)

Da fühlte sie, (a) daß hier sich etwas vollenden sollte, (b)
und wurde nicht gewahr, wie lange sie so stand; Viertelstunden,
      Stunden..
..die Zeit lag <u>reglos</u>,
                  von <u>unsichtbaren</u> Quellen gespeist,
                  wie ein <u>uferloser</u> See (c) <u>ohne</u> Mündung und
                              Abfluß
     um sie.
Nur einmal, irgendwann, glitt
       irgendwo
     von diesem <u>unbegrenzten</u> Horizont (d) her
             etwas Dunkles durch ihr Bewußtsein, (e)
      (f)   ein Gedanke,
             ein Einfall,

---

a) Here the pronoun is a provisional mark of identity for a person
whose self-perception, as we see towards the end of the passage (see
note (m) below), is anything but secure.

b) The verb 'sich vollenden' suggests the slow working-out of some
process; the passage relies more heavily on verbs than on nouns, and
so gives an impression of change, movement and, thereby, elusiveness.
The verb 'sich vollenden' stands out as a reminder of the title of the
story and also anticipates the verbal noun 'Vollendung' later in the
passage.

c) Musil establishes a word-link between two areas of human
experience which defy accurate measure: time is seen through the image
of the sea. Both are formless - Musil, unlike Newton, sees time as
an unfathomable element.

d) The oxymoron 'unbegrenzte(..) Horizont' gives precise form to the
problem which Musil is exploring here.   The subject is looking for
some context, a boundary within which to find a measure of security -
she finds none.   Here the mystery of the context of things is
expressed in the image of space which knows no bounds, which has
neither beginning nor end; above it was expressed in the element of
time which stretches from the tip of her perception to eternity.

e) Musil here gives expression to his sense of the unpredictability
of this thought, which arrives unbidden from its unknown origin.

f) Here, by juxtaposing words and phrases, Musil does not state
categorically 'she had an idea'; rather he 'conveys' the idea with
reverence and caution, as if to say: 'Look what linguistic lengths I
have to go to in order to make the reader aware of what a strange
thing it is when an idea occurs to a person'.   He uses the same
technique at several points in this extract, indeed throughout the two
'Novellen' juxtaposition of this kind is found repeatedly.

... und wie es an ihr vorbeizog, erkannte sie die Erinnerung darin an
      lang versunkene Träume ihres früheren Lebens
- sie glaubte sich von Feinden gefangen (g) und war gezwungen,
      demütige Dienste zu tun -
und währenddessen begann es schon zu entschwinden
         und schrumpfte ein
und aus der dunstigen Unklarheit der Weite hob sich ein letztesmal,
      wie gespenstisch klar geknotetes Stangen- und Tauwerk
      eins nach dem andern darüber hinaus,
und es fiel ihr ein, wie sie sich _nie_ wehren gekonnt,
        wie sie aus dem Schlaf schrie,
        wie sie schwer und dumpf gekämpft,
     bis ihr die Kraft und die Sinne schwanden,
        dieses ganze _maßlose,_
           formlose Elend ihres Lebens, (h)
...und dann war es vorbei
und in der wieder zusammenfließenden Stille
     war nur ein Leuchten,
        eine veratmend zurückstreichende Welle, (i)
als wäre ein _Unsagbares_ gewesen, (j)
... und da kam es jetzt plötzlich von dort (k) über sie

---

g) The sense of the violation of the inwardness of the self from
external forces is essential, not only to this passage, but to Musil's
thinking as a whole; this memory leads into the phrase below in the
text 'dieses (...) formlose Elend ihres Lebens', symbolising her sense
of helplessness and vulnerability.

h) within the structure of the passage 'dieses (...) formlose Elend'
is the expression towards which the words and phrases at points d) and
f) are pointing; in terms of the meaning of the passage, it appears
that 'dieses formlose Elend' is the source of the idea which we have
just seen taking shape in her consciousness.

i) Here the image of the wave which, as Jacqueline Magnou shows, is
implicit in the structure of the passage, is made explicit.

j) Musil makes explicit the problem of expression which has been
pursuing him throughout this passage and throughout the work as a
whole.

k) This 'dort' is not a place but an absence of any place - it refers
to the 'unbegrenzten Horizont' above, the unnameable source of the
subject's thinking and feeling.

- wie einstens diese schreckliche Wehrlosigkeit ihres Daseins
  hinter den Träumen, fern,
      unfaßbar,
      im Imaginären, (1)
  noch ein zweitesmal lebte -
eine Verheißung,
ein Sehnsuchtsschimmer,
eine niemals gefühlte Weichheit,
ein Ichgefühl, (m) das - von der fürchterlichen Unwiderruflichkeit
  ihres Schicksals nackt,
     ausgezogen,
     seiner selbst entkleidet -
während es taumelnd nach immer tieferen Entkräftungen
       verlangte,
sie dabei seltsam wie der in sie verirrte,
     mit zielloser Zärtlichkeit seine
       Vollendung suchende
  Teil einer Liebe (n)
verwirrte,
      für die es in der Sprache
des Tags und des harten,
    aufrechten Ganges noch kein Wort gab. (o)
    (GWII,173-174)

---

1) Here the technique of juxtaposition is more patent than elsewhere
in the passage - the narrator casts around repeatedly for the words
that will fit the sensation, but, to judge from the words at the end
of the sentence, is not successful.

m) This apparently substantial 'Ichgefühl' will be partially 'rubbed
out' in the words and phrases which subsequently qualify it.

n) 'Liebe' is both the subject of the work as a whole and the climax
of this passage.

o) Here, Musil gives yet another reminder of the narrator's intrinsic
problem in dealing with such subject-matter.

Then she felt (a) that here something was to be completed, (b) and was
not aware how long she stood like that; whole quarters of an hour,
     hours..
..time lay <u>without</u> moving,
              fed from <u>unseen</u> springs,
              like a lake with <u>no</u> sides (c) <u>without</u> mouth
                                    or outlet
     around her.
Only once, at sometime or other, slid,
         somewhere or other,
     from this horizon <u>without</u> limits (d)
         something dark into her consciousness, (e)
     (f)   a thought,
                an idea,

---

a) Here the pronoun is a provisional mark of identity for a person
whose self-perception, as we see towards the end of the passage (see
note (m) below), is anything but secure.

b) The passage relies more heavily on verbs than on nouns, and so
gives an impression of change, movement and, thereby, elusiveness.
The expression 'to be completed' stands out as a reminder of the title
of the story and also anticipates the verbal expression 'to become
complete', later in the passage.

c) Musil establishes a word-link between two areas of human
experience which defy accurate measure: time is seen through the image
of the sea. Both are formless - Musil, unlike Newton, sees time as
being like the sea; both are elements which noone can fathom.

d) The oxymoron 'horizon without limits' gives precise form to the
problem which Musil is exploring here.   The subject is looking for
some context, a boundary within which to find a measure of security -
she finds none.   Here the mystery of the context of things is
expressed in the image of space which knows no bounds, which has
neither beginning nor end; above, it was expressed in the element of
time which stretches from the tip of her perception to eternity.

e) Musil here gives expression to his sense of the unpredictability
of this thought, which arrives unbidden from its unknown origin.

f) Here by juxtaposing words and phrases Musil does not state
categorically 'she had an idea'; rather he 'conveys' the idea with
reverence and caution, as if to say: 'Look what linguistic lengths I
have to go to in order to make the reader aware of what a strange
thing it is when an idea occurs to a person'.   He uses the same
technique at several points in this extract - indeed, throughout both
'Novellen', juxtaposition of this kind is found repeatedly.

... and as it passed by her she recognised a memory within it of
        long submerged dreams of her life earlier
- she believed she was captured by enemies (g) and was forced,
        to perform humble services -
and, meanwhile, it was already starting to recede
                and wither away
and from the misty vagueness far away arose, for a last time, with
        ghostly clarity,
                what seemed like a network of poles and ropes
                        one after the other emerging above it,
and it occurred to her how she had never been able to resist,
                how she screamed from her sleep,
                how she fought hard and indistinctly,
        until strength and senses disappeared,
                this whole, measureless,
                        formless wretchedness that was her
                                        life, (h)
... and then it was over
and in the stillness flowing in again there was only
        a glow,
        a receding breath of a retreating wave, (i)
as if something unsayable had been there (j)
and then, suddenly, something from there (k) came over her

----

g) The sense of the violation of the inwardness of the self from
external forces is essential, not only to this passage, but to Musil's
thinking as a whole; this memory leads into the phrase below in the
text 'this (...) formless wretchedness that was her life', symbolising
her sense of helplessness and vulnerability.

h) Within the structure of the passage 'this (...) formless
wretchedness' is the expression towards which the words and phrases at
points d) and f) direct the reader's attention; in terms of the
meaning of the passage, it appears that 'this (...) formless
wretchedness' is the source of the idea which we have just seen taking
shape in her consciousness.

i) Here the image of the wave which, as Jacqueline Magnou shows, is
implicit in the structure of the passage, is made explicit.

j) Musil makes explicit the problem of expression which has been
pursuing him throughout this passage and throughout the work as a
whole.

k) This 'there' is not a place but an absence of any place - it
refers to the 'horizon without limits' above, the unnameable source of
the subject's thinking and feeling.

- as once that dreadful <u>defencelessness</u> of her existence
      behind the dreams, far off,
             beyond all reach,
             in the realm of the imaginary,   (1)
      lived for a second time -
a message of promise,
a shimmer of longing,
a softness <u>never</u> felt before,
a feeling of 'I' (m) that - from the fearsome irrevocability
      of her fate, naked,
             without any clothing,
             stripped of itself -
      while, reeling, it begged for ever more profound states
                       of <u>powerlessness</u>,
      left her in strange confusion
                 like some part of a love (n)
      which, lost within her, was searching with <u>aimless</u>
                 tenderness to become complete,
      and for which, in the language of the day
            and of hard,
                   upright onward-marching there is
still <u>no</u> word. (o) (my emphases)

----

1) Here the technique of juxtaposition is more patent than elsewhere
in the passage - the narrator casts around repeatedly for the words
that will fit the sensation, but, to judge from the words at the end
of the sentence, is not successful.

m) This apparently substantial sense of the 'I' will be partially
erased in the words and phrases which subsequently qualify it.

n) 'Love' is both the subject of the work as a whole and the climax
of this passage.

o) Here Musil gives yet another reminder of the narrator's intrinsic
problem in dealing with such subject-matter.

'Die Versuchung der stillen Veronika'

The narrative

'Die Versuchung der stillen Veronika' is commonly regarded as a 'Novelle'. [18] This prose form is frequently compared, in structural terms, with drama.   Here, in 'Die Versuchung der stillen Veronika', there are, to keep to this idiom, four 'dramatis personae'. Veronika, a young woman who fears that she may be on the way to becoming an old maid; Veronika's aunt, an old maid; Johannes, a young man who has a priestlike and somehow anaemic air about him; Demeter, a vigorous, earthy fellow.   The elements of dramatic action appear to be present: Johannes, after desperate heart-searching with Veronika whom he loves and who seems to love him, goes off to commit suicide and Veronika is left in the house with the other male who, in close-fitting riding breeches, exudes a seemingly irresistible sexuality.   The stage is set for a dramatic unfolding of action. Will Johannes commit suicide?   What will Veronika do if he does? Will the vigorous Demeter have his way with poor Veronika?   But such questions, only the first two of which are explicity answered, focus attention on the wrong issue - namely the action.   In this narrative Musil is concerned, as we have seen, with what his characters think and feel rather than with what they do.   Indeed, one has the impression that, if that had been possible, he would have dispensed with the 'characters' altogether as entities that tend to divert the reader's attention from his central concerns. [19]

Musil admitted that, in narrative terms, he had gone too far in 'Die Versuchung der stillen Veronika'. He explains: 'Die Schwäche war, daß in diesem Nichtgeschehen, das eine immer länger werdende Motivkette umspannen mußte, das Äußere überdehnt wurde' (GWII,973) ('The weakness was that, given the "non-action" which had to embrace a chain of motives which got longer and longer, the externals were stretched too far'). It was to be expected that there would be tension between Musil's demanding work and readers with orthodox and leisurely expectations of prose writing. In 'Die Versuchung der stillen Veronika' there are barely two dozen lines of narrative action. (Surely Musil must have reckoned with this kind of response? He knew what he wanted to achieve, but the vast majority of his readers did not. It would not be unfair to accuse him of negligence. Musil makes no concessions, leaving his readers struggling in the unfamiliar element of this strange writing.) [20] The readers tend to seize hold of the few fragments of narrative action with relief, as familiar landmarks in a sea of feelings and reflections. More than a page elapses before the first modest 'landmark' appears: '(Johannes und Veronika) glitten in dem dunklen Haus aneinander vorbei' (195) ('(Johannes and Veronika) glided past each other in the dark house'). Even now, the reader, grown insecure and suspicious, wonders whether this is really what it seems - is 'Haus' perhaps a chiffre for the enclosed man-made restrictive setting that we found in Törleß's institute; does 'aneinandervorbeigleiten' ('gliding past each other') symbolise the frustrations of the attempts by human beings to penetrate the mystery of each other's existence? This may be so as well, but the reader finally does identify it, with relief, as a fixed point. Johannes and Veronika do indeed live in the same house. This narrative is partly, perhaps largely, about their relationship, but the relationship is so elusive that even further fixed points in the narrative seem to add very little to our understanding of it. 'Sie gingen aneinander vorbei; sie sahen einander an; sie wechselten belanglose oder suchende Worte - täglich' (202) ('They went past each other; they looked at each other; they exchanged inconsequential or searching words - each day'). They are evidently in love, but they part: 'Und dort stand, der heute noch abreisen sollte, Johannes, und da stand sie' (206) ('And there stood he who was to depart that day, Johannes, and there she stood'). Why do they part? The narrative provides no answer. Johannes has not been called away, he goes apparently of his own volition to take his own life. What is it that causes Veronika's feelings for Johannes to change to the point where her interest shifts towards Demeter even though she has received a letter from Johannes to say that he is still alive? Again, the narrative offers no satisfaction; there is just the vaguest hint, conveyed in the 'noch' ('yet') in the following statement, that Veronika's attention has now shifted decisively towards Johannes' rival: 'Und nach einer Weile gingen (Veronika und Demeter) weiter, ohne noch gesprochen zu haben' (223) ('And after a while (Veronika and Demeter) went on, without yet having spoken').

The reader, as we have seen, tends to be attached to aspects of narrative which Musil considers of minor importance; from Musil's perspective, the reader is like a visitor in an art gallery who insists on admiring the frames rather than the paintings. The reader is disposed by previous experience of narrative to ask about motivations: What prompts Johannes to want to commit suicide? Why does Veronika transfer her attentions from Johannes to Demeter? Musil expects him or her to look at experiences 'per se'; the reader wants to produce an image of them according to the kind of criteria that he or she uses in daily life: what do they look like, what sort of things do they do, are they good or bad? Musil wants the reader to concentrate on aspects of experience that usually remain hidden, even from those directly concerned – the subtle play of consciousness itself. Veronika, in this respect, is out-of-the-ordinary; she expresses Musil's point of view when she says: 'es kommt ja nur darauf an, daß man wie das Geschehen ist und nicht wie die Person, die handelt' (201)) [21] ('it is only a question of being like the action and not like the person who is involved in the action'). Thus this is a 'Novelle' written against the tide of current literary, and indeed social, practices: against the concern with outward actions at the expense of inwardness, with personality rather than the person, with the reasons behind behaviour rather than with behaviour itself. Unfortunately for the reception of Vereinigungen, the traditions which Musil was attacking remained very vigorous and indeed still inhibit an appreciation of the work today.

Imagery

The primary vehicle for conveying experience to the reader in
this narrative is the image. In a letter to Franz Blei, an author who
later became a close friend, Musil explains the vital role which
images have in Vereinigungen. 'Die Bilder gehören zum Knochenbau des
Buchs, nicht zu seiner Oberfläche, sie sind Bedeutungsträger' (Briefe
I,87) ('The images are not on the surface but part of the bone
structure of the book, they are carriers of meaning'). He goes on to
explain that the images are not analogies, in a common sense –
artificial constructions plucked by the author from his imagination to
expound something that might otherwise evade capture in words – he
claims that they are authentic and spontaneous elements of the inner
lives of the characters concerned: 'Die Vergleiche, Bilder, den Stil
diktiert nicht der Autor, sondern sie sind psychische Konstituenten
der Personen, deren Gefühlskreis sich in ihnen umschreibt' (GWI,87)
('The similes, images, style are dictated not by the author but are
rather psychic constituents of the people whose emotional field is
rendered by them'). Even when we have subtracted from this statement
a certain amount of credibility to compensate for its touch of
neo-Romantic inflation – and, after all, Musil's characters must be to
some extent creatures of his imagination, despite what he says here –
something important still remains. For Musil asserts here that at
least some of the images which appear in the work are lifted directly

from the emotional life of the people on whom the characters are
modelled: namely himself, Martha, and possibly some of the men she
knew. This, Musil claims, is literature that keeps unusually close to
life.

The images are of two kinds: implicit and explicit. The images
we have just discussed are explicit and we shall consider them more
closely below, but we must also be aware of images implicit in the
narrative. The house in which 'Die Vollendung der Liebe' is partly
set is not merely a location but something enclosed, man-made, with
walls separating one space from another. [22] Allied to the image of
the house is another implicit image, that of darkness and light - a
legacy perhaps of Musil's study of Manichaeism. Musil examines the
full range of intensities from the clear light of morning through to
the black depths of darkness after the last candle has guttered out;
within these extremes he records the gradations and intensities of
light that constantly change around the shape and feel of things that
are part-illuminated or shade into nothingness. This, we feel, is a
world where there are no 'things-in-themselves' - no essences beyond
the fallible and shifting perceptions of individuals. Here all is
pure phenomenon.

Far more common, however, are the explicit images that interrupt
the narrative, many of which are presented as similes. In fact, the
implicit imagery of house and light sometimes becomes explicit. Here
Veronika uses both in a single sentence: '<<Und oft fühle ich dann

unser Haus (...), seine Finsternis mit den knarrenden Treppen und den klagenden Fenstern, den Winkeln und ragenden Schränken und manchmal irgendwo bei einem hohen, kleinen Fenster Licht, wie aus einem geneigten Eimer langsam sickernd ausgegossen, und eine Angst, als stünde einer mit einer Laterne dort (...)>>' (200) ('<<And often I feel our house (...), its darkness with the creaking stairs and the moaning windows, the corners and the looming cupboards and sometimes, somewhere by a high, small window, light as if spilling slowly out of a bucket and a sense of fear as if someone were standing there with a lantern (...)>>'). Here Veronika's fear seems to signal a primitive mode of experience as if she were awakening, utterly disorientated, to the unfathomable strangeness of phenomena where 'Haus' ('house') and 'Licht' ('light') are only approximations for sense impressions that have lost their roots in any familiar setting. Less orthodox, indeed with a most intriguing perspective which seems chosen to unhinge the reader's human orientation, is the following passage in which Veronika gives expression to the animal power which Demeter exerts on her: '<<(...) Er tat sich bloß vor mir auf wie ein großer mit Zähnen bewehrter Mund, der mich verschlingen konnte, als Mann blieb er mir so fremd wie alle, aber es war ein Hineinströmen in ihn, was ich mir plötzlich vorstellte und zwischen den Lippen in Tropfen wieder Zurückfallen, ein Hineingeschlucktwerden wie von einem trinkenden Tier, so teilnahmslos und stumpf (...)>>' (201) ('<<(...) He simply opened up before me like a large mouth armed with teeth which was able to devour me, as a man he remained as much a stranger as all others but there was (a sense of) streaming into him which I suddenly

97

imagined, and a falling back in drops between his lips, (a sense of)
being swallowed up as if by an animal drinking, it was just as
uninvolved and apathetic as that (...)>>'). It is interesting to
note that, in this statement, the images which are most sharply
focussed - 'ein großer mit Zähnen bewehrter Mund' ('a large mouth
armed with teeth'), '(das) trinkende(..) Tier' ('(the) animal
drinking') - are those which are identified specifically as similes,
whereas the actual feelings to which the similes refer are verbs, or
verbal nouns indicating unspecific changes of state: 'tat sich (...)
auf' ('opened up'), 'Hineinströmen' ('streaming in'),
'Hineingeschlucktwerden' ('being swallowed up').

On many occasions Veronika is seized by a mood of dull despair:
'häufig kroch lautlos ein zäher Ekel durch diese Welt, der alle
Gefühle wie mit einer Teermaske verschmierte' (207) ('often, without a
sound, a viscous loathing crept through this world which smeared all
feelings as if with a mask of tar') - every reader can supply the
requisite personal experiences for this 'objective correlative'.
Also ready to be charged with the potential of the reader's
experiences is the following image - as arresting as it is grotesque -
in which the narrator compares Veronika's longing to hold Johannes
with that of a 'weiche wunde Schnecke, die mit leisem Zucken nach
einer zweiten sucht, an deren Leib es sie verlangt, aufgebrochen und
sterbend zu kleben' (210) ('soft sore snail which, with silent
convulsions, looks for another snail on whose body it desires to
stick, broken open and dying'). Musil sets the drama of tragic love

among the garden pests. Even a more conventional image for love –
that of the sea – is transformed here by its association, in
Veronika's imagination, with Johannes' anticipated suicide by
drowning: 'Zuweilen aber lag ihre Liebe nur weit und sinnlos über ihm
wie das Meer, müd schon, manchmal wie das Meer vielleicht über seiner
Leiche lag' (217) ('But sometimes her love merely lay over him, broad
and senseless like the sea, tired now already, sometimes in the way
that the sea perhaps lay over his corpse'). Here the sense of
formlessness which we find elsewhere is linked with the death, and
accompanying dissolution, of the individual.

It is difficult to avoid being affected by such unusual imagery.
Musil seems to want to make his narrative an utterly faithful record
of emotions whatever they may be. He seems to be as unflinching in
his record of perceptions and feelings as was Rilke in his novel, <u>Die
Aufzeichnungen des Malte Laurids Brigge</u>, which Musil read in 1910. [23]
In the following extract, Rilke sets down the evidence of human
activity on ruined walls which are all that has survived of a
demolished building:

> Und aus diesen blau, grün und gelb gewesenen Wänden, die
> eingerahmt waren von den Bruchbahnen der zerstörten
> Zwischenmauern, stand die Luft dieser Leben heraus, die zähe,
> träge, stockige Luft, die kein Wind noch zerstreut hatte. Da
> standen die Mittage und die Krankheiten und das Ausgeatmete und
> der jahrealte Rauch und der Schweiß, der unter den Schultern
> ausbricht und die Kleider schwer macht, und das Fade aus den
> Munden und der Fuselgeruch gärender Füsse. Da stand das Scharfe
> vom Urin und das Brennen vom Ruß und grauer Kartoffeldunst und der
> schwere, glatte Gestank von alterndem Schmalze. Der süße, lange
> Geruch von vernachlässigten Säuglingen war da und der Angstgeruch
> der Kinder, die in die Schule gehen, und das Schwüle aus den

Betten mannbarer Knaben. [24]

(And from these walls that had been blue, green and grey, that
were framed by the lines along which the ruined partition walls
had broken came the air of these lives, the viscous, sluggish,
fetid air which no wind had yet dissipated.   There stood the
midday (meals) and the illnesses and the exhaled breaths and
years-old smoke and the sweat which breaks out in armpits and
makes clothes heavy, and the stale smell of mouths and the rot-gut
reek of fermenting feet.   There stood the sharp taint of urine
and the burning one of soot and grey potato steam and the heavy
smooth stink of ageing lard.   The long sweet smell of neglected
babies was there, and the smell of frightened children going to
school, and the humid fug from the beds of pubescent boys.)

Musil felt a strong bond of sympathy for Rilke. As he expressed it in

his Berlin 'Rede zur Rilke-Feier' ('Funeral Oration for Rilke') Musil

sensed that Rilke felt as he did that at the most fundamental level in

human experience there are no compartments, no things that it is not

proper to mention, for all things flow in and through all other

things. [25] It seems that in Musil's narrator, and in Veronika too,

the censor for civilised attitudes has been put to sleep; both

remember what - to borrow Freud's theory - they were brought up to

forget.   So it is that, for Veronika, the experience of love is

compounded on unexpected elements: the sensation of the thick coat of

a St. Bernard, her companion in early adolescence; the thought of a

peasant woman and her supposed sodomy with her hounds; the blow and

humiliation that Johannes suffered at the hands of the stronger

Demeter; even the vision of Johannes' corpse claimed by the sea. The

Wilhelmine critic who found Musil's first book perverse must have had

his opinion confirmed by the second. Yet, just as in the case of

Rilke, the reader senses that the author's unceasing contemplation of

the things of this world, whatever they may be, this unremitting

watchfulness that does not spare the watcher, springs from some
unspecified conviction which views human life as a precious trust.

Johannes is more conventional than Veronika.   He wants to keep
things in their place and hates it when Veronika talks of the woman
and her dogs: '<<Es ist Sünde, was du sprichst, es ist Unflat.>>'(199)
('<<What you say is sinful, it is lechery.>>').   By condemning
Veronika's thoughts he keeps them at a distance from himself, but she
will not leave his position unchallenged.   They talk often of God:
'einmal hatte er zu Veronika gesagt: es ist Gott; er war furchtsam und
fromm, es war lange her und war sein erster Versuch, das
Unbestimmbare, das sie beide fühlten, fest zu machen' (195) ('once he
had said to Veronika: it is God; he was fearful and pious, it had
happened long ago and was his first attempt to fix the indefinable
sense that they both felt').   Veronika does not believe in such
simplistic naming; she makes litte attempt to interpret, to impose
order on, the partially incoherent data of her impressions and
feelings:

> <<Also ist etwas auch in dir, das du nicht klar fühlen und
> verstehen kannst, und du nennst es bloß Gott, außer dir und als
> Wirklichkeit gedacht, von dir, als ob es dich dann bei der Hand
> nähme? (...)   Und du bedienst dich (...) solcher Worte wie Gott,
> weil sie in ihren dunklen Kleidern aus einer andern Welt
> dahingehen mit der Sicherheit von Fremden aus einem großen,
> wohlgeordneten Staate, wie Lebendige (...) und weil du es um jeden
> Preis als wirklich fühlen möchtest?>> (196).

> (<<So there is also something in you that you cannot feel and
> grasp clearly and you simply call it 'God', (it is) outside you
> and perceived as reality, (it is) from you as if it would then
> take you by the hand (...)   And you use such words as 'God'
> because they go past like living people in their dark clothes from

another world with the self-assurance of strangers from a great
well-ordered state (...) and because you want, at any price, to
feel it is real?>>)

Veronika records her perceptions of herself and of things around

her - though these are, of their nature, vague and elusive - in a far

more precise way than does Johannes.   Whole sequences of images are

used to express them.   On the day when Johannes leaves, Veronika

senses how much she has changed, how she has lost the intensity of

youth.   In the passage in question she focusses successive

perceptions in images (which are clearly identified as analogies in

the text, and which accordingly stand for the things they represent

without 'standing in their way'):

Und es mußte bloß irgendwann einmal gewesen sein, daß sie dem
Leben näher stand und es deutlicher spürte, wie mit den Händen
oder wie am eigenen Leibe, aber schon lange hatte sie nicht mehr
gewußt, wie das war, und hatte nur gewußt, daß seither etwas
gekommen sein mußte, was es verdeckte. (...)   Denn inzwischen
hatte sich ihr schwaches alltägliches Leben über diese Eindrücke
gelegt und hatte sie verwischt wie ein matter, dauernder Wind
Spuren im Sand; nur mehr seine Eintönigkeit hatte in ihrer Seele
geklungen, wie ein leise auf und ab schwellendes Summen (...) Die
Tage gingen einer wie der andere dahin und eines gleich dem
anderen kamen die Jahre; (...) sie hatte ein unklares, fließendes
Gefühl von sich selbst, und wenn sie sich innerlich betastete,
fand sie nur den Wechsel ungefährer und verhüllter Formen, wie man
unter einer Decke etwas sich bewegen fühlt, ohne den Sinn zu
erraten.   Es war allmählich, wie wenn sie unter einem weichen
Tuche lebte, geworden oder unter einer Glocke von
dünngeschliffenem Horn, die immer undurchsichtiger wurde.   Die
Dinge traten weiter und weiter zurück und verloren ihr Gesicht und
auch ihr Gefühl von sich selbst sank immer tiefer in die Ferne.
Es blieb ein leerer, ungeheurer Raum dazwischen und in diesem
lebte ihr Körper; er sah die Dinge um sich, er lächelte, er lebte,
aber alles geschah so beziehungslos und häufig kroch lautlos ein
zäher Ekel durch diese Welt, der alle Gefühle wie mit einer
Teermaske verschmierte (206-7) (my emphases).

(And it must simply once have been the case that she stood closer

to life and felt it more distinctly <u>as if with her hands or as if
on her own body</u> but she had long since forgotten how that felt and
had only known that, in the meantime, something must have come and
covered it (...)   For, meanwhile, her weak daily life had
overlaid these impressions and wiped them away <u>just as a slight
but constant breeze wipes away traces in sand;</u> it was now only
its monotony that sounded in her soul <u>like a humming, rising then
falling</u> (...)   Days went by, one after the other, and the years
came, each like the other; (...) she had an unclear flowing
feeling of herself and whenever she went groping through her inner
self she found only changing, approximate and veiled forms <u>as when
one feels something moving under a blanket without recognising the
meaning.</u>   Gradually it had become <u>as if she were living under
soft cloth or under a bell made of horn carved thin and becoming
more and more opaque.</u> The things retreated further and further
off and lost their face, and her sense of herself also sank ever
deeper away into the distance.   There remained a vast, empty
space between, and in this lived her body; it saw the things
around itself, it smiled, it went on living, but all happened
without any context and frequently a viscous loathing crept
without a sound through the world and smeared all feelings <u>as if
with a mask of tar</u>. (my emphases).)

Here the images are equivalent to a set of still pictures taken of

some action; they are not the action itself, but only a

representation of aspects of the action artificially frozen in a

moment of time.   But in the above passage Musil records Veronika's

habitual mode of self-awareness as a backcloth for her singular

perception at this moment: 'Und nur als diese seltsame Bewegung in ihr

entstand, die sich heute erfüllte, hatte sie daran gedacht, ob es nun

nicht vielleicht wieder wie vordem werden könnte' (207) ('And only

when this strange movement, which today was being fulfilled, took

shape in her had she wondered if life could not perhaps be again what

it had been before').   In this way, the present moment of awareness

is set in relief against a previous state of awareness which in turn

has replaced a former state, long forgotten, but now brought to mind

once more.   Musil's 'mindscapes' are delicate tissues of time and
space.

As we have seen, it is apparent that Musil was working from
direct perception of living consciousness, as he made efforts to
record - with the greatest conceivable accuracy - his own [26] and,
above all, Martha's experiences at decisive phases in their lives.
Now, of course, only the record of the experiences survives - they
cannot be compared with their originals or even the memory of the
originals.

But to say that Robert and Martha Musil are behind these
sketches is, in one sense, misleading.   Vereinigungen provides not
only images of particular persons.   It is true that we can tell that
the portrait of Johannes is of a cautious person while Veronika is
more bold and daring, but we know so little about them that we would
find it impossible, for example, to give any kind of useful
description of their appearance.   Apart from one passage in which
Johannes imagines Veronika standing before him, when we are given
isolated details - he sees her 'hohe(n) Wuchs' ('tall frame'),
'große(n) wollüstigen Mund' ('big, sensual mouth'), 'den leichten
Flaum schwarzer Haare, der ihre Arme bedeckte' (203-4) ('the light
down of black hair which covered her arms') - they both have the
anonymity of the masked figures of Ancient drama.   Such masks had the
effect of distancing the audience from too close an involvement with
the character as an individual.   In the absence of the realistic

detail of portraiture it was easier for the member of the audience to
sense that here something more than an individual fate was being
enacted; they were not being invited to identify with one man or
woman but rather to see more clearly, through the masked figure, what
it is to be a human being. Though the conception of Vereinigungen
may start with the relationship of two individuals, the finished text
mobilises free-flowing sensations, fears, loathings and attractions
that are perpetual elements in human experience below the threshold of
personality: the many images in the text focus on such feelings in
the reader and divert their amorphous energy into the channel of the
narrative. Musil wants the figures that were, in their 'raw' state,
himself and his wife to be enmeshed with the feelings of the reader.
Accordingly, he makes far heavier demands than most readers are used
to. Reading Vereinigungen is an activity requiring effort and
stamina.

'Die Vollendung der Liebe'

Narrative perspective

The main theme of 'Die Vollendung der Liebe' - which Musil
describes as the more important [27] of the two 'Novellen' in the
collection Vereinigungen - is, once again, love and sexuality, the
polarity of the near-spiritual and the near-bestial as experienced by
a woman.   Here, however, a clearer literary shape emerges.   In 'Die
Versuchung der stillen Veronika' Veronika is in the process of falling
out of love with one man and is about to take up with another.   This
transition complicated Musil's depiction of what are in any case
elusive states of mind.   The broad shift from more spiritual to more
carnal feelings in Veronika is partly blurred, from the reader's
perspective, by the differences in character between Demeter and
Johannes;   furthermore, the shift away from Veronika to Johannes who
becomes at one point the central consciousness in the narrative
detracts from the intensity of this inner portraiture.   In 'Die
Vollendung der Liebe', on the other hand, there is greater unity of
perspective;   after a brief introductory section the narrator follows
the flow of thoughts and feelings in Claudine with almost unbroken
concentration, focussing particularly on her love for her husband and
the ways in which the anticipation of adultery illuminates that love;
the third figure in this love triangle, a 'Ministerialrat' - the

shadowy stereotype of an opportunist, a spare-time seducer - scarcely commands any attention from the reader.

As a narrative, 'Die Vollendung der Liebe' is more accessible to the reader; although the sections which provide a continuous commentary on the inner moods, feelings and thoughts of the central character are no less demanding and indeed are sometimes more prolonged than in 'Die Versuchung der stillen Veronika' they are relieved by more frequent, if still short, passages of external action which help with orientation. A snatch of conversation at the start of the story gives the reader some indication of what is happening:

> <<Kannst du wirklich nicht mitfahren?>>
> <<Es ist unmöglich; du weißt, ich muß trachten, jetzt rasch zu Ende zu kommen.>>
> <<Aber Lilli würde sich so freuen ...>>
> <<Gewiß, gewiß, aber es kann nicht sein.>>
> <<Und ich habe gar keine Lust ohne dich zu reisen ...>> (156).

> (<<Can you really not come, too?>>
> <<It is impossible; you know I must do my best to finish as quickly as I can.>>
> <<But Lilli would be so pleased ...>>
> <<Yes, certainly, but it cannot be.>>
> <<And I simply have no desire to travel without you ...>>)

In the scene which follows the two speakers are identified as man and wife; they are taking tea in their home. They are deeply in love: 'Die Frau setzte den Tee ab, ihre Hand legte sich auf den Tisch; wie erschöpft von der Schwere ihres Glücks, sank ein jedes in seine Kissen zurück und während sie sich mit den Augen aneinander festhielten, lächelten sie wie verloren und hatten das Bedürfnis nichts von sich zu

sprechen' (157) ('The woman put down the tea, her hand was lowered
onto the table; as if exhausted by the weight of their happiness,
each sank back into the cushions and, fixing their eyes upon each
other, they smiled as if they were lost and felt the need to say
nothing about themselves'). Musil, in evoking the quality of this
experience for the lovers, seems to be producing a mood painting which
might be entitled 'and time stood still...'. He gives expression to
their desire to prolong the moment for an eternity; their combined
effort of will, projected onto their immediate surroundings, produces
a curious Musilian pathetic fallacy - their mood seems to penetrate
the objects around them:

> Die Gegenstände hielten umher den Atem an, das Licht an der Wand
> erstarrte zu goldenen Spitzen, .. es schwieg alles und wartete und
> war ihretwegen da; .. die Zeit, die wie ein endlos glitzernder
> Faden durch die Welt läuft, schien mitten durch dieses Zimmer zu
> gehen und schien (...) plötzlich einzuhalten und steif zu werden,
> ganz steif und still und glitzernd, .. und die Gegenstände rückten
> ein wenig aneinander' (157).

> (The objects around them held their breath, the light on the wall
> froze in golden lacework,.. all was still, waiting, and was there
> for their sake; .. time, which runs like an endless shimmering
> thread through the world, seemed to run through the middle of this
> room and seemed (...) suddenly to pause and become stiff, quite
> stiff and still and shimmering ... and the objects moved a little
> closer to each other.)

Here Musil is successful in conveying a kind of inverted
psycho-kinesis - a state in which, through a spiritual effort, time is
frozen and objects seem to hold their breath in response to the wish
of the people in the room.

Time, of course, does not stand still - not even in this
narrative.   A few pages later we follow the woman - her name is
Claudine - as she takes a train to visit Lilli, who is identified as
her thirteen-year-old daughter;   Lilli was conceived in a casual act
of sex with a dentist in his surgery.   (This I interpret as a
deliberately provocative element in the narrative - this act of
promiscuity, which no doubt confirms many readers in their rejection
of the heroine, underscores the central paradox of the work:
'behaviour which contemporaries condemn as immoral', Musil seems to
say, 'is transformed in this tale into a vision of goodness, or at
least of love.')   Though much of the section of narrative which
corresponds to the time spent on the train is taken up with Claudine's
reflections, we are also introduced, against an appropriately darkened
background, to a stranger who is later identified as the
'Ministerialrat' ('Ministerial Counsellor'): 'Sie sah heimlich zu dem
Fremden hinüber.   Er zündete in diesem Augenblick ein Streichholz an;
sein Bart, ein Auge leuchteten auf' (170) ('She looked secretly across
at the stranger.   He was at this moment lighting a match;   his beard,
an eye, were illuminated');   the school where Claudine's daughter
boards and the small town where Claudine stays have some substance in
the text as does the inn where she lodges in the company of her
pursuer.   Here the outer action of the narrative reaches its climax.
 Claudine has retired for the night, she has undressed 'Und mit
einemmal hörte sie verheimlichte Schritte, ein Knarren der Treppe, ein
Stehenbleiben; vor ihrer Tür ein leise auf der Diele knarrendes
Stehenbleiben' (188) ('And suddenly she heard the sound of hushed

footsteps, the creaking of the stairs, a standing-still; in front of her door a quiet standing-still on the landing'). The 'Ministerialrat' has arrived.

So the external action of the narrative leads directly, and economically, from the harmony of a profound love affair to a squalid act of adultery by one of the lovers. Another author might have made of it something totally different. He might have stressed the drama of psychological conflict: matrimonial bliss, one partner fatally flawed by sensuality, the heroine tempted by the seducer-villain, her inward struggles against illicit passion, her yielding and the subsequent self-torturings of conscience. This would all have been framed in scenes which point up what might be conceived to be the central problem, the clash between loyalty and morality on the one hand, passion and immorality on the other; the text would have recorded the slow, vertiginous slipping of the heroine over the precipice into the abyss. Such a play would then have conformed to Aristotle's prescription of unity of dramatic action. [28] Perhaps this is precisely how the 'Ministerialrat' would have accounted for what happened. Casting himself no doubt in the role of the enviable Don Juan, he would have cited his own 'irresistible masculinity' and Claudine's sensuality and 'feminine fallibility' as parts of the mechanism of the drama. But this is certainly not how the author saw the development of his narrative.

Here, as in 'Die Versuchung der stillen Veronika', the emphasis

is not on external action, nor is it concerned with notions about the
psychological laws of character; it examines what passes through the
mind of the woman at the centre of the narrative.   The effect of this
inner commentary is to present the action in a quite different light -
not as the destruction of a love but as a 'Vollendung', a
'completing', 'rounding-out', perhaps even a 'perfecting' of a love.
A close examination of one segment of the inner commentary will help
to identify the elements that make up Claudine's love for her husband
in the context of her inner life as a whole.   Any interpretation
necessarily involves concentration on some aspects at the expense of
others;   in following one path, I am very aware of leaving others
unexplored.

From love to infidelity

> 'eine Untreue kann in einer tieferen
> Innenzone eine Vereinigung sein'
> (TbI,232)
> ('An act of infidelity, in a deeper
> inner realm, can be an act of union')

The passage in question is that corresponding to Claudine's journey in the train to visit her daughter. This covers some ten pages of text and is largely taken up with Claudine settling into her seat and spinning herself into a cocoon of private reflections and sensations. The passage starts with a record of her earlier promiscuity:

> sie beging und erlitt Handlungen von einer Stärke der Leidenschaft bis zur Demütigung und verlor doch nie ein Bewußtsein, daß alles, was sie tat, sie im Grunde nicht berühre und im Wesentlichen nichts mit ihr zu tun habe. Wie ein Bach rauschte dieses Treiben einer unglücklichen, alltäglichen, untreuen Frau von ihr fort und sie hatte doch nur das Gefühl, reglos und in Gedanken daran zu sitzen (160-161).

> (she performed and suffered actions of intense passion to the point of humiliation and yet never lost a sense that everything she was doing basically did not affect her and, of its nature, had nothing to do with her. Like a stream, these urgent acts of a mundane, unhappy, unfaithful wife rushed away from her and yet she still only had the feeling of sitting there thinking about it all.)

This sense of an impenetrable inwardness behind all that she does - which may be compared with the way Törleß dissociates his 'real' self and the homosexual act - coexists with a complementary sense that there is no centre to what she does. Thus when she meets her

daughter's teachers she steps outside herself in imagination, at once
contemplating her own image from the perspective of the other
passengers and confronting her own inward insubstantiality: 'Sie
fühlte eine eigentümlich traurige Lust, hier mit ihrem unnahbaren
Lächeln der fremden Dame, in ihr Aussehen verschlossen, vor ihnen
sitzend, bei sich selbst nur ein Zufälliges zu sein, nur durch eine
wechselbare Hülle von Zufall und Tatsache, die sie umfing, von ihnen
getrennt zu sein' (179) ('Wrapped in the unapproachable smile of the
unknown woman, closed up in her appearance as she sat before them, she
felt a curiously sad pleasure in being only something produced by
chance, separated from them only by the changeable veil of chance and
fact which surrounded her').

From a more conventional perspective people appear as
self-consistent; here they do not. In Claudine's world, opposites
coexist – we are reminded of dreams, interpreted by Freud, where love
and hatred merge in scenes of strange ambiguity. [29] But, despite
this, Claudine, even before she fell in love with her husband, sensed
that within her was something all-of-one-piece, an identity which
resisted impermanence and was never affected by her immorality:

> Hinter allen Verknüpfungen der wirklichen Erlebnisse lief etwas
> unaufgefunden dahin, und obwohl sie diese verborgene Wesenheit
> ihres Lebens nie noch ergriffen hatte und vielleicht sogar
> glaubte, daß sie niemals bis zu ihr hin werde dringen können,
> hatte sie doch bei allem, was geschah, davon ein Gefühl wie ein
> Gast, der ein fremdes Haus nur ein einziges Mal betritt und sich
> unbedenklich und ein wenig gelangweilt allem überläßt, was ihm
> dort begegnet (161).

> (Behind all the connections of real events something ran on

undiscovered and, although she had never caught hold of this
hidden essence of her life and perhaps had already come to believe
that she would never get through to it, she had a feeling,
accompanying everything that happened, of being a guest who, on
one occasion only, enters a strange house and lets himself be
swept up unthinkingly and with a trace of boredom into everything
that happens to him there).

Musil, as so often and particularly in <u>Vereinigungen</u>, makes use of the

image of the house to imply an area bounded by walls that restrict the

individual, forcing him or her to take a particular direction and

coercing a free-flowing human consciousness into a hard and fixed

environment made by other brains and hands.   Beneath the analogy we

glimpse a wider critical position: that the public world as a whole is

the enemy of each private self, forcing upon it through blunt reality

a host of expectations and rules that circumscribe it and deny it that

intuitive self-expression which Musil saw as the essence of freedom

and, thereby, of authentic action. [30]

    The relationship with her husband has changed her life: 'es kam

nicht mehr darauf an, was vordem gewesen war, sondern nur auf das, was

jetzt daraus wurde, und alles schien nur dazu dagewesen zu sein, daß

sie einander stärker fühlten' (161) ('what had happened before was no

longer of importance but only what was going to follow on from it now,

and everything seemed to have been present solely to make them even

more intensely aware of each other').   A little earlier the narrator

identified the quality of the relationship in a striking, if somewhat

grotesque image - a variant on Aristophanes' reflections on love.

The lovers are 'wie zwei wunderbar aneinandergepaßte Hälften, die,

zusammengefügt, ihre Grenze nach außen verringern, während ihr Inneres
größer ineinanderflutet' (159) ('like two halves miraculously fitted
together which, when joined, decrease their external surface area
while, inside, they flood into each other more completely'). This
reflection, in the hands of Aristophanes, was an elaborate joke; for
Musil it is not. The simile is his equivalent for the formula with
which a scientist represents a chemical reaction; Musil, like the
scientist, recognises that the formula is not a perfect image of the
real thing, but it is the closest correlation of observation and sign
that he can provide.

Despite the security of the love she feels for her husband,
Claudine's memories of her promiscuous past provoke a sensation of
vague unease. This is somehow connected with the turmoil at the
station where she has been pushed about at the centre of the crowd -
the impersonal sexual suggestiveness of the contact with other bodies
fills her at once with repugnance and passion: 'Die Gefühle, die
ringsum auf den morgendlich geöffneten, bleichen Gesichtern lagen,
schwammen auf ihnen durch den dunklen Raum wie Laich auf fahlen
Wasserflächen. Es ekelte ihr' (161) ('The feelings which lay on the
pale faces, open to the morning, floated on them through the dark
space like spawn on unlit stretches of water. She felt disgust').
The reader may note here the correspondence between the outer world
and inner response: from the personal and private love-relationship
with its refinement of feeling she moves to the anonymous crowd scene
with its free-floating animal energy and hectic sensuality. The

feelings engendered by the crowd are too powerful and immediate to
allow her to find her way back to the calm and security of her bond
with her husband: '(sie suchte) das Gestern zu erreichen; aber (...)
(sie) gewann davon bloß ein Bewußtsein, als trüge sie heimlich etwas
Kostbares und Zartes' (162) ('(she tried) to find the past; but (...)
all (she) captured of it was an awareness which was as if she were
secretly carrying something precious and delicate'). But even behind
the thought of her husband there is another awareness, something she
cannot quite catch hold of, that has an elusive haunting quality 'wie
ein Kinderlied, wie ein Schmerz' (162) ('like a nursery-rhyme, like a
pain'). The telegraph-poles and fields rushing past provide a
setting of impermanence quite different in mood from the static scene
at her home when she took tea with her husband and where the two had
had a sense 'als spannte (etwas) sich zwischen ihnen wie eine Strebe
aus härtestem Metall und hielte sie auf ihren Plätzen fest und
verbände sie doch, trotzdem sie so weit auseinander waren, zu einer
Einheit, die man fast mit den Sinnen empfinden konnte' (156) ('as if
(something) like a strut of the hardest metal were held in tension
between them, holding them fast to their seats and yet joining them,
although they were so far apart, into a whole which was almost
perceptible to the senses'). This image, from Musil's perspective,
is disturbingly ambiguous: their love is as strong, as hard as this
metal strut, yet its very hardness identifies it as something which
belongs in the external world that imposes itself on human
consciousness, contrasting with the fluidity of inwardness. Love, in
this shape, is restrictive. The rhythmic motion of the railway

carriage which is taking her further and further away from her husband
indicates a mood of what, from the perspective of a normal view of
love, seems a perverse relief: 'es war etwas Lustiges und Leichtes,
ein Weitwerden, wie wenn Wände sich auftun, etwas Gelöstes und
Entlastetes und ganz Zärtliches' (163) ('it was something light and
gay, a widening as when walls open, it was something unloosed and
disburdened and quite tender').   Here the reader observes a
volte-face of feeling, recorded in the now-familiar image of the house
with its obtrusive substantiality and emphatic divisions: love with
its association with fixity is here transformed into something quite
different, indeed almost a polar-opposite.   It seems that Claudine
has reached a point where her perception is so profound that she
grasps some underlying ambiguity of love and is bewildered at the
implications of this discovery:

(sie empfand) fast eine Sehnsucht, diese große Liebe, die sie
besaß, zu verlassen, als dämmerte vor ihr der Weg einer letzten
Verkettung und führte sie nicht mehr zum Geliebten hin, sondern
fort und schutzlos in die weiche, trockene Welkheit einer
schmerzhaften Weite.   Und sie merkte, daß das von einer fernen
Stelle kam, wo ihre Liebe nicht mehr bloß etwas zwischen ihnen
allein war, sondern in blassen Wurzeln unsicher an der Welt hing
(164-165).

((she experienced) almost a longing to abandon this great love
that she possessed as if she were dimly making out before her the
path of a final concatenation which was leading her not towards
her lover but away, defenceless, off into the soft, dry withering
of a painful distance.   And she noticed that this came from a
distant part where her love was no longer merely something that
existed between them alone but hung, with pale roots, insecurely
from the world.)

What Musil seems to say here is that the love between two people is

exclusive and thereby restrictive. In escaping from her loved one
while taking the experience of love locked within her, Claudine is
exploring love in a deeper and wider context.

In a kind of visionary day-dream she looks back on herself and
her husband walking transfigured in twilight: 'als ob sich mit
einemmal die stummen, folgsamen Dinge von ihnen losgemacht hätten und
seltsam würden, und sie waren hoch und aufgerichtet in dem halben
Licht, wie Abenteurer, wie Fremde, wie Unwirkliche, von ihrem
Verhallen ergriffen, voll Stücken eines Unbegreiflichen in sich, dem
nichts antwortete, das von allen Gegenständen abgeschüttelt wurde
(...)' (165) ('as if, suddenly, the dumb, obedient things had detached
themselves from them and become strange and they were tall and erect
in the half-light like adventurers, like strangers, like unreal
people, stirred by their vanishing echo, full of elements of something
incomprehensible within themselves, to which nothing responded and
which was shaken off by all objects'). Claudine seems to be leaving
all material things behind and entering a limbo where she is free from
the influence of the earth. The divorce of spiritual and physical
realms is here complete. Just as an ascetic subjects the body to
intense discomfort to prove that it is of no consequence to him, so
Claudine, in her present state of mind, sees promiscuity as an act of
spiritual defiance against the flesh: 'Dann vermochte sie zu denken,
daß sie einem andern gehören könnte, und er erschien ihr nicht wie
Untreue, sondern wie eine letzte Vermählung, irgendwo wo sie nicht
waren, wo sie nur wie Musik waren, wo sie eine von niemandem gehörte

und von nichts widerhallte Musik waren' (165) ('Then she was able to
conceive of belonging to another and he seemed to her not like an act
of infidelity but like a final wedding rite somewhere other than where
they were, where they were only like music, where they were music
heard by noone, reechoing from nothing'). In the intensity of the
experience is an exquisite suffering as if the music were the pure
embodiment of the absolute will behind the universe which Schopenhauer
presents in Die Welt als Wille und Vorstellung [31] where pleasure is
merely a refinement of pain: '(sie wünschte) daß sie einander erst mit
der Lautheit des einen leisen, fast wahnsinnig innigen, schmerzlichen
Ton Nicht hörenwollens liebten (...); und mit dem Schmerz des einsamen
nebeneinander Dahineinragens (....) liebte sie ihn, wenn sie dachte,
ihm das letzte erdschwere Weh zu tun' (165) ('(she desired) them to
love each other with the intensity of tone of a soft, almost madly
inward, painful note of not wanting to hear (...) and, with the pain
of a lonely jutting-out-into-space next to each other, she loved him
as she thought of inflicting on him the ultimate heavy, earth-bound
woe'). The coming act of infidelity, marking the separation of
husband and wife in the flesh, will seal - through the pain that it
inflicts on them both - the pact that unites them in spirit, their
common understanding of the wider context of love and morality.

When she looks out of the train window again, however, the mood
has changed once more: 'schal und unnachgiebig lag (draußen) ein
Widerstand darüber, als sähe sie durch eine dünne, milchige Widrigkeit
hindurch' (166) ('flat and unyielding there lay over it (outside) a

resistance as if she were looking through a thin, milky repulsion');

the earlier sensaton of lightness has yielded to one of claustrophobic

oppression by the rigidity and stale order of her life:

> Und mit einemmal fiel ihr ein, daß auch sie (...) in sich gefangen
> und auf einen Platz gebunden dahinlebte, in einer bestimmten
> Stadt, in einem Hause darin, einer Wohnung und einem Gefühle von
> sich, durch Jahre auf diesem winzigen Platz, und da war ihr, als
> ob auch ihr Glück, wenn sie einen Augenblick stehen bliebe und
> wartete, wie solch ein Haufen gröhlender Dinge davonziehen könnte
> (166).

> (And suddenly it occurred to her that she, too, lived trapped
> within herself and bound to one place, in a particular town, in a
> house in that town with a residence and a feeling of selfhood,
> year after year in this tiny place, and then it seemed to her as
> if her happiness, too, if she were to stand still and wait for a
> moment could go rushing away like some mob of yelling things.)

This provides further evidence of that inconstancy of inner moods

where sensations are juxtaposed or follow closely on their antitheses.

Since the narrator has tuned the reader's attention to a

Schopenhauerian perception of the powerlessness of a mind in an

objective world of unalloyed wilfulness, the reader accepts more

readily the moment where Claudine relaxes her own will and submits to

the relentless energy of forces which, though foreign to her, will

work through her: 'es begann allmählich unter dem Druck des ungeheuer

Fremden ihr Geist sich aller Abwehr und bezwingenwollenden Kräfte zu

schämen und ihr war, als besänne er sich, und es ergriff ihn leise

jene feinste, letzte, geschehenlassende Kraft der Schwäche und er

wurde dünner und schmaler als ein Kind und weicher als ein Blatt

verblichener Seide' (167) ('gradually, under the pressure of this

immense strangeness, her mind ('Geist') began to be ashamed of all

resistance and all efforts to overcome and it seemed to her as if it
was beginning to pause, to reflect, and that most fine, final,
indolent power of weakness took gently hold of it and it became
thinner and more slender than a child, and softer than a leaf of faded
silk'). The energy of her secret insights seems to drain away,
leaving her helpless in the face of the pitiless onslaught of
externality.

In these pages Musil provides a unique record of a woman in
love. Elements of her emotional life are doubtless bound up with a
particular historical epoch - a modern reader would be unlikely to be
tempted to interpret experiences under the influence of Schopenhauer,
nor, given the more relaxed attitude to morality, would so much
opprobrium attach to infidelity - thus something of the scandalous
force of the work is lost today. Nonetheless, the contemporary
reader will still appreciate the skill with which Musil traces the
inner path that Claudine follows as she leaves the warmth and security
of conjugal love and gives way to extramarital lust. We have seen
that Musil deliberately underplays the action of these 'Novellen', but
this does not mean that the reader is completely disorientated here.
In the following passage there is a strong sense of the real - we feel
that the train, the passengers, the darkened landscape are no less
objectively present than they would be in a novel by Theodor Fontane.
It is Musil's particular achievement to merge this sense of the
substance of material things with the consuming inner preoccupations
of this strange and fascinating woman. [32] This merging of outer and

inner worlds - a narrative blend of aspects of realism and expressionism - [33] can best be appreciated by quoting at length from this section of the 'Novelle':

Draußen tobte lautlos die Landschaft. Ihre Gedanken fühlten die Menschen so groß und laut und sicher werden, und sie schlüpfte davor in sich hinein und hatte nichts als ihr Nichtssein, ihre Schwerlosigkeit, ein Treiben auf irgend etwas. Und allmählich begann der Zug ganz still, in weichen, langen Schwingungen durch eine Gegend zu fahren, die noch in tiefem Schnee lag, der Himmel wurde immer niedriger und es dauerte nicht lange, so fing er schon auf wenige Schritte an, in dunklen, grauen Vorhängen von langsam dahintreibenden Flocken auf der Erde zu schleifen. In den Wagen wurde es dämmrig und gelb, die Umrisse ihrer Mitreisenden hoben sich nur mehr ungewiß vor Claudine ab, sie schwankten langsam und unwirklich hin und her. Sie wußte nicht mehr, was sie dachte, nur ganz still faßte sie eine Lust am Alleinsein mit fremden Erlebnissen; es war wie ein Spiel leichtester, unfaßbarster Trübungen und großer, danach tastender, schattenhafter Bewegungen der Seele. Sie suchte sich ihres Mannes zu erinnern, aber sie fand von ihrer fast vergangenen Liebe nur eine wunderliche Vorstellung wie von einem Zimmer mit lange geschlossenen Fenstern. Sie mühte sich, das abzuschütteln, aber es wich nur ganz wenig und blieb irgendwo in der Nähe wieder liegen. Und die Welt war so angenehm kühl wie ein Bett, in dem man allein zurückbleibt.... Da war ihr, als stünde ihr eine Entscheidung bevor, und sie wußte nicht, warum sie es so empfand, und sie war nicht glücklich und nicht entrüstet, sie fühlte bloß, daß sie nichts tun und nichts hindern wollte, und ihre Gedanken wanderten langsam draußen in den Schnee hinein, ohne zurückzusehen, immer weiter und weiter, wie wenn man zu müd ist um umzukehren und geht und geht (167-168).

(Outside, the landscape raged without a sound. Her thoughts felt people becoming so tall and loud and secure and, in the face of this, she slipped into herself and had nothing but her non-being, her weightlessness, a drifting towards something indefinite. And gradually the train began to travel quite silently in soft, long oscillations through a region which lay in even deeper snow, the sky came lower and lower and before long it began, as close as a few feet away, to drag along the ground in dark grey curtains of slowly drifting flakes. In the carriages a yellow dusk fell, the contours of her fellow-passengers were only imperfectly distinguishable in front of Claudine, they swayed slowly and unreally to and fro. She no longer knew what she was thinking, and it was only very gently that she was seized by excitement at being on her own with strange experiences; it was like a game of the lightest, most intangible opacities and of large, shadowy movements of her psyche (Seele) reaching out for them. She tried

to remember her husband but of the love which had almost gone she
found only a curious image as if of a room with windows that had
long been shut.   She tried to shake this off but it only
retreated slightly and lay still, somewhere close by.   And the
world was as pleasantly cool as a bed in which one is left behind
on one's own.... Then it seemed to her as if she were faced with a
decision and she did not know why she felt this way and she was
neither happy nor annoyed, she felt only that she wanted neither
to start nor to stop anything, and her thoughts wandered slowly
out into the snow without looking back, moving further and further
away, as when one is too tired to turn back and keeps walking on
and on.)

Vereinigungen is fed by many sources in Musil's life: his

studies in philosophy and psychology in Berlin; the overwhelming

emotion generated by his falling in love with Martha; a deep ambition

to make his mark in literature by devoting himself without reservation

to the writing of one work.   This work was undertaken after years of

what would now be considered extremely unhealthy preoccupation with

his own inner life - such narcissism was then, of course, the

affectation of many of his generation.   To these sources were added

ingredients that were later conspicuously absent in Musil's life:

leisure, freedom from financial worries and no publisher's deadlines

to meet (or rather, not to meet and to have to renegotiate!).   Given

the energy thus generated and the undoubted talent which the author of

Die Verwirrungen des Zöglings Törleß had displayed, something special,

indeed something extraordinary, was almost bound to emerge.

It would be wrong, however, to describe Vereinigungen as a

'masterpiece' for that term implies the existence of other pieces - by

Musil or by others - with which it could be compared.   There are no

others. Neither Musil nor, to my knowledge anyone else, ever wrote anything comparable. In Vereinigungen Musil brings to a literary genre the same concern for precision that he had been taught to demand in any scientific context. Most 'Novellen' mobilise the reader's capacity for vicarious involvement in the lives of others; Musil, as we have seen, is more than usually specific in this respect. By the use of images, he makes deliberate sorties into the reader's subconscious to prompt and prod particular feelings, shaping them to his own ends. Some readers are irritated by the undisguised self-consciousness of this text; others are not willing to suspend their own moral scruples and so they turn down the chance to explore Musil's world in the way that the narrative requires - namely without preconceptions. But those who put themselves into the author's hands are rewarded with a rare experience.

In a short study in Nachlaß zu Lebzeiten, Musil describes two ancient sarcophagi in Italy where man and wife, sculpted in stone, gaze lovingly at each other: 'Dieser treue, brave, bürgerliche, verliebte Blick hat die Jahrhunderte überstanden; er ist im alten Rom ausgesandt worden und kreuzt heute dein Auge' (GWII,486) ('This faithful, upright, bourgeois, loving gaze has withstood the centuries; it was sent out in Ancient Rome and falls upon your eye today'). Though Musil's Vereinigungen has not lasted two thousand years, its historical durability is beyond question; it provides for us, more than half a century on, direct access to the mind of an extraordinary woman who lived before World War I, via a word-bridge fashioned by an extraordinary man.

Chapter 4   'DIE SCHWÄRMER'

In 1911 Musil moved to Vienna and started work as a librarian in
the 'Technische Hochschule' there; in April of the same year he and
Martha were married.   Though his library duties took up only a couple
of hours a day he found them very irksome because they interfered with
his creative work.   In 1913 he left to become an editor of Die neue
Rundschau, a Berlin journal; this work was brought to an end by the
outbreak of World War I.   Musil served in the Austrian Army on the
Italian front and distinguished himself for his bravery.   In 1916,
after a period of illness, he was made the editor of Die
Soldatenzeitung, a newspaper for the armed forces; when this ceased
publication he worked on another War Ministry propaganda paper,
Heimat, until the end of 1918.   Later he became an archivist in the
press section of the Foreign Office until 1920 when he was made an
educational adviser to the Austrian Army.   Although he was offered a
permanent position in 1922 he decided to devote himself full-time to
creative writing.

The uncertainties and disturbances of these years help to
explain the long gap between major literary works: Vereinigungen was
published in 1911, and it was not until 1921 that the play, Die
Schwärmer, appeared.   It was performed once only in Musil's lifetime
- in 1929 in a small theatre in Berlin - and the production was a
disaster.   The critic of the Steglitzer Anzeiger wrote: 'man saß

ratlos zweieinhalb Stunden lang vor einem wirren Gedankenknäuel,
qualvoll bemüht, irgendeinen Zipfel zu erhaschen, auf daß einem
wenigstens ein Schimmer von Erleuchtung werde.   Noch selten ist die
Geduld des Zuschauers derart auf die Probe gestellt worden' [1] ('for
two and a half hours one sat before a confused knot of thoughts, not
knowing what was happening, and desperately trying to pick up some
thread which might lead to at least a glimmer of illumination.
Seldom has the patience of an audience been so sorely tried').
Musil's other play, the farce, Vinzenz und die Freundin bedeutender
Männer, (Vinzenz and the Girl-friend of Important Men) was performed a
number of times and was a qualified success.   Musil did not consider
it an important work; it does introduce, however, themes which Musil
was to explore more deeply in Die Schwärmer and is, accordingly, of
some interest here.

Vinzenz und die Freundin bedeutender Männer

In writing Vinzenz und die Freundin bedeutender Männer, Musil
seems to have set aside his customary seriousness: 'Die Laune (...),
in der ich diesen Spaß schrieb, war die des doppelten
Nichternstnehmens, weder der Welt, viel weniger noch des Theaters'
(Briefe I, 325-6) ('The mood (...), in which I wrote this frolic was
one of not-caring-less for the world, even less for the theatre').
There were three productions in less than a year: the first, in
Berlin in December 1923, was quite well-received by audiences and

critics alike as was the second, in a provincial theatre in Bohemia,
in June 1924; however, when the play was brought to the 'Deutsches
Volkstheater' in Vienna in August, 1924, not only were most critics
scornful, but a vociferous minority of one of the audiences booed and
hissed so much that the police were called. [2] Vinzenz und die
Freundin bedeutender Männer has been described as companion piece to
Die Schwärmer - a 'satyr-play' [3] counterbalancing the 'tragedy' of
Musil's later and far more substantial piece - but it is less than
that. Though it would be wrong to overlook it entirely, it deserves
no more than our passing attention. [4]

Vinzenz, the hero, is a figure who prompts some of the action in
the play rather than becoming directly implicated. (In a letter to
his mentor, the critic Alfred Kerr, Musil says that he imagines the
figure 'melancholisch-komisch, in Moll, lebensenttäuscht-lustig'
(Briefe I, 327) ('melancholically-comical, in a minor key, expressing
disappointment with life, yet amusing').) He has come to visit a
former girl-friend, Alpha, on the pretext of finishing a conversation
which they had been conducting many years previously! (Musil
apparently wanted the audience to see such contrived elements in the
plot for what they were: the author of the farce reminding the
audience that they were watching a farce.) [5] However, there can be
no doubt that he also hoped that the audience would recognise that
Vinzenz and Alpha, though surrounded by characters which were
grotesquely exaggerated, were themselves expressing ideas which Musil
did take seriously. Musil put his finger on a central flaw of the

work when he pointed out to the director of the original production,
Berthold Viertel: 'Das eigentliche Stilproblem ist (...) die
Verschmelzung (des) flachgehaltenen dadaistischen Untergrunds der
Posse mit den dreidimensionalen Figuren des Vinzenz und der Alpha'
(Briefe I,320) ('The real stylistic problem is (...) the merging (of
the) deliberately flat, dadaist background of the farce with the
three-dimensional figures of Vinzenz and Alpha').

Alpha, deserted by Vinzenz many years ago at the very moment
when their love blossomed, has become a promiscuous society woman,
surrounded by a coterie of admirers, some rich, some famous, who are
led on by her sensuality and held in thrall by her wit and tactical
skill. (Musil felt that he had not quite got this figure right: 'die
Alpha braucht viel von Gnaden der Schauspielerin' (Briefe I,320)
('Alpha needs a good deal of help from the actress').) But one of
the fraternity threatens to be too much for her to handle: Bärli, a
business-man who owes his success to a ruthless wilfulness, brooks no
resistance. He asks her to choose between marrying him, or dying
with him by the gun. With deliberate improbability, Musil has
Vinzenz eavesdrop on the scene - Vinzenz stops Bärli from killing the
woman whom he so desperately loves and from taking his own life. [6]

In view of the grotesque elements in the plot, contemporary
audiences must surely have failed to identify Musil's passionate
concern with the phenomenon of love. Musil does not lay sufficient
stress on the time, now fifteen years in the past, when hero and

heroine were in love; but, since the audience is not forced to
consider this dimension, they became disorientated and the work loses
its force.   The play seems to be nothing more than a depressing
reflection on the meaninglessness of life in general, although Musil
was, in fact, trying to express something else: the meaninglessness
of an adult life which betrays youthful feelings.   Youth is a time
when one feels unique; with maturity, too many people surrender this
sense of uniqueness and join the herd – they adjust their hopes,
desires and their fulfilments to sterile contemporary stereotypes.
The image with which this process is expressed is that of the theatre.

In this play, theatre does not copy life, life imitates
theatre. [7]   Alpha and her admirers – as Vinzenz, Musil's mouthpiece,
explains – are all involved in more or less elaborate games of
pretence.   They act out their lives in a world of appearances,
neglecting what they really feel inside.   The initial dramatic
mechanism – Bärli's dangerous passion for Alpha – is used by Vinzenz
as an object-lesson; he secretly persuades the impetuous lover to
substitute blanks for the bullets which he proposes to use on Alpha
and himself.   The subsequent charade – which Alpha believes is real –
is as cathartic for Bärli as murder and subsequent suicide would have
been.   If, to keep to the image used above, this energetic
businessman is, in emotional terms, just another animal in the herd,
why should he make himself into a scape-goat?   Why should he draw
down the wrath of society on his head by committing murder, when
murder would be nothing more than a theatrical response to the

stereotype, the tired cliché of the blind anger of a frustrated lover?

While avoiding the unpleasant consequences of the actions he originally intended, Bärli experiences the emotions that those actions would have entailed, finds that they mean far less to him than he thought they would, falls as quickly out of love with Alpha as he had fallen in love with her and leaves a wiser, though not a happier, man.

Vinzenz 'stage-manages' a parallel disabusing of Alpha: her excitement at the prospect of the immeasurable wealth that seems to be within her reach when Vinzenz tells her of a new gambling system he has invented kindles in the heroine a passion which Musil invites us to treat with suspicion - 'Mach mit mir, was Du willst' (432) ('Do with me what you will') she cries in that suspiciously self-interested abandon, which can only come with a failure to know not what the self wants but what it needs. She realises what that money will mean to the outer course of her future life, but does not realise that money will leave her inner self unchanged and as unfulfilled as she is even now. In fact, Vinzenz has not invented any gambling system - he has merely fabricated a situation to teach Alpha the futility of all anticipation, whether passionate or otherwise. Towards the end of the play it becomes clear that Alpha, like Bärli, has adopted Vinzenz's cynicism - she decides to accept the offer of marriage of the ugliest, and richest, of her suitors. Vinzenz, with a cheque from Bärli in his pocket and having scotched for good the yearnings which he once stirred in Alpha, leaves to find a post in some other household.

The reader who knows Musil's other works will recognise familiar
themes in <u>Vinzenz und die Freundin bedeutender Männer</u>: the hero
(though uncharacteristically world-weary and stoical) condemning a
society preoccupied with the non-essential; the sense that no
subsequent experience can match the intensity of first love; the
intricate playing on the notion that the contemporary world is a stage
and that all the people on it are merely going through the motions of
living. But all these themes are left at what in terms of Musil's
normal standards is a primitive level of development. Most of the
people in those early audiences must surely have left with the
impression that, for all his skill with words, the author was just
another shallow cynic.

Die Schwärmer

As we have seen, <u>Vinzenz und die Freundin bedeutender Männer</u> was
not a successful work; Musil felt that <u>Die Schwärmer</u> (translated as
<u>The Enthusiasts</u>) was. In 1923 he described the play, which had first
appeared in print in 1921, as 'den höchsten Punkt, den meine Linie
bisher erreichte' (<u>Briefe</u> I,333) ('the highest point which I have
touched on my course thus far') - it was awarded the prestigious
Kleist Prize in that year.   Thereby the zenith of its course in the
world had been reached and passed.   For, as a play, it had serious
shortcomings.   Above all it was almost too much for any audience,

however sophisticated, to digest.   Shortly after completing the play,
Musil tried to persuade several theatres to put it on but not one
accepted the challenge.   It was eventually staged in 1929 but, as we
saw above, was a complete flop. (It must be stressed, however, that
this production went ahead without Musil's permission and against his
bitter protest.) [8]   After a performance in 1955 in Darmstadt one
bewildered critic wondered whether it was Musil or the audience who
had 'not come up to the mark'! [9]   Productions of the work in Vienna
(in 1980) and Berlin (in 1981) were given a mixed reception by critics
- we read: '"Die Schwärmer" sind (...) moderne Gedankenriesen, Masten
einer Hochspannungsleitung, durch die die gleiche verzweifelte
Sehnsucht fließt' ('The "Schwärmer" are (...) modern giants of
thought, pylons for high voltage current through which flows the same
desperate longing'); [10] but elsewhere it is bluntly dismissed as
'dieses als tot nachgewiesene Unstück Musils' ('this un-play of
Musil's which has now been given its death certificate'). [11]
Audience reaction seems to have been positive, on the whole, but this
may have been partially in deference to Musil's reputation, partly the
audience's sympathy for the author and knowledge of his other works,
rather than appreciation of the play itself. [12]

We have seen above how, in Vinzenz und die Freundin bedeutender
Männer, the plot was of only minor importance; this is so for Die
Schwärmer, too. [13]   In fact it might have helped if Musil had had a
prologue in which he had an actor explain what was about to happen,
leaving the audience to concentrate on what the characters say.   Such

an actor, taking the role of the author himself, might have said
something like this:

'The plot of my play is, briefly, as follows: Anselm, a married
man, without a job or any sense of purpose in life, has seduced
Regine, the wife of a leading academic, Josef; the action of the play
starts after the adulterers have taken refuge in the home of another
university teacher, Thomas, whose promotion to professor depends on
Josef's support, and his wife, Maria. Anselm and Thomas are close
friends, Regine and Maria are sisters and all four lived together in
this very house as adolescents some fifteen years ago - these are the
'Schwärmer' of my title (and, by the way, what this title means you
will discover only by paying close attention to my play as a whole, I
cannot bring myself to spare you this effort of concentration by
giving the game away now!); years ago, Regine married Johannes, the
fifth 'Schwärmer', but he committed suicide . Regine's memory of her
dead first husband, always keen to the point of neurosis, is sharpened
by the sense that he died in the house she is now visiting. Josef,
her wronged and outraged second husband, arrives only to discover that
Regine has been unfaithful not just this once but many times before.
He leaves without her. In the meantime, Anselm has turned away from
Regine and started to pay court to his hostess, Maria - she, despite
the pleadings of her husband, succumbs. Anselm, the seducer, leaves
and Maria, his new conquest, follows. Only two 'Schwärmer' are
left: Regine, deserted by her most recent lover, haunted by her first
husband and abandoned by her second, and Thomas, his wife gone and his

promotion chances dashed.

 All of the characters who you will see before you on the stage are
suffering life's most intimate entanglement - they are in love; this
means that they become caught in the stresses of marriage, seduction,
threats of suicide, deception and revelation - in short, the tale is
as sordid and banal as any of you could desire for your evening's
entertainment.   What could be more familiar, you may say?   Familiar?

Well, here we disagree because, for me, love is a profoundly strange
and puzzling thing.   Perhaps those of you who have been in love will
say that you know all about it.   But, if you pause for a moment, can
you honestly say that you are able to give a precise account of what
it is to be in love and what it is to experience all the other
emotions which tend to be tangled up with love: jealousy, anger,
self-doubt, anxiety, despair?   Forgive me, but I don't think that any
of you could do so, at least not with the accuracy, the precision
that, in my view, such a theme demands.   I have spent many years
exploring ways of expressing such things.

 You have come, no doubt, to be entertained.   But, as Schiller
is my judge, I offer not entertainment, but enlightenment. [14]   I have
designed the action to bring together people who are going through
crises: Thomas and Anselm struggling for the love of Maria like two
human stags, pitting words against words, attitude against attitude,
self against self; Regine, in whom the anguish of degradation is
added to the torment of remembered passion, and Maria, wanting to be

the dutiful wife but demanding a conventional demonstrative affection
which Thomas is too honest to give her; finally, Josef, who in losing
Regine is also losing face and finding this latter loss, if anything,
more painful than the former. You will find that most of my
characters, most of the time, speak with a frankness that is more
bracing than amusing; the words they utter express directly what is
going on inside them. This means that what they say does not sound
like normal dialogue: first, because, as each of you knows, when you
are in company, you do anything but say what you think, except in
moments of extreme emotional stress; second, because most of you,
unlike my 'Schwärmer', would not be able to give a precise account of
what you think and feel at any given moment.

Why have I written the play, you wonder? Well, I believe it is
the task of members of the intelligentsia like myself - and here I
quote from one of my own essays - 'neue geistige Impulse aufzunehmen
und ihnen den Weg in Tiefe und Breite möglichst zu bahnen' [15] ('to
pick up new spiritual impulses and, if possible, prepare a way for
them that has both a wide and a profound effect'). So you see, it
is really quite simple: in my play I am making propaganda for
'Geist'.'

* * * * *

As we saw above, Musil was unsuccessful in his attempts to
persuade theatres to perform his play. [16] He records, scornfully,
the response of one official from the 'Burgtheater' in Vienna: 'Er

fühlt nicht den Menschen, nicht die Hauptsachen, nicht das Pathos,
nicht das Ethos; er muß mir sozusagen alles Eigentliche des Werks für
die paar Stellen konzedieren, die ihm näher gingen, die aber in
Wahrheit meine Konzessionen sind, mit einem Wort, er sieht an meinem
schönen Käs nur die Löcher und findet, daß der Käs zu wenig Löcher
habe' (Briefe I,202-203) ('He feels neither the man, nor the main
points, nor the pathos, nor the ethos; he is forced, so to speak, to
concede all the essentials of the work in exchange for the few
passages that affected him but which, in fact, are my concessions; in
a word he sees only the holes in my cheese and thinks the cheese has
too few holes'). Musil fails to realise here that it is scarcely
likely that the public at large would respond more intelligently to
the work than the expert whom he scorns. But let us examine things
from Musil's perspective.

In this play he attempts to change people's perception of the
world. His intention might be compared with that of the
Impressionist painters whose works were a statement about how they saw
the world. They were convinced that their paintings were closer to
reality than the works of more traditional painters; but the public
had to be reeducated to see as clearly as they did. Musil's field of
interest is not the world as seen through the eyes, but the world of
the emotions. He requires the audience to revise their interpretation
of what is going on in the minds of characters on the stage; he also
expects that this will result in their revising their interpretation
of what is happening within their own minds.

It is perhaps easiest to approach Musil's work from his
perception of conventional behaviour. In Die Schwärmer, as in
Vinzenz und die Freundin bedeutender Männer, he examines bourgeois
society in the early twentieth century; in Vinzenz und die Freundin
bedeutender Männer, as we saw, he turned on its head the idea that the
theatre reflects the external world, arguing that the bourgeois tends
to be an actor, modelling what he does according to stereotypes of
acceptable behaviour: the bourgeois plays at being a bourgeois. In
Die Schwärmer Musil does not use this image, but does stress the
extent to which bourgeois conduct is shaped by conventional behaviour;
the play is designed as a vehicle to estrange the audience from such
rituals. In a world where appearances are paramount, life runs
according to stereotypes: 'faithful wife', 'constancy in friendship',
'undying love'; this is true also for negative images, as we see, for
example, when Josef arrives: 'pillar of society' confronts 'adulterous
wife' and 'Don Juan'. Thomas, who is Musil's 'persona', determines
to arrange a special reception for Josef which will mirror his rage;
Thomas intends to 'stage' a dramatic scene: 'The Arrival of the
Wronged Husband'. In this way, Thomas wants to make explicit the
'theatre' that is now playing in Josef's mind. But Thomas proposes
to substitute for the bourgeois trappings of law-suits and injured
pride an alienating African context. (Musil was fascinated by African
art and artefacts.) In other words, it will be made clear to Josef
that his anger is only a social ritual which, when set in the context
of another culture, is unmasked as merely a ridiculous piece of

acting. 'Was es an leer gewordenen Kokons gibt, aus denen je der
Schmetterling der menschlichen Verzückung emporgetaumelt ist, hänge
ich rings um ihn auf! Negertanztrommeln, Gefäße für den göttlichen
Urinrausch, Federtalare, in denen das Männchen vor dem Weibchen
tanzt!' (319) ('I shall hang up around him whatever empty cocoons
there are out of which the butterfly of human ecstasy has ever come
reeling forth! Negro dance-drums, vessels for the divine
urine-frenzy, feather capes in which male dances before female!').

Musil is not merely making the point that all human activity is
conditioned by the society in which it originates (providing a
delicately ridiculous spectacle for whatever divinity, whatever cosmic
sociologist, may be looking on). He was trying to present Josef's
stereotyped response in absolute terms - from the perspective of
'Geist'. Die Schwärmer, in my view, throws some more light on what
Musil understood by this concept.

Musil had no time for Stefan George [17] and yet the youthful
'Schwärmer', fifteen years before the action of the play, seem to have
acknowledged Thomas' leadership, in the way that George's disciples
followed their 'Master's' guidance in all important aspects of their
lives. Regine and, to a lesser extent, Maria still accept Thomas's
preeminence, only Anselm has rebelled. Thomas owes his position to
his intellectual brilliance, to his being on the most intimate terms
with 'Geist'. In his commentary on the production of Die Schwärmer
in 1929 (which had gone ahead without his authorisation), Musil

discusses the original intentions behind the play; he writes of:

> die Forderung eines schöpferischen Theaters (...), in der sich die
> Tatsache spiegelt, daß wir in der Hauptsache aus Geist bestehn.
> Keine Angst, wir dürfen trotzdem Hummer essen, Politik machen und
> sonst tun, was menschlich ist (sollen es!), und meinetwegen mag
> man sich den Geist so materialistisch vorstellen, wie man will.
> Aber wir wollen nicht leugnen, daß die lebenswertesten Augenblicke
> die sind, wo das, was wir tun, von irgendeinem heimlichen, aber
> über uns hinausgehenden, in die Weite des Allgemeinen tragenden
> Gedanken belebt wird (GWII,1191).

> (the demand for a creative theatre (...), in which the fact is
> reflected that we are made up mainly of spirit (Geist). Don't be
> alarmed, we can still eat lobster, we can still be politically
> active and still do (indeed, we should do) all the other things
> that are part of human life and, as far as I'm concerned, one can
> have as materialistic a view of spirit (Geist) as one likes. But
> we won't deny that the most valuable moments in our lives are
> those where what we do is given vital impetus by some kind of
> secret thought which goes beyond us into the far reaches of the
> universal.)

Musil, despite suffering from what many commentators - and
indeed the author himself - considered a surfeit of thought, was not a
philosopher. Had he been he might have been tempted to construct a
system, or at least compose a discursive tract, in which he expounded
what he saw 'Geist' to be. In the absence of any such system or
work, readers of his play can only speculate on what he meant by
'Geist'. In a way, Musil tried to square the circle: he wanted
positivism [18], and he wanted mysticism. In addition to his
commitment to empiricism, Musil was strongly influenced by the dualism
inherent in Idealist thought - in fact, in those moments in this play
and in other texts where we are permitted a glimpse of Musil's vision
of 'Geist' it is possible to detect a kind of informal Platonism, a
radical disjunction between the things that are of this world and an

inner realm to which human beings have access.   Take, for example, a
remark by Thomas at the end of the play.   '(Wir Schwärmer sind) auf
der unbestimmten Bettlerfahrt des Geistes durch die Welt' (407) ('(We
"Schwärmer" are) on an undetermined journey with the spirit (Geist) as
it begs its way through the world').   'Geist' is not at home in this
world;   'Schwärmer' are more receptive than most people to a
meta-world.   They have '(ein) richtungsloses Gefühl ohne Neigung und
Abneigung zwischen den Erhebungen und Gewohnheiten der Welt.   Ein
Heimweh, aber ohne Heimat' (330) ('(a) sense without any direction,
without inclination or disinclination among the elevations and usages
of the world').   Above all the final words of this quotation set the
tone of Musil's mysticism.   Though Musil was not religious in any
conventional sense, I believe that he experienced the alienation of
'Geist' from material things almost in the way that a Christian
visualises the Fall of Man.   We are, and are not, part of this world.
Our senses may be ensnared by the world in its present form;   yet,
something within us always remains free of material things.   This
faculty represents all that is finest in our nature.   Unfortunately
it is no easier to present 'Geist' in dramatic form than it would be
to persuade the unbeliever that some happening was the result of
divine grace.   To see 'Geist' one must believe in it, or be young
enough to perceive its working through every fibre of one's being.
Again it is Thomas who keeps alive the conviction which pulsed through
the band of 'Schwärmer' when they were young:

Als wir jung waren, wußten wir, daß alles, wofür die Alten <<im
Ernst>> leben und sterben, im Geist längst erledigt und

entsetzlich langweilig ist (...) Als wir jung waren, wußten wir,
daß das, was wirklich geschieht, ganz unwichtig ist neben dem, was
geschehen könnte.   Daß der ganze Fortschritt der Menschheit in
dem steckt, was nicht geschieht.   Sondern gedacht wird; ihre
Ungewißheit, ihr Feuer (330).

(When we were young we knew that everything which the old live and
die for <<in earnest>> is, from the point of view of spirit
(Geist), long since redundant and dreadfully boring (...)   When
we were young we knew that what happens in reality is quite
unimportant when set against what could happen.   That all
progress for humanity lies in things which do not happen - but
which are thought.   This is humanity's uncertainty, her fire'.)

Here the energy and passionate potential of youth - mocking the dead

stereotypes of conventionality - celebrate 'Geist', which links the

human and the divine.

In Musil's view of the world, nothing is substantial; the more

substantial a thing appears to be, the less it belongs to the realm of

'Geist'.   When Josef, as the representative 'Bürger' says: 'Ich

brauche eine feste, verläßliche Grundlage, um existieren zu können'

(389) ('I need a firm reliable foundation to make it possible for me

to exist'), [19] he is demonstrating how far his position is from

Thomas's.   Regine, so says Thomas, has never been able to understand

all the things that give Josef's life its weight and predictability:

'Für dich (Josef) gibt es Gesetze, Regeln; Gefühle, die man

respektieren muß, Menschen, auf die man Rücksicht zu nehmen hat.   Sie

hat mit all dem geschöpft wie mit einem Sieb; erstaunt, daß es ihr

nie gelingt' (399) ('For you (Josef) there are laws, rules; feelings

that one must respect, people one has to consider.   It was as if she

were scooping around in all these with a sieve; astonished at never

being successful'); later in the same scene, still in conversation
with Josef, he makes the point again: 'Du gehst auf einem ausgelegten
Balkennetz; es gibt aber Menschen, die von den dazwischenliegenden
Löchern angezogen werden hinunterzublicken' (399-400) ('You walk on a
structure of interlocking beams; but there are people who are tempted
by the holes between to look down'). For Regine and for Thomas, the
'ausgelegte(s) Balkennetz' ('structure of interlocking beams') is not
secured to anything - it is suspended in space. For them, no thing,
no idea, no ideal has lasting weight or substance. Josef's line of
thinking is self-evident: he sees the damage that Anselm has done to
him, invading the sacred relationship of man and wife, destroying the
reputation which he has earned in academic work and in the order of
his life up to this point. The damage cannot only be felt, it can be
measured in terms of the transgression of moral principles which Josef
and the majority of the people whom he knows accept as absolute. The
audience feels Josef's irritation and anger at Thomas' failure to
realise that Anselm is about to destroy his (Thomas') marriage in the
way that he has destroyed Josef's:

THOMAS: (...) (Anselm) kann nicht gekommen sein, um mir Übles zu
tun!
JOSEF: Aber du Narr! Du eingebildeter Narr! Du meinst, die
einfache Wahrheit sei für dich nicht gut genug; das Einmaleins
der Tatsachen, für dich gilt es nur, wenn es zugleich eine
<<höhere Wahrheit>> ist! (366).

(THOMAS: (...) (Anselm) can't have come to do me harm!
JOSEF: You fool! You deluded fool! You think that simple truth
isn't good enough for you; the one-times table of facts is valid
for you only if, at the same time, it's a higher truth!)

Josef is not able to grasp how Thomas sees things; I suspect that his irritation must have been shared by a large section of the original audience, who were similarly puzzled by the attitude of the 'Schwärmer'. It might have helped them if, in their programme notes they had been able to read the table which Musil drew up for himself in 1920 while he was writing the play:

Schöpferische Menschen	Unschöpferische
Unbestimmt	Bestimmt
Transwahr	Wahr
Transrechtlich	Rechtlich
Fühlloser Träumer	Mitfühlend
Ungesellig	Gesellig
Metaphysisch unruhig	M(etaphysisch) ruhig
Ausgeschlossen	Eingeschlossen
Passiv aus Widerwillen geg. das Bestehende wie das Verbessern	Aktiv
Wirklichkeitsverachtend	Wirklich
Antiideale	Sonntagsideale
Antiillusionen	Illusionen: Realitäten, (TbI,365)

(Creative People	Uncreative People
Undetermined	Determined
Trans-truthful	Truthful
Trans-just	Just
Dreamers without feelings	Feelings of sympathy
Metaphysically unstable	M(etaphysically) inert
Excluded	Included
Passive out of distaste for what exists and for improving things	Active
Despising reality	Real
Anti-ideals	Sunday-ideals
Anti-illusions	Illusions: realities.)

Can we detect the hidden criteria which prompted Musil in devising this table? On the right we find people such as Josef whose attention is focussed on this world, and, on the left, the 'Schwärmer'

- for surely this is who Musil had in mind with the designation,
'schöpferische Menschen' ('creative people') - [20] who approach the
world with a 'mental reservation' (hence the proliferation in the
'Schöpferische Menschen' column of what we might call the prefixes of
dissent or escape: 'trans-', 'meta-', 'un-', 'anti-').   Musil also
invites us to be sceptical about terms such as 'wahr' ('true'),
'rechtlich' ('just') and 'wirklich' ('real'), by indicating that
'Schwärmer' cannot accept these, seeing them not so much as indicators
of the status of some content, but as bourgeois value judgments which
are debased by being set alongside the synonymous concept:
'Illusionen: Realitäten' ('Illusions: realities').   Of course, the
rather nebulous nature of the '"Schwärmer"-outlook' is intimated by
the extent to which it is seen as a negation of the bourgeois, rather
than something readily identified in its own right.

The time when Thomas was the undisputed leader of a small band
which included Anselm, Regine and Maria is now, as we have seen, only
a fifteen-year-old memory.   As they have grown older, the 'Schwärmer'
have responded differently to bourgeois life - they have all made
compromises, and now that the group has reassembled Thomas tries to
assert his authority again.   This means a confrontation with Anselm
who has ideas of his own.   The dramatic business unfolds in a
struggle for dominance between Thomas and Anselm, in the course of
which there emerge the new pairings of Thomas and Regine, representing
the '"Schwärmer"-orthodoxy', and Anselm and Maria, as the 'revisionist
off-shoot' of the movement which wants to make peace with the enemy.

In the contest with Anselm, Thomas uses the weapon of a truth
too blatant for the bourgeois.   Thomas speaks with a bluntness that
cuts through convention.   In the following extract we find him not
only wrapped up in the struggle with Anselm for Maria, but
simultaneously a spectator at that struggle with perceptions as sharp
as they are uncensored.   Thomas addresses Maria: 'nun ist es wie in
der Welt der Hunde.   Der Geruch in deiner Nase entscheidet.   Ein
Seelengeruch!   Da steht das Tier Thomas, dort lauert das Tier Anselm.

Nichts unterscheidet sie vor sich selbst, als ein papierdünnes
Gefühl von geschlossenem Leib und das Hämmern des Bluts dahinter'
(360) ('now it's like being in a world of dogs.   The smell in your
nose is decisive.   A spiritual smell!   Here stands Thomas, the
animal, there the animal, Anselm, lies in wait.   Nothing
distinguishes them from their own point of view except a paper-thin
sense of an enclosed body with the hammering of the blood behind it').
Thomas has caught the animality of the moment in a striking analogy.
This is also the case for another moment later in the same act.   Here
again there is a confrontation 'in the flesh' viewed through the prism
of 'Geist', it is the drama of man against man seen without
presupposition.   In this moment of almost manic anger, as Thomas sees
and feels the powerful psychic and sexual attraction between Anselm
and Maria, his words are those of one who is at once involved, and
also just an onlooker: 'legt euch doch auf die Erde....(...) Tut es
ab, bevor wir weiterreden!   Blut durchqualmt euch den Kopf!   Das
noch nicht vereinigte Mark steht in der Tiefsee der Körper wie

Korallenwald!   (...)   Du und Ich pressen sich geheimnisvoll
vergrößert ans Kugelglas der Augen!' (370) ('Go on, lie down on the
ground!.... (...)   Get it over with before we go on talking!
Blood-mist is seething in your heads!   The bone-marrow, still
ununited, is like a forest of coral in the sea-depths of your bodies!
(...)   Thou and I press in mysterious magnification against the
convex glass of the eyes!') Here it is even more evident than
elsewhere in this play that Thomas, like the other 'Schwärmer', speaks
a language of his own.   It owes much to Expressionism, all the more
because what it describes belongs within an inner rather than to an
outer frame of experience.   In this explosion, Thomas vents an anger
which is not blind but sharp-eyed with jealousy.   It recalls
Büchner's Woyzeck ranting at the shameless lust of his mistress and
her powerful soldier-lover.   It expresses that protest of a man,
thwarted in his love for a woman, which becomes a cry of agony over
the ways of the flesh and an emphatic rejection of creation as well as
procreation.   It is 'Geist' in its bitter lament at being lost in
existence.

Maria feels this hiatus between feeling and thinking in Thomas'
relationship with her;   it disturbs her profoundly - she wants love
unspoilt by reflection, but, Anselm sneers, Thomas's 'Gefühle sitzen
im Kopf' (335) ('feelings are located in his head').   A profession of
love by Thomas is not sweet nothings whispered in Maria's ear but
eccentric self-observings which are meaningless until one realises
that Thomas is giving an account of what it is like to be not one

person, but two – namely, man and wife:

> Wenn man solang verheiratet ist und immer auf vier Füßen geht und
> immer Doppelatemzüge macht und jede Gedankenstrecke zweimal geht
> und die Zeit zwischen den Hauptsachen doppelt voll mit Nebensachen
> geräumt ist: Da sehnt man sich natürlich manchmal wie ein Pfeil
> nach einem ganz luftdünnen Raum. Und fährt auf in der Nacht,
> erschreckt von den eignen Atemzügen, die eben noch so gleichmäßig
> dahingegangen waren ohne einen selbst. (...) Und da liegt noch
> so einer in Fleisch gewickelt. Das erst ist Liebe (321).

> (When you have been married for a long time and always walk on
> four legs and always draw double breaths, think each thought out
> twice and the time between the main things is doubly full with
> minor things: then, sometimes, it's natural to ache like an arrow
> for a space where the air is quite thin. And you jump up in the
> night, frightened by your own even breathing which had just been
> going on without you (...) And there another like you lies
> wrapped in flesh. Only then is it love.)

Thomas seems oblivious to the effect which such words have on Maria,
who, after so many years of this kind of comment, yearns for a more
normal lover, perhaps with more than a touch of the conventionally
romantic about him. (As Anselm puts it, '(Maria) braucht Lyrik,
geradezu mit der Butterspritze' (344) ('(Maria) needs lyricism laid on
with a trowel').)

Anselm's understanding of Maria's emotional needs provides the
opportunity he wants to assert himself over Thomas. Perhaps, even at
an early age, Anselm desired Maria and was jealous of Thomas' success
with her, linking this unconsciously with Thomas' intellectual
dominance of the group. But intellectual superiority, viewed from
another point of view, can be seen as an Achilles' heel. Men like
Thomas, says Anselm, who desire to change the world 'müssen

wahrscheinlich gefühllos sein; wer die Welt um hundertachtzig Grad
drehen will, darf nicht inniger als durch Gedanken mit ihr verflochten
sein' (328) ('probably have to be without feeling; whoever wants to
turn the world through a hundred and eighty degrees must not be
entwined with it in any more intimate a way than through ideas').
Anselm works at developing a talent which Thomas has neglected: the
ability to know intuitively what another person wants to hear. Even
Josef ruefully remembers how delightfully sympathetic Anselm was when
they first met, how Anselm seemed to understand exactly what he wanted
to express, to know exactly what was going on in his mind. [21] The
audience will probably feel sympathy for Maria, for whom the daily
deceits of conventional living (precisely the kind of life that Musil
tries to lay bare in all its duplicity in Die Schwärmer) must seem a
blessed haven after years of living with a man who has compulsively
recorded and analysed all that has passed between them with no regard
for the occasion and no consideration for her 'feelings'. We see
this in the following exchange between Thomas and Maria:

> MARIA: (...) Du hast mich den Mut zu mir selbst verlieren lassen!
> THOMAS: Und Anselm gibt dir einen gefälschten!! Du wirst eine
> ungeheure Enttäuschung erleben!
> MARIA: Vielleicht fälscht er. Aber ich habe ein Recht darauf,
> daß man mir vorredet: so ist es! Daß – und wenn es nur eine
> Täuschung wäre! – etwas stärker als ich aufwächst. Daß man mir
> Worte sagt, die nur wahr sind, weil ich sie höre. Daß mich Musik
> führt, nicht daß man mir sagt: vergiß nicht, hier wird ein Stück
> getrockneten Darms gekratzt! Nicht, weil ich dumm bin, Thomas,
> sondern weil ich ein Mensch bin! So wie ich ein Recht darauf
> habe, daß Wasser rinnt und Steine hart sind und Schweres in meinen
> Rocksaum genäht, damit er nicht schlottert! (369).

> (MARIA: (...) You have made me lose confidence in myself!
> THOMAS: And Anselm gives you counterfeit confidence!
> MARIA: Perhaps he is a counterfeiter. But I've a right to have

people say to me: that is so! So that - even if this is only a
deception - something stronger than I am grows up! That someone
speaks words to me that are only true, because it is I who am
listening to them. That I lose myself in music, not that someone
says to me: don't forget that this is a piece of dried gut being
scraped! Not because I'm stupid, Thomas, but because I'm a human
being! Just as I have a right to the fact that water flows and
stones are hard and weights are sewn into the hem of my skirt to
stop it flopping about!)

Maria's will to illusion is nothing less than 'Schwärmer'-heresy.

But Thomas seems powerless to influence her now: [22] 'Wir reden

aneinander vorbei. Wir sagen das gleiche, aber bei mir heißt es

Thomas und bei dir Anselm' (369) ('We are talking at cross-purposes.

We are saying the same thing but with me it's called Thomas and with

you Anselm').

Just as Anselm has studied Thomas, so Thomas has studied Anselm.

Anselm may be, unlike him, a 'Schwindler' (318 and 360)

('swindler'), [23] a seducer and a dealer in illusion. But, at root,

he remains a 'Schwärmer', marked with their mark: '(Anselm) lockt

unter betrügerischen Versprechungen Menschen an, weil er mitten in der

Unendlichkeit allein auf seiner eigenen Planke treiben muß!' (362)

('(Anselm) attracts people to him with deceitful promises because he

has to drift all alone on his own plank in the midst of eternity').

Under the surface of the performance that he is giving we find not

Josef's 'ausgelegte(s) Balkennetz' ('structure of interlocking beams')

but existential anguish which comes from the sense of the

insubstantiality of all things. Thomas places 'brackets' around

perceptions thus expressing doubt about them and considering the possibility of change. Anselm hates his rival for this intellectual

virility for he, Anselm, tends to lose himself in the world; even a

tree can capture his labile emotions (it is curious to reflect that

Musil evidently wants the audience to see this as a performance which

is, at one at the same moment, both exaggerated and serious!):

Ich wurde einmal von einer Weide –: ergriffen.   Auf einer weiten
Wiese und außer mir stand nur dieser Baum.   Und ich konnte mich
kaum aufrecht erhalten, denn was sich in diesen Ästen so einsam
verzerrt und verknotet hatte, diesen gleichen schrecklichen Strom
Lebens, fühlte ich in mir noch warm und weich und er wand sich.
Da warf ich mich auf die Knie! (325).

(Once a willow-tree positively reached out and grabbed hold of me.
 It was in a wide meadow, and apart from me the only thing that
stood there was this tree.   And I could scarcely stand upright
for what, in this lonely place, had twisted and knotted itself in
these branches, this same frightening current of life, I could
feel still warm and soft in me, and it writhed.   Then I threw
myself down on my knees!)

Of course, the woman whom he loves (at least for the moment!) exerts a

power which is even stronger: 'Maria, ich bin manchmal so durchflutet

(von den Kräften, die in Ihnen wirken), daß ich unter der Angst leide,

meine Glieder und Gesichtszüge könnten wider Willen die Bewegungen der

Ihren nachahmen wie Pflanzen, die am Grund eines fließenden Wassers

stehn' (334) ('Maria, sometimes (the powers which are present in you)

flood through me so strongly that I am afraid that my limbs and the

features of my face might, against my will, imitate movements of your

limbs and face like plants on the bed of a fast-flowing river').   The

sensuous world is always reaching out and grasping hold of Anselm; he

is a gifted coiner of images, above all of moments of intensely

uncomfortable involvement.   So, of his experience of trying to get

out of Thomas' field of domination, he says: 'ich (muß) mich losreißen
(...) wie eine Heuschrecke, die ihr gefangenes Bein in der Hand eines
Stärkeren läßt' (328) ('I (have to) tear myself away (...) like a
grasshopper which leaves its trapped leg in the grip of a stronger
one'); of Regine, as she screams out a nameless suffering, he says:
'Wie sie sich festklammert; wie eine kleine Katze, die ertränkt
werden soll!' (352) ('How she clings on tight; like a kitten which is
to be drowned!').

Although it is her elopement with Anselm which sets the dramatic
mechanism in motion, Regine is only peripheral to the play. She
presents an example (and a warning) of the way in which Thomas'
attitude to the world works out in practice. She has his immediacy
of perception. She cries out: 'Liebe ist gar nie Liebe! Ein
körperlich Antreffen von Phantasien ist es! Ein Phantastischwerden
von (...) Stühlen ...Vorhängen...Bäumen...Mit einem Menschen als
Mittelpunkt!' (321) ('Love isn't love at all! It's a meeting-place
in bodies for fantasies. A nascent fantasia of (...)
chairs...curtains...trees...With a person as the centre'); she is
surrounded, in Anselm's words, by a 'gespenstischen Luftleere' (335)
('ghostly vacuum'); for her, too, the physical universe is only the
threshold to another one. Her actions in this world, as for Claudine
in 'Die Vollendung der Liebe', involve an abasing of the physical
body, self-flagellation for the good of her spirit. Anselm, with
his extraordinary empathy, feels this distinctly: he links her
tendency as a child to swallow earth, stones and earthworms with her

adult sense that dirt and obscenity will somehow be transformed:
'Einmal wird plötzlich etwas ganz Wunderbares daraus entstehn! (...)
Männer, das ist ja nichts andres, das ist doch auch nur - das
Geheimnis, das man in den Leib nimmt' (354) ('Sometime, something
quite wonderful will suddenly emerge from that! (...) Men, they're
nothing but..., they're just simply - the mystery one takes into one's
body').

Her visions of her dead lover, Johannes, (who actually appears
before her in Hans Neuenfels's film version of the play) [24] function
as a reminder of transcendence. Thus Regine, the antithesis of the
bourgeois ideal of the virtuous wife, is presented as a sign from
another realm; when threatened by Stader, a private detective and a
former lover, with the exposure of her promiscuity, Regine replies:
'Man kann innen heilig sein wie die Pferde des Sonnengotts und außen
ist es das, was Sie in Ihren Akten haben (...) Man tut etwas und es
bedeutet innen etwas ganz andres als außen' (343) ('Inside one can be
as holy as the horses of the Sun God and outside it's what you've got
in those files of yours (...) One does something and inside it means
something quite different from outside').

Up to this point in her married life she has kept private and
public worlds apart. Josef knows nothing of her affairs. The
anticipation of being unmasked plunges her into fear; she takes
refuge in a prolonged fit of screaming (a vivid reminder that, for the
'Schwärmer', life can reach a pitch of intolerable intensity). But

once it is seen to be inevitable that her shame will come out, Regine
fiercely resists that public orderliness which her husband embodies;
she also fights to stop Anselm making his peace with that order,
seeing the humiliation of exposure which they share in the second act
as something positive, a confirmation that they have broken out of
what she calls the 'Kerker der Vernunft' (347) ('dungeon of Reason').
Suffering humiliation is, she asserts, 'das Schicksal des Geistes in
der Welt' (365) ('the fate of the spirit in the world').   'Laß dich
nicht mit ihrer Vernunft ein!' (373) ('Don't have anything to do with
that Reason of theirs!') she screams at Anselm as the secrets of their
relationship are revealed.

* * * * *

The final scenes of the play are almost bare of outward action
and it is here that we are given the clearest insight into what Musil
conceives the life of the 'Schwärmer' to be.   Thomas and Regine are
interrupted in an innocent kiss by Frl. Mertens, a middle-aged
spinster and a paragon of respectability.   She assumes that their
relationship is adulterous and contrasts their 'promiscuity' with her
'fidelity': 'Denn (wie Regine habe) auch ich (...) einst den
Geliebten verloren; aber ich habe ihm durch einundzwanzig Jahre reine
Treue gewahrt bis heute' (405) ('For (like Regine) I too (...) once
lost my loved one; but I have been completely faithful to him for the
past twenty years').   Frl. Mertens takes her final leave and Thomas,
with sad irony, sums up her attitude: 'Da hast du's!   Das Laster ist
Schmutz.   Aber die Tugend ist auch nur frisch genießbar!' (405)

('There you have it! Vice is dirt. But virtue can only be
appreciated when fresh!'). Thomas and Regine want to find an
alternative to the kind of behaviour that Frl. Mertens epitomises;
they want to strip away pretence and get back to basic human
experience. This is not easy or pleasant for the fictions of
bourgeois behaviour serve to reduce the tension and the pain of
living.

Regine remembers one instance of such living. This was the
terribly slow passing of the hours after Johannes' death: 'ein
endloses Quellen von leeren Stunden' (405) ('an endless welling-up of
empty hours!'). Now that their loved ones have gone, it seems that
they are both left with the prospect of that kind of unending
emptiness. Thomas offers no consolation, no balm for suffering - for
it is fear of suffering that makes people shut their eyes and minds to
experience, making them 'Schwindler' ('swindlers'), like Anselm.
Regine says: 'Ich verstehe einfach nicht, wie die andren Menschen es
machen, (die Stunden) richtig auszufüllen' (405) ('I just don't
understand how other people arrange to fill (the hours) properly');
Thomas replies: 'Sie schwindeln natürlich; sie haben einen Beruf,
ein Ziel, einen Charakter, Bekannte, Manieren, Vorsätze, Kleider.
Wechselseitige Sicherungen gegen den Untergang in den Millionen Metern
Raumtiefe' (405) ('They cheat, of course; they have a career, a goal,
a character, acquaintances, manners, intentions, clothes. Mutual
safe-guards against going under in millions of metres of deep space').
Thomas can offer Regine no help in coming to terms with life - he

tells her 'Man muß einfach die Kraft haben, diese Widersprüche (des
Lebens) zu lieben (...)' (406-407) ('One must simply have the strength
to love these contradictions (of life)').   Regine and he can have no
comfort from the illusions that satisfy others, for they are both
'Träumer' (407) ('dreamers');   as Thomas says: 'Das sind scheinbar die
gefühllosen Menschen.   Sie wandern, sehn zu, was die Leute machen,
die sich in der Welt zu Hause fühlen.   Und tragen etwas in sich, das
die nicht spüren.   Ein Sinken in jedem Augenblick durch alles
hindurch ins Bodenlose.   Ohne unterzugehn.   Den Schöpfungszustand'
(407) ('Such people seem to be without feeling.   They wander,
watching what the people do who feel at home in the world.   And have
within them something that others do not sense.   At each moment, a
feeling of sinking through everything into the void.   Without going
under.   The state of creation').

* * * * *

It is easy to understand why Musil was tempted to write the two
plays.   The theatre offered him large assemblies of people who might
be moved by his critical message and might, like his 'Schwärmer', dare
to consider new ways of living.   However, he seems to have
underestimated the difficulty of changing a settled view of the world.
Musil was attacking, in the course of works lasting only a couple of
hours, the sum of many years of experience by each member of the
audience - namely, the mental habits which were implanted into each of
his contemporaries in the long process of integration into adult

society. Moreover, unlike the dramatic works of a Brecht, for
example, Musil's alienating plays were not presented within the
framework of a familiar ideology which required no introduction - the
ideology in Musil's dramas was simply the sum of personal insights
gathered through years of private observation and reflection and
supplemented by specialised reading in philosophy, psychology and
other more esoteric fields. The most important 'Schwärmer' is one
who does not appear in the play - Musil himself.

In the case of both his plays, but particularly with Die
Schwärmer, Musil fails to assess realistically his lines of
communication with his audience. During the thirties Musil wrote in
one of his notebooks: 'Schwärmer, Grundunterschied: Die meisten
Dramatiker schreiben, wie die Schauspieler sprechen; ich verlange,
daß sie sprechen, wie ich schreibe' (TbI,881) ('Schwärmer, basic
difference: most dramatists write as actors speak; I demand that
they speak as I write'). This is an arrogant attitude to take to the
process of writing for the stage - a public medium demands concessions
to public expectations. The appropriate medium for Musil's more
private reflections was clearly that of narrative prose. Here,
through the subtle propaganda of a powerful mind acting on receptive
readers, prejudices could be revealed, mental habits attacked and
outdated attitudes recast. [25] As a play for public performance, Die
Schwärmer was bound to be a failure; [26] its more important function,
from the perspective of literary history, was as a proving ground for
some of the ideas that would be vital to Der Mann ohne Eigenschaften.

Chapter 5   'DREI FRAUEN'

Drei Frauen, published by Rowohlt in 1924, is a collection of
three 'Novellen', each of which had been published separately earlier:
'Grigia' in 1921, 'Tonka' in 1922/3, 'Die Portugiesin' ('The Woman
from Portugal') in 1923. [1] These are quite different from earlier
creative works. The philosophical and psychological interests of the
author, though still strongly represented, are less obtrusive; here
the story as such comes into its own. The plots are quite simple.

In 'Grigia', a scientist with the unlikely name of 'Homo' has
decided to spend some time away from his wife, whom he loves, and his
son; he accepts an invitation to take part as a geologist in an
American-sponsored expedition to reopen old gold workings in the
mountains to the North of Venice; in the village where the expedition
is based he has an affair with a peasant woman, is trapped with her in
a cave by the woman's husband and dies at the moment when the
expedition is abandoned.

In 'Die Portugiesin', Ketten, a medieval knight, woos and weds a
Portuguese lady and brings her back to his castle.   When he arrives
he is called away to fight a campaign that drags on for eleven years –
during which time his wife bears him two sons but remains almost a
complete stranger to him – before he is able to defeat the enemy.   On

his return to civilian life, Ketten falls ill.   His recovery stops
part way.   A cat comes to the castle, befriends the inhabitants,
amazing them with its all-but-human qualities, then sickens and dies;
somehow the cat seems to be connected with Ketten and his fate.
Ketten, exerting himself with a last irrational effort, climbs the
unclimbable sheer rock-face of his mountain fortress, and in so doing
regains his strength and, apparently, the love and respect of his
wife.

'Tonka', set like 'Grigia' in the early part of this century,
presents the relationship between a working-class girl and a young man
of good family.   The girl, Tonka, has worked for a short time as
nurse to the young man's grandmother, when the grandmother dies.
Tonka is paid the very small amount that is her legal due and
dismissed.   The young man, who is both sexually attracted to Tonka
and feels a sense of shame at the shabby way she has been treated by
the family, offers to protect her.   She accepts and becomes his
mistress.   Some years later Tonka becomes pregnant and is found to
have contracted venereal disease.   All the doctors whom the young man
consults agree that it is virtually certain that he is neither the
source of the infection nor the father of the child.   Despite his own
doubts about Tonka's faithfulness and his mother's urgings to desert
Tonka, the young man, who is intensely involved with scientific work,
continues to support her.   Tonka eventually dies as a result of the
combined stresses of disease, pregnancy and social disgrace.

Though the decision to publish the stories in a single volume
may have been prompted by the publisher they have common features:
each is a love story seen broadly from the man's perspective; each is
firmly based in Musil's own experience; each suggests that life is
set in a framework of which human beings are aware only intermittently
and imperfectly - in short, each gives expression to Musil's
fascination with mystical experience.   In the following thematic
examination of the stories we shall see these features emerging
clearly;   they express some of Musil's vital concerns.

Autobiographical roots

The autobiographical roots of the 'Novelle', 'Tonka', the
longest of the three stories of Drei Frauen, can be traced back to
Musil's early manhood. The diary-'Hefte' provide evidence of Musil's
preoccupation with this material in the early years of the century. [2]
 Probably in 1901, during his year of voluntary military service,
Musil met a girl, Herma Dietz, who was working as a nurse for his
grandmother. [3] When his grandmother died, Herma, like Tonka in the
'Novelle', was dismissed and Musil took her as his mistress.   Herma
later went with him to Berlin.   Like Tonka she contracted a venereal
infection - for which, as doctors assured Musil, he was not
responsible - and became pregnant.   Despite the evidence of
infidelity Musil supported Herma until her death in 1907. [4]   The
diaries contain the record of Musil's obsession with the question of

whether or not Herma had been unfaithful to him; [5] though Musil was
repeatedly assured that she must have been unfaithful he was never
able to accept the fact of her guilt.   His reaction, as he recognised
himself, was modelled on his earlier refusal to believe that Heinrich
Reiter was his mother's lover despite all the circumstantial evidence
to this effect. [6]   In his diary in the early 1900s Musil wrote:
'Zwischen der Mutter u. (Herma) besteht eine versteckte Parallele.
Auch die Mutter war einmal ein Mädchen, das mehr noch als (Herma) zu
(Robert Musil) gepaßt hätte (TbI,96) ('Between Mother (and Herma)
there is a hidden parallel.   Mother, too, was once a girl who would
have been a better match than (Herma) for (Robert)').   His
relationship with Herma was a continuation of the one with his mother;
it was based on an unwritten and unspoken contract of trust which,
though not excluding suspicion of adultery, constantly rejected it as
unworthy. [7]   It was as if the vision of the purity of the woman in
question - a vision defended all the more vigorously because of the
'versteckte Parallele' ('hidden parallel') between mistress and mother
- rejected and repressed all actual evidence of impurity, however
strong that might be.   'Tonka' is about integrity.   Musil, in
protecting the integrity of his mistress was protecting the memory of
childhood;   equally, as we shall see, Musil protects the integrity of
the intuition of divine intervention in this world against the inroads
of sceptical positivism represented by the medical men who shook their
heads when he attempted to find some other explanation for Herma's
condition.

'Die Portugiesin', with its medieval setting, seems on first reading to have little to do with Musil's own life. [8]   Closer inspection, however, reveals that it is based on Musil's relationship with Martha Musil and on experiences which Musil had as an officer on the Italian front. [9]   One diary entry tells of a meeting with Martha after Musil had been ill; with horror and amazement they discovered that a cap which once fitted tightly now slips down to Musil's ears - this extraordinary detail is recounted in 'Die Portugiesin'. [10] During this period of sickness Musil had experienced the gentle ecstasy of the loss of will, the passive acceptance of death [11] which is attributed to Ketten in 'Die Portugiesin'.   Even the diseased cat from 'Die Portugiesin' made its first appearance at the house where Musil stayed with Martha when on a short break from military duty. The cat suffered all the symptoms later recorded in 'Die Portugiesin'. [12]   As in the case of Herma Dietz, so here with Martha, Musil is caught up in the way that intense emotions jolt the human being beyond this world, making him or her receptive to signs from another realm - to be in love is to be near death and near God, too.

'Grigia', like 'Die Portugiesin', is based on Musil's experiences during World War I as an officer on the Italian front; Musil carried with him then a little pocket book in which he recorded many of the experiences that were later to be attributed to Homo - some of the language of the fictional narrative closely resembles, indeed in some cases is all but identical to, the war-time notes. [13]

Homo, like Musil, is fascinated by the peasant women with their
unself-conscious and unladylike ways. They sit astride donkeys with
no thought for decorum, squat like Africans by the roadside, spit into
little bunches of hay which they then tuck away out of sight and their
method of binding the hay itself involves flinging themselves down and
embracing it in a manner which reminds Musil of the actions of the
scarab beetle. [14] Nor is it only the peasant women whom Musil meets
during the war who find their way into 'Grigia'. Many other
experiences first noted in the war diary find their place there, too:
the dog that bites a piece off the hand of a cook who is giving him
food; a pig dying in terror; horses forming groups that seem to have
been arranged by a painter; samples of the idiosyncrasies of the
local German dialect. [15] Permeating all this is Musil's sense of
being a man of the city who, despite his relative wealth and civilised
skills, is, by contrast with these peasants, deprived of close links
with the natural environment and of intuitive knowledge of its ways -
in short he represents an age that has exchanged a strong instinctive
grasp of life for a weak, reflective knowledge about aspects of life.

Musil makes only minimal changes in autobiographical data,
behaving rather as if it would be unethical to tamper with the
existential evidence on which his work rests. Musil offers in Drei
Frauen images of himself drawn from different phases of his life: in
'Tonka' as the young man emerging into adulthood and asserting his
independence of the family; in 'Grigia' as a civilised, indeed
effete, modern man in early maturity who finds his scientific training

and urban skills anaemic by comparison with peasant ways and peasant lore; in 'Die Portugiesin', as the soldier in the prime of life, separated from his wife for interminable periods, then reunited for brief interludes and puzzling over intense experiences for which he can find no rational explanation. The irrational is the common denominator here.

What F.G.Peters says of 'Tonka' holds true for all these stories: 'an abyss yawns between the scientific perspective that demands objective verification by empirical evidence and a realm of truth beyond reason that demands nothing more or less than simple faith'. [16] It is in 'Grigia' that Musil identifies the problem most explicitly. Homo and the members of his expedition have imported the twentieth century, with its mix of technical skills and existential ineptitude, into the timeless community of mountain peasants. By day, they impress the local inhabitants with their energy and expertise, at night, left to themselves, they are plagued by the modern ill that they have brought to this remote valley - a sense of total loss of any vital centre to their lives:

Es war die überall gleiche Einheitsmasse von Seele: Europa (...) Sehnsucht nach Weib, Kind, Behaglichkeit. Und zwischendurch immer von neuem das Grammaphon. Rosa, wir fahr'n nach Lodz, Lodz, Lodz ... und Komm in meine Liebeslaube (...). Unanständige Witze zerknallten zu Gelächter (...); nur einmal fragte einer: Wieviel Rattenschwänze braucht man von der Erde zum Mond? (...) Von einem der vielen langen Fliegenpapiere, die von der Decke herabhingen, war vor (Homo) eine Fliege heruntergefallen und lag vergiftet am Rücken, mitten in einer jener Lachen, zu denen in den kaum merklichen Falten des Wachstuchs das Licht der Petroleumlampe zusammenfloß (...) Homo sagte leise vor sich hin: 'Töten, und doch Gott spüren; Gott spüren, und doch töten?' und er schnellte

mit dem Zeigefinger dem ihm gegenübersitzenden Major die Fliege
gerade ins Gesicht, was wieder einen Zwischenfall gab, der bis zum
nächsten Abend vorhielt (244-245).

(Everywhere was the same uniform psychic mass: Europe (...)
longing for wife, child, comfort. And, intermittently, constantly
repeated, the gramophone. Rosa, we're going to Lodz, Lodz,
Lodz... and come to my bower of love (...) Obscene jokes
exploded in laughter (...); once someone asked: how many rats'
tails do you need from the earth to the moon? (...) From one of
the many long pieces of fly paper which hung from the ceiling a
fly had fallen down in front of (Homo) and lay poisoned on its
back in the middle of one of those puddles in which the light of
the paraffin lamp collected in the scarcely perceptible folds of
the wax-cloth (...) In a low voice Homo said to himself: 'To
kill and yet feel God; to feel God, and yet to kill?' and with
his index finger he flicked the fly right into the face of the
major who was sitting opposite him, and this gave rise to another
incident which lasted until the next evening.)

What are such men, products of modern civilisation, to make of these
fragmented experiences? If there is any message, then they
certainly do not understand it. But perhaps the message is not
directed to their understanding at all? In 'Grigia', as in the
other two 'Novellen', the protagonist is in a transitional phase of
his life; he is moving from one kind of awareness to another in a
process of inner growth which he cannot account for but can only feel.

The structure of the narratives in 'Drei Frauen'

In a short essay which he wrote in August 1914, Musil argued
that a good 'Novelle' was to be recognised not by its adherence to
formal criteria but rather by the success with which it recorded
something that shook the author to the very fibre of his or her
Weltanschauung - it was 'etwas, das über (den Dichter) hereinbricht,

eine Erschütterung; (...) eine Fügung des Geschicks' (GWII,1465)
('something that breaks in upon the (creative writer), a shock; (...)
a dispensation of fate').

In each of these 'Novellen' this 'etwas' ('something') takes
explicit shape. In two it forms the climax: in 'Grigia' it is the
protagonist being walled in to die in the cave; in 'Die Portugiesin',
Ketten's defiance of death in scaling the sheer face of the mountain
on which his castle stands; with 'Tonka', on the other hand, it is
the continuing mystery that surrounds the girl's illness and
pregnancy. In each story Musil demonstrates a single-minded
attention to these symbols of commitment beyond the reach of reason;
the sense of mystery is deepened by the succinctness of the style.

Just as in a mathematical proof, economy of argument is an
object of admiration, so in these 'Novellen' the narrator seems to be
impelled by a desire to present what it is that has been shaken by
some settled order with few circumlocutions; as Musil expresses it:
'Außer dem Zwang, in beschränktem Raum das Nötige unterzubringen,
bedingt kein Prinzip einen einheitlichen Formcharakter der Gattung'
(GWII,1466) ('Except for the pressure to fit everything into a
restricted space there is no principle which determines a homogeneous
form or character for the genre'). In 'Grigia' even the hay is ripe
with significance:

> Die Heuställe hatten sich gefüllt. Durch die Fugen zwischen
> den Balken strömt silbernes Licht ein. Das Heu strömt grünes

Licht aus.   Unter dem Tor liegt eine dicke goldene Borte.
    Das Heu roch säuerlich.   Wie die Negergetränke, die aus dem
Teig von Früchten und menschlichem Speichel entstehn.   Man
brauchte sich nur zu erinnern, daß man hier unter Wilden lebte, so
entstand schon ein Rausch in der Hitze des engen, von gärendem Heu
hochgefüllten Raums.
    Das Heu trägt in allen Lagen.   Man steht darin bis an die
Waden, unsicher zugleich und überfest gehalten.   Man liegt darin
wie in Gottes Hand, möchte sich in Gottes Hand wälzen wie ein
Hündchen oder ein Schweinchen.   Man liegt schräg, und fast
senkrecht wie ein Heiliger, der in einer grünen Wolke zum Himmel
fährt (249).[17]

    (The hay barns had filled up. Through the joins between the
beams silver light streams in. From the hay, green light streams
out. Under the gate is a thick golden border.
    The hay smelt a little sour. Like the negro drinks which are
made from a paste of fruits and human spittle. One only had to
remember that one was living here among barbarians and straight
away one felt intoxicated in the narrow space piled high with
fermenting hay.
    The hay offers support in all positions. Standing in it up
to one's calves, one is both insecure yet held all too firmly.
One lies in it as if God's hand, one would like to wallow in God's
hand like a puppy or a little pig. One lies at an angle, almost
vertically, like a saint being borne up to Heaven in a green
cloud.)

Musil does not digress here at all from his central concerns in the
'Novelle'; the hay, presented as the product of the intermingling of
the light of the sun with the earth, is also the bed for Homo and
Grigia's love making; this natural substance sets Homo's mind along
the track of the thoughts worked into this extract and is a stage in
that strange initiation which will eventually lead to his being
reconciled to becoming a suborganic part of the universe.

    The extraordinary climb in 'Die Portugiesin' is narrated with no
deviation from the essential: the effort of the climb is in the
continuum of Ketten's vital energy, traced from the sinews of the

fingers through the network of nerves into the brain:

> Tief beim Fluß bog er ab; über Blöcke, zwischen denen das
> Wasser trieb, dann an Büschen hinauf in die Wand. Der Mond
> zeichnete mit Schattenpunkten die kleinen Vertiefungen, in welche
> Finger und Zehen hineingreifen konnten. Plötzlich brach ein
> Stein unter dem Fuß weg; der Ruck schoß in die Sehnen, dann ins
> Herz. Ketten horchte; es schien ohne Ende zu dauern, bevor der
> Stein ins Wasser schlug; er mußte mindestens ein Drittel der Wand
> schon unter sich haben. Da wachte er, so schien es deutlich, auf
> und wußte, was er getan hatte. Unten ankommen konnte nur ein
> Toter, und die Wand hinauf der Teufel. Er tastete suchend über
> sich. Bei jedem Griff hing das Leben in den zehn Riemchen der
> Fingersehnen; Schweiß trat aus der Stirn, Hitze flog im Körper,
> die Nerven wurden wie steinerne Fäden: aber, seltsam zu fühlen,
> begannen bei diesem Kampf mit dem Tod Kraft und Gesundheit in die
> Glieder zu fließen, als kehrten sie von außen wieder in den Körper
> zurück. Und das Unwahrscheinliche gelang; noch mußte oben einem
> Überhang nach der Seite ausgewichen sein, dann schlang sich der
> Arm in ein Fenster (268-269).

> (Deep down by the river he turned off; over slabs of stone
> between which the water drove, then up past bushes and up to the
> cliff-face. The moon marked, with patches of shadow, the little
> hollows in which fingers and toes could find a hold. Suddenly a
> stone broke away under a foot; the jolt shot into the sinews,
> then into the heart. Ketten listened; it seemed to be an age
> before the stone hit the water; he must have climbed at least a
> third of the face already. It seemed clear to him that it was
> then that he woke up and realised what he had done. Only in
> death could one get to the foot of the face again, only the Devil
> could get to the top. He felt around above him. With every
> hand-hold life hung in the ten little straps that were the finger
> sinews; sweat stood out on his brow, warmth raced in his body, the
> nerves became like threads of stone: but, in a strange sensation
> which accompanied this struggle with death, strength and health
> began to flow into his limbs as if they were returning to the body
> from without. And the improbable was accomplished. There was
> still an overhang to skirt around, then the arm reached through an
> open window and held on.)

Here Musil, at the vital centre of his 'Novelle', with barely a
metaphor, captures the deed that makes manifest Ketten's essential
wilfulness. The man, even in his weak state, conceives the deed, and
in doing the deed, recovers - recovers his former self. 'I shall do

it,' he seems to be saying, 'because the rock is there, because I want to do it.' No reason is needed for this reaffirmation by Ketten that, despite the important insights that have come to him in the passive condition of illness, his natural state is activity. He is not a watcher but a doer.

In 'Tonka' we find a sentence whose length belies its significance: 'Sie sagte nicht ja und nicht nein und nicht danke' (281) ('She did not say yes, nor no, nor thank you'). This exercise in negation, following immediately on the young man's offer to care for Tonka after she has lost her job as a nurse, marks the moment in the 'Novelle' where Tonka, by accepting, passes from independence of him to total dependence on him. For Musil's reader it may seem to have the strange appeal of an oracular utterance; for Musil its resonance was even stronger. He recorded it first in his diary shortly after the turn of the century and it evidently marks the moment when Herma accepted his offer of protection. [18] The sense of depth which attaches to much of Musil's language can often be traced to such a sensitive psychic origin in the author's own life; the reader is left with the impression that Musil has lived for a long time not just with the memory but also with the formulation in which that memory is held.

The imagery which Musil uses is similarly suggestive; the 'wie' ('like') or 'als' ('as') with which the most striking images are introduced lift the narrative into a different dimension, bringing the reader's own world into direct contact with Musil's own. The effect is almost that of a dialogue - Musil seems to invite the reader to join in a common enterprise by saying: 'By exploring what this image suggests to you, you will no doubt be able to find a corresponding emotion within your own field of experience.' This invitation, though open-ended, is closely linked to the narrative as 'Novelle'.

An image from 'Tonka' will illustrate this process: 'Tonka liebte er, weil er sie nicht liebte, weil sie seine Seele nicht erregte, sondern glatt wusch wie frisches Wasser' (284) ('He loved Tonka because he did not love her, because she did not arouse his soul, but washed it smooth as fresh water'). The image, 'seine Seele (....) glatt wusch wie frisches Wasser' ('washed his soul (...) smooth as fresh water'), though it reaches into the reader's store of private emotional experience, is held firmly within the field of the paradox, the 'abstract oxymoron': 'Tonka liebte er, weil er sie nicht liebte' ('He loved Tonka because he did not love her'). The image of fresh water, a union of purity and the absence of any strong sensation of taste, makes meaningful a statement which holds the attention because of its surface denial of meaning. It will only be when Tonka is dead - in other words, in the terms of the image, when the young man's soul is denied her cleansing presence - that he will realise what she means to him. This image anticipates the sensation which overwhelms the young man towards the end of the narrative when full awareness that Tonka is dead comes to him - [19] a Proustian appreciation of experience through retrospection.

In 'Grigia' we find a similarly economical use of images. The geographical setting, the interrelations of peasants and the land they till, is crucial to the 'Novelle'; Homo's growing appreciation of the natural cycle of things, of man's primeval link with the soil, will reconcile him to his immurement later in the living rock of the old mine-workings – the geologist will become one with his subject. Consider the following image, part of that narrative line which leads to this death – a fate whose horror is attenuated by Homo's being inwardly reconciled to it – which is integral to the passage where Grigia herself is introduced: 'Sie saß dann, mit ihrem violett braunen Rock und dem gesprenkelten Kopftuch, am Rand ihrer Wiese, die Spitzen der Holländerschuhe in die Luft gekrümmt, die Hände auf der bunten Schürze verschränkt, und sah so natürlich lieblich aus wie ein schlankes giftiges Pilzchen' (245) (my emphasis) ('She was sitting wearing her violet and brown skirt and the spotted head-scarf, at the edge of her meadow, with the tips of her Dutch clogs curving upwards, hands folded on her brightly-coloured apron, and she looked as natural and inviting as a slim poisonous toadstool'(my emphasis)).

The image fits into the immediate context – the colours of the traditional costume suggest the pigmentation of a toadstool; but it also fits the wider context: the sense of the organic interdependence of mankind and nature, just as the toadstool is merely the spore stem of a network of tubules under the surface of the soil where it makes its brief and fragile appearance. [20]

In 'Die Portugiesin' Ketten and his lady are presented, through images, in terms of the characteristic by which - so the reader imagines it - each recognises the other. Ketten comes from a line of fighting men: 'Und bös wie Messer waren sie, die gleich tief schneiden' (253) ('and they were bad-tempered as knives which straight away cut deep'). Small wonder that the lady from Portugal rears a wolf whose presence reminds her of her husband as he was before his illness. Ketten cannot see through the veil of his wife's foreign beauty to the depths of her inner self, her dark eyes do not reveal her soul but only reflect his image. [21] She has borne him two sons but he still cannot penetrate her mystery: 'Es war wie Zauberei. Ruhig saß, in ihrem reichen Gewand, mit dem Rock, der in unzähligen Faltenbächen herabfloß, die Gestalt, nur aus sich heraussteigend und in sich fallend; wie ein Brunnenstrahl' (259) (my emphasis) ('It was like sorcery. This figure sat there calmly, in its rich gown, with its skirt flowing down in a stream of countless folds, rising up from itself and falling back into itself; like the water-jet of a fountain'(my emphasis)). The image expresses Ketten's sense of the perhaps alien forces playing without apparent effort behind the familiar mask of his wife's foreign face. These images underpin the reader's awareness of the dangerous instability of this marriage. To the wife, the husband appears as a being of menacing vigour; to the husband, the wife appears as an inscrutable sorceress with occult powers.

We have examined how Musil uses linguistic means to shape the
disparate and discrete elements of experiences he has had into
coherent literary form.   There are other means at his disposal as
well: one is the inherent suggestiveness of the setting of each of the
'Novellen'.

'Tonka' is set in a city.   It is a story that revolves around
the different expectations and rules that govern the lives of members
of different social classes.   Though Musil was by upbringing and
inclination a liberal, there are passages in this 'Novelle' that might
have been written by a Marxist; [22]   this city, as one critic puts it,
is 'la Ville-Monstre'. [23]   When the fact that Tonka is pregnant comes
to the attention of her employer - she is an assistant in a big shop
in a workers' quarter - she is dismissed on the spot.   The narrator
comments:

(...) eines Tages wurde Tonka ins Kontor gerufen und rund heraus
gefragt, wie es mit ihr stünde.   Sie brachte keine Antwort
hervor, bloß die Tränen traten ihr in die Augen.   Und den
vernünftigen Mann rührte es nicht, daß sie nicht sprechen konnte;
er zahlte ihr den Gehalt für einen Monat aus und entließ sie auf
der Stelle.   So böse war er geworden, daß er donnerte, er sei
jetzt verlegen um einen Ersatz, und es sei Betrug von Tonka
gewesen, ihren Zustand zu verheimlichen, als sie die Stellung
annahm;   nicht einmal das Kontorfräulein schickte er hinaus, als
er ihr das sagte.   Tonka kam sich danach sehr schlecht vor, aber
auch er bewunderte heimlich diesen schäbigen, kleinen, namenlosen
Kaufmann, der nicht eine Minute lang geschwankt hatte, seinem
Geschäftswillen Tonka zu opfern, und mit ihr ihre Tränen, ein Kind
und weiß Gott welche Erfindungen, welche Seelen, welches
Menschenschicksal, denn das alles wußte er ja nicht und fragte
nicht danach (292-293).

((...) one day Tonka was summoned to the office and asked straight
out if she was pregnant or not. She couldn't get an answer out,
the tears just welled in her eyes. And this man of reason was
not moved by her not being able to speak; he paid her a month's
salary and dismissed her on the spot. He had become so angry
that he thundered that he would now have difficulty finding a
replacement and that it was deception on Tonka's part to have
concealed her condition when she took the job; he didn't even
send the office-girl out when he told her this. Afterwards Tonka
felt that she was very bad but he, too, felt a secret admiration
for this shabby little nameless merchant who had not hesitated for
a moment to sacrifice Tonka to his business interests and, with
her, her tears, a child, Lord only knows what intentions, what
souls, what human fate, for he knew nothing of all this, nor did
he ask about it.)

Lack of support from his family forces the young man to share

Tonka's destitution, though his clothes mark him out as belonging to a

higher social class: 'Er machte eine sonderbare Figur in seinen

vornehmen Kleidern zwischen den Gehilfen und Geschäftsdienern, ernst,

schweigsam, treu zur Seite seiner schwangeren Gefährtin und

unzertrennlich' (293) ('In his elegant clothes he cut a strange figure

among the shop assistants and workers, serious, silent, faithful and

inseparable by the side of his pregnant partner').

The young man's actions give the lie to the assumption made

explicit by the shopkeeper's behaviour and in his family's action when

they paid Tonka simply what was her legal due - that human commitments

can be measured and discharged in hard cash. This 'capitalist

morality' surfaces again in the 'Novelle' when the young man's mother

appears and suggests a business transaction to 'pay off the debt' of

the girl's pregnancy and predicament: '(Die Mutter hatte) den Vater

trotz aller Schwierigkeiten bewogen, eine gewisse Summe zu opfern.

Man werde damit, eröffnete sie wie eine große Güte, das Mädchen samt
den Ansprüchen des Kindes abfinden' (291) ('(The mother had), in spite
of all the difficulties involved, persuaded the father to sacrifice a
certain sum. It would be possible, she said, as if it were an act of
great kindness, to reach a settlement with the girl, and meet the
claims of the child').

The young man, prompted by his innate humanity, refuses to
accept this and is thereby reduced to chancing his luck, quite
literally, in city lotteries. His failure to win any prize and his
sense that it is as unthinkable for someone of his station to look for
a menial job as it would be to marry his plebeian mistress, the
consequent cheap accommodation, poor food, the loss of self-respect,
drive Tonka steadily down the spiral of urban poverty to her death.
For all the young man's honourable self-sacrifice on Tonka's behalf he
gets off lightly, with sad memories, chastened but not broken. He is
overwhelmed for a moment by the sense of having lost Tonka, but that
passes. He apparently feels no remorse for what he has done or left
undone. In the narrative, which closely follows the young man's own
sensations, the retrospective third-person, past-tense perspective
imbues what happens with an air of inevitability. This contrasts
sharply with the mood of Der Mann ohne Eigenschaften where the
narrative attacks the complacency of such fatalism; but in 'Tonka'
the narrator seems to imply 'this is what happened because this was
meant to happen' - and such a mood is admirably suited to the
'Novelle' form, which thrives on the sense of the action being

rounded-off and complete.

In 'Grigia' Homo steps from the city into the world of mountain
peasants. Where, before, the urban environment surrounded him on all
sides with artefacts, now, with heightened awareness, he sees human
life in its natural setting. In the following passage the narrator
describes the moment when Homo and his companions, riding up a valley
high in the mountain, first set eyes on the place where they will base
their operations:

> (Der seltsame Ort) hing an der Lehne eines Hügels; der Saumweg,
> der sie hingeführt hatte, sprang zuletzt förmlich von einem großen
> platten Stein zum nächsten, und von ihm flossen, den Hang hinab
> und gewunden wie Bäche, ein paar kurze, steile Gassen in die
> Wiesen. Stand man am Weg, so hatte man nur vernachlässigte und
> dürftige Bauernhäuser vor sich, blickte man aber von den Wiesen
> unten herauf, so meinte man sich in ein vorweltliches Pfahldorf
> zurückversetzt, denn die Häuser standen mit der Talseite alle auf
> hohen Balken, und ihre Abtritte schwebten etwas abseits von ihnen
> wie die Gondeln von Sänften auf vier schlanken baumlangen Stangen
> über dem Abhang (236).

> ((The strange place) hung on the slope of a hill; the path, which
> had brought them there along the edge of the hill had finally made
> great leaps from one large flat stone to the next, and a few short
> steep alleys, meandering like streams, flowed down from it into
> the meadows. If one stood next to the path one only had before
> one some humble, neglected farm houses, but if one looked upwards
> from the meadows below one felt transported back in time to some
> primeval village on stilts, for on the side facing the valley the
> houses stood on high beams and their privies which were set a
> little way apart from them, swayed over the slope like
> litter-carriages on four thin poles as tall as trees.)

Given the proximity of earth and stone the villagers have an affinity
to these elements which is, at the outset, quite foreign to Homo

(whose very name is an impersonal scientific label, suggesting the
self-alienation which Homo feels). The women of the village are a
revelation to the hero. Their unconscious actions and uninhibited
mannerisms fascinate and sexually stimulate this city man who is used
only to the coy propriety of over-dressed ladies of civilised society:

> Wenn (diese Weiber) warten mußten, setzten sie sich nicht auf den
> Wegrand, sondern auf die flache Erde des Pfads und zogen die Knie
> hoch wie die Neger.   Und wenn sie, was zuweilen geschah, auf
> ihren Eseln die Berge hinanritten, dann saßen sie nicht auf ihren
> Röcken, sondern wie Männer und mit unempfindlichen Schenkeln auf
> den scharfen Holzkanten der Tragsättel (239).

> (When (these women) had to wait, they didn't sit by the wayside
> but on the flat earth of the path itself, drawing up their knees
> like negroes. And when, as sometimes happened, they rode up the
> mountains on their donkeys they did not sit on their skirts but
> sat like men and with insensitive thighs, on the sharp wooden
> sides of the saddles.)

The peasant girl, Grigia, whom Homo takes as his mistress, represents
for him the contiguity of earth and human flesh.   Sometimes when he
goes to look for her he finds her crouching in a potato field, the
narrative catching a stab of sexual desire: 'Er wußte, sie hat nichts
als zwei Röcke an, die trockene Erde, die durch ihre schlanken, rauhen
Finger rann, berührte ihren Leib' (249) ('He knew, she has nothing on
but two skirts and the dry earth which ran through her slim, rough
fingers touched her body').

The reader approaches this strange community from Homo's angle,
and tries with him to puzzle out their tribal attitudes, the habits
and rituals into which their alien minds are set.   There are no

answers, just implicit questions.   How is the sexual freedom of these

women, expressed in deed as well as word, [24] to be squared with the

terrible penalty for adultery exacted from Homo at the end of the

'Novelle'?   At what point did a liaison which appeared to be

tolerated by the villagers break some secret irrational taboo?   To

this stranger no answers are given, only an ultimate final initiation

into tribal practice.   To 'know' the secrets of this community there

are only two ways: to live here, or to die here - either to grow up

with these people, in this place where survival is to scrape a living

from the soil and to feel, by instinct as much as by admonition, how

one has to behave, or to experience the power of their ways and their

lore through their deep anger.   No doubt the manner of his dying

makes Homo a part of folk lore, but it does not bring either him or

the reader any closer to understanding it.   But to feel irritated at

this is to miss an important message from the text: 'understanding' is

something for folk from the city;   for these peasants there is only

the unwritten code of life in their mountains.   The mystery which

this community holds for the protagonist, and thereby the narrative

tension vital to the 'Novelle', is maintained to the end.

In 'Die Portugiesin' the setting is even wilder and more

mountainous; it is remote not only in space but in time.   By placing

the action in the medieval world Musil gives freer rein to

imagination: the immediate is seen with the detail of that sharper

sense perception which is associated with primitive people, the more

distant is lost in vague recollection, rumour and myth.   Here the narrator describes Ketten's castle:

Wild stieg das Schloß auf.   Da und dort saßen an der Felsbrust
verkümmerte Bäumchen wie einzelne Haare.   Die Waldberge stürzten
so auf und nieder, daß man diese Häßlichkeit einem, der nur die
Meereswellen kannte, gar nicht hätte zu beschreiben vermögen.
Voll kaltgewordener Würze war die Luft, und alles war so, als
ritte man in einen großen zerborstenen Topf hinein, der eine
fremde grüne Farbe enthielt.   Aber in den Wäldern gab es den
Hirsch, Bären, das Wildschwein, den Wolf und vielleicht das
Einhorn.   Weiter hinten hausten Steinböcke und Adler.
Unergründete Schluchten boten den Drachen Aufenthalt.   Wochenweit
und -tief war der Wald, durch den nur die Wildfährten führten, und
oben, wo das Gebirge ihm aufsaß, begann das Reich der Geister.
Dämonen hausten dort mit dem Sturm und den Wolken; nie führte
eines Christen Weg hinauf (...) (255).

(The castle rose up wildly. Here and there at the cliff's breast
were little stunted trees like single hairs. The wooded mountains
hurled themselves downwards and upwards in a way that would have
been impossible to describe to one who knew only the waves of the
sea.   The air was full of the cooled fragrance of herbs and it
all seemed like a ride into a big pot containing a strange green
paint which had burst open.   But in the woods there were deer,
bears, wild boar, wolves and perhaps unicorns.   Further on ibexes
and eagles lived.   Unfathomed canyons offered dragons shelter.
The woods, crossed only by the trails of animals, were weeks-wide
and weeks-deep and above the point where they were topped by the
mountain range began the realm of the spirits.   Demons dwelt
there with the clouds and the storm; never did a Christian turn
his steps that way.)

To its inhabitants, this castle is at the threshold of the beyond.

They are not solid early twentieth-century positivists, certain that,

were they able to circle the whole globe, all things which they

encountered would, in time, yield up their secrets and their

strangeness; rather they are natural mystics, conscious of the limits

of their human understanding and ever on the watch for signs that

indicate the influence of the divine.   In such a setting why should

not a cat with symptoms of the mange have been sent by God as a

warning or a sign?   A beautiful woman from a land immeasurably
removed from this place might she not be at least a necromancer,
perhaps even the Devil himself?   What could be more understandable
here, what more fitting as a test of knightly resolve, will and
self-reliance than a 'trial' or 'ordeal' - Ketten's flinging down the
gauntlet to fate with the challenge which will decide whether or not
he is to be master of his own house, setting off before he has fully
recovered from his illness to scale the sheer face of the mountain on
which his castle-home stands.   Ketten is not like the male
protagonists of the two other 'Novellen'.   They are essentially
passive figures - scholar/observers by trade and by inclination;
Ketten is a man of action who, though incapacitated by illness, finds
his way back to his old active self.   In view of this, is it possible
to maintain that the three men who have been captivated by these three
women are all expressions of sides of Musil's own psychic personality?

Narrator as observer

Ketten, as we saw, when healthy hardly pauses to draw breath.
The language with which this man of action is described bristles with
his unreflective energy: having scarcely arrived home with his new
bride: 'Zwei Tage später saß er wieder im Sattel. (..) Und elf Jahre
später tat er es noch' (256) ('Two days later he was again in the
saddle. (..) Eleven years later he was still on horseback').   Even a
wound scarcely slows him down:

'Fünf Tage nach der Kunde von seiner Verwundung kam er erst zu (seiner Frau) und blieb bloß einen Tag. Sie sah ihn an, ohne zu fragen, prüfend, wie man dem Flug eines Pfeils folgt, ob er treffen wird.

Er zog seine Leute herbei bis zum letzten erreichbaren Knaben, ließ die Burg in Verteidigungszustand setzen, ordnete und befahl. Knechtlärm, Pferdegewieher, Balkentragen, Eisen- und Steinklang war dieser Tag. In der Nacht ritt er weiter' (256).

(It was only five days after the news of his being wounded that he came to (his wife) and then he stayed only one day. She looked at him, without asking anything, watching closely in the way one follows the flight of an arrow to see if it will hit the target.

He gathered his men, down to the very last boy who could be reached, put the castle in a state of defensive readiness, organised and issued orders. Noisy retainers, neighing of horses, baulks of timber, the sound of iron and stone being struck, filled this day. That night he rode on.)

Then, having brought generations of feuding to a successful end, Ketten contracts a disease that leaves him a changed man; with the disease comes reflection (provoking a suspicion that this symptom may be a secret, symbolic cause): 'Er schlief viel und war auch mit offenen Augen abwesend; wenn aber sein Bewußtsein zurückkehrte, so war doch dieser willenlose, kindlich warme und ohnmächtige Körper nicht seiner, und diese von einem Hauch erregte schwache Seele seine auch nicht' (262) ('He slept a great deal and his eyes, when open, had a vacant stare; but when his consciousness returned this powerless body, warm as a child's and without any will, was not his, nor was this mind his, which a mere breath could arouse').

Stripped of the central concern of his life and reduced to lassitude by illness, Ketten is a different being. It is true that, even while he is ill, he makes ineffectual attempts to recover his vitality: he orders the wolf which his wife is rearing as a pet to be

killed; he strikes across the face a chaplain who insults him, but it
is only when he undergoes the final 'trial' on the cliff-face that he
becomes himself again. But during his illness we find him brooding
over his inability to comprehend his wife:

> In den Nebeln der Krankheit, die ihn umfangen hielten, erschien
> ihm die Gestalt seiner Frau weicher, als es hätte sein müssen;
> sie erschien ihm nicht anders als früher, wenn es ihn gewundert
> hatte, ihre Liebe zuweilen heftiger wiederzufinden als sonst,
> während doch in der Abwesenheit keine Ursache lag.   Er hätte
> nicht einmal sagen können, ob er heiter oder traurig war; genau so
> wie in jenen Tagen der tiefen Todesnähe.   Er konnte sich nicht
> rühren.   Wenn er seiner Frau in die Augen sah, waren sie wie
> frisch geschliffen, sein eignes Bild lag obenauf, und sie ließen
> seinen Blick nicht ein (265).

> (From the mists of the sickness that surrounded him the figure of
> his wife seemed softer to him than it ought to have been; she
> seemed to him to be just as she had been earlier on occasions when
> he had been surprised to find her love more violent than usual
> when, after all, in his absence there was no reason for this.   He
> would not even have been able to say whether he was happy or sad;
> just like in those days when he had sunk so close to death.   He
> could not move.   When he looked into his wife's eyes they seemed
> newly polished, his own image lay on top and they did not let his
> gaze in.)

His interrogatory gaze, heavy with thought, seems bound to be
reflected unanswered; now that he is ill he has become the 'brother
in perception' of the male protagonists in the other stories - a
hesitant, anxious, uncertain man.

Homo, in 'Grigia', enters the village, as we have seen, as an
outsider, skilled in science but unversed in the ways of simpler
people.   He knows how to observe but is, so to speak, existentially
illiterate.   He records the data of consciousness as they register in

his brain, whether the datum is a pig about to be slaughtered, a group
of women resting in a field or a fly expiring on the tablecloth.   But
the very precision of his perception of objects throws into relief the
isolation of Homo's self as subject;   it identifies him as man
detached from life.   His anguish verges on the religious: he seems
to be searching for the link that will absorb him, the alienated
subject, into this world of objects that will not yield up its secrets
to his probing psyche − he does not realise that it is the probing
psyche itself that denies meaning.   Here Musil creates a character
who expresses the problem which Husserl saw as the dilemma of the
scientific viewpoint: in a world of objects, where is the subject to
stand?   Later Homo does find his place but, in so doing, surrenders
his life.   The process which takes place within Homo is described in
the following extract; it starts with a description of the way in
which Homo feels the outside world is swallowing him up:

(...) dann kann es geschehen, daß diese fremden
Lebenserscheinungen Besitz von dem ergreifen, was herrenlos
geworden ist.   Sie gaben ihm aber kein neues, von Glück ehrgeizig
und erdfest gewordenes Ich, sondern sie siedelten nur so in
zusammenhanglos schönen Flecken im Luftriß seines Körpers.   Homo
fühlte an irgend etwas, daß er bald sterben werde, er wußte bloß
noch nicht, wie oder wann.   Sein altes Leben war kraftlos
geworden; es wurde wie ein Schmetterling, der gegen den Herbst zu
immer schwächer wird (248).

((...) then it can happen that these alien phenomena of life take
possession of that which is without a master.   But they did not
give him a new "I", endowed by happiness with ambition and a sense
of earthbound substantiality, but just took up residence, within
the airy outline of his body, in patches of incoherent beauty.
Then somehow Homo had a feeling that he would soon die, he just
didn't know how or when.   His old life had become powerless; it
became like a butterfly getting weaker and weaker as autumn
approaches.)

The price which Homo pays for dividing the world sharply into subject
and object is, in his case, death. (Was ever the feeling which Freud
has given the name 'thanatos' expressed in a more delicate way?)

In 'Tonka', the isolation of subject and object is portrayed
with even greater emphasis. This is seen perhaps most clearly at the
beginning of the work. Musil spent a great deal of time working on
the opening paragraph. In an early draft the tone is conversational,
though something of the effect of the discontinuity of experience can
be identified:

> Ich sage es ist eine banale Geschichte. Sie begann, als
> Nestor.. sein Freiwilligenjahr bei den Nikolausdragonern
> abdiente, auf einem Spazierritt. An einem Zaun. Abends. Die
> Sonne war schon irgendwo hinter den Bäumen. Ein Vogel sang. Er
> saß auf dem Zaun und sang. Dann schwieg er. Und die
> Bauernmädchen kamen singend über die Felder zurück. Tonka stand
> vor der Tür eines städtischen Häuschens, dem vordersten im Dorf
> gegen die Stadt zu (TbII,859).

> (As I said, it's a banal kind of story. It began when
> Nestor .. was doing his year's voluntary service with the Nikolaus
> Dragoons, on a ride. Next to a fence. In the evening. The
> sun was already somewhere or other behind the trees. A bird was
> singing. It sat on the fence and sang. Then it fell silent.
> And the peasant-girls came singing back across the fields. Tonka
> stood in front of the door of a municipal cottage, the first one
> in the village when one comes from the town.)

In the finished version Musil has cut back the descriptive detail and
added strange observations which imply that a message is hidden in the
phenomena presented for scrutiny:

184

An einem Zaun. Ein Vogel sang. Die Sonne war dann schon
irgendwo hinter den Büschen. Der Vogel schwieg. Es war Abend.
Die Bauernmädchen kamen singend über die Felder. Welche
Einzelheiten! Ist es Kleinlichkeit, wenn solche Einzelheiten
sich an einen Menschen heften? Wie Kletten!? Das war Tonka.
Die Unendlichkeit fließt manchmal in Tropfen (270).

(Next to a fence. A bird was singing. The sun was then already
somewhere behind the bushes. The bird fell silent. It was
evening. The peasant-girls came singing across the fields.
What details! Is it pettiness if such details cling to a person?
 Like burrs!? That was Tonka. Infinity sometimes flows in
droplets.)

What, the reader wonders, has happened to the observer-narrator who
was identified in the original passage? [25] Now in the final version
he is conspicuous by his absence. Phenomena are what they are and no
more; as presented here they are things untouched by meaning and
syntax. Man may try to put his mark on them - they can be moved
around in the imagination into different patterns - but, Musil seems
to suggest here, they are indifferent to the probing of scientific
method. Musil expresses the hopelessness of the scientist's search
for certainty within the phenomenal world; the story itself documents
the young man's interrogation of Tonka and medical men in unceasing
but fruitless attempts to reach absolutely objective knowledge about
her innocence or guilt. [26] Certainty, if it is to be found at all,
does not come from the mode of enquiry characteristic of science.

The climax of each 'Novelle' represents, in different ways, the
triumph of an anti-objective, non-rational perspective: Ketten
recovers not through finding out what is going on behind his wife's
dark eyes but by indulging an impulse of folly; Homo lets himself be

led into the mountainside as a scapegoat for sins committed against an order that he does not understand; the young man in 'Tonka', after months of intense scientific work and months of obsessional questioning of Tonka, must face the fact of her recent death. His frantic energy drains away : 'Die Spannung der letzten Wochen, die Spannung seiner Erfindung (...), hatte sich gelöst, er war fertig (...)' (306) ('The tension of the last few weeks, the tension of his invention (...) had relaxed, he had finished'). The sight of a child's face suddenly triggers off an overpowering response in him at this moment of passivity and receptivity: '(...) da schrie die Erinnerung in ihm auf: Tonka! Tonka! Er fühlte sie von der Erde bis zum Kopf und ihr ganzes Leben. Alles, was er niemals gewußt hatte, stand in diesem Augenblick vor ihm, die Binde der Blindheit schien von seinen Augen gesunken zu sein' (306) ('(...) then memory shouted out within him: Tonka! Tonka! He felt her and her whole life go right through him from head to foot. Everything that he had never known stood before him in this moment, the scales of blindness seemed to have dropped from his eyes'). A fragment from the realm of the transcendental breaks through into a human life; it is not accidental that this happens through the agency of love.

Love, death and beyond

Love is linked with death. This link is an echo of Novalis whom Musil actually mentions in 'Tonka'. [27] In the year when Drei Frauen was published both his mother and father died and, though these events can have had no direct effect on the 'Novellen' which were completed before 1924, Musil's anticipation of the death of his parents no doubt did leave its mark on his narratives.   Death, like illness and the metaphysical, exerts a strong fascination on Musil; he strains senses and intellect to grasp its meaning.

Since death reaches out to the individual through sickness, sickness provides a guide to at least the threshold of death.   Musil was evidently recording his own state of high fever in 1916, when he drafted the description of Ketten's illness:

> (...) Er schlief viel und war auch mit offenen Augen abwesend; wenn aber sein Bewußtsein zurückkehrte, so war doch dieser willenlose, kindlich warme und ohnmächtige Körper nicht seiner, und diese von einem Hauch erregte schwache Seele seine auch nicht. Gewiß war er schon abgeschieden und wartete während dieser ganzen Zeit bloß irgendwo darauf, ob er noch einmal zurückkehren müsse. Er hatte nie gewußt, daß Sterben so friedlich sei; er war mit einem Teil seines Wesens vorangestorben (...) (262). [28]

> ((...) He slept a great deal and his eyes, when open, had a vacant stare; but when his consciousness returned this powerless body, warm as a child's and without any will, was not his, nor was this mind his which a mere breath could arouse.   It was certain that he had already departed and throughout this whole period was just waiting to see if he would have to return again.   He had never known that dying was so peaceful; a part of his being had gone on before in anticipation of death (...))

Here, again, Musil succeeds in giving a precise account of a state which is intrinsically resistant to language.   Ketten, formerly a man of will and action, is unrecognisable here.   In this moment of weakness Ketten sees his wife bending over him:

Während die Knochen noch im Bett lagen, und das Bett da war, seine
Frau sich über ihn beugte, und er, aus Neugierde, zur Abwechslung,
die Bewegungen in ihrem aufmerksamen Gesicht beobachtete, war
alles, was er liebte, schon weit voran.   Der Herr von Ketten und
dessen mondnächtige Zauberin waren aus ihm herausgetreten und
hatten sich sacht entfernt: er sah sie noch, er wußte, mit einigen
großen Sprüngen würde er sie danach einholen, nur jetzt wußte er
nicht, war er schon bei ihnen oder noch hier.   Das alles aber lag
in einer riesigen gütigen Hand, die so mild war wie eine Wiege und
zugleich alles abwog, ohne aus der Entscheidung viel Wesens zu
machen.   Das mochte Gott sein (262).

(While the bones still lay in bed and the bed was there, with his
wife bending over him and as he - from curiosity, to pass the time
- observed the movements in her attentive face, everything that he
loved was already far on ahead.   Lord von Ketten and his moon-lit
night-sorceress had detached themselves from him and had gently
moved off: he could still see them, he knew that afterwards he
would catch up with them with a few great leaps, only now he did
not know if he was already with them or still here.   But it all
lay in a huge kindly hand which was as gentle as a cradle and at
the same time weighed everything up without making much fuss about
the decision.   That may have been God.)

To be ill is to draw close to death but thereby, Musil implies, close

to God, also.   Illness brings a surrender of vitality and of the

energy of wilfulness;   the onset of organic dissolution predisposes

the individual to be receptive to the divine.   What we observe in

'Die Portugiesin' we find in a modified shape in 'Grigia' and 'Tonka'.

Homo is not sick, it is true, but he suffers from a weakness that

will prove fatal.   By comparison with the peasants his hold on life

is feeble.   This hold is further weakened by his decision to spend

the summer away from his wife and son;   this decision he sees: 'als

eine große Selbstsucht, es war aber vielleicht eher eine

Selbstauflösung, denn er war zuvor nie auch nur einen Tag lang von

seiner Frau geschieden gewesen' (234) ('as an intense selfishness, but

188

perhaps it was rather a self-dissolution, for he had never before been parted from his wife even for one day'). He receives a letter from his sick son and, as he wanders on his own across meadows and through the trees of this remote place, something strange comes over him:

> (....) er erkannte jetzt erst, was er getan hatte, indem er sich für diesen Sommer absonderte und von seiner eigenen Strömung treiben ließ, die ihn erfaßt hatte. Er sank zwischen den Bäumen mit den giftgrünen Bärten aufs Knie, breitete die Arme aus, was er so noch nie in seinem Leben getan hatte, und ihm war zu Mut, als hätte man ihm in diesem Augenblick sich selbst aus den Armen genommen (240).

> ((...) he now, for the first time, realised what he had done, in isolating himself for this summer and letting himself drift with his own current which was now carrying him off. He sank down on his knees between the trees with their beards of poisonous green, spread his arms out, something which he had never done before in all his life, and he felt as if he himself had, at this moment, been taken out of his own arms.)

Here, again, love and death are intermingling:

> Er fühlte die Hand seiner Geliebten in seiner, ihre Stimme im Ohr, alle Stellen seines Körpers waren wie eben erst berührt, er empfand sich selbst wie eine von einem anderen Körper gebildete Form. Aber er hatte sein Leben außer Kraft gesetzt. Sein Herz war demütig vor der Geliebten und arm wie ein Bettler geworden, beinahe strömten ihm Gelübde und Tränen aus der Seele. Dennoch stand es fest, daß er nicht umkehrte, und seltsamerweise war mit seiner Aufregung ein Bild der rings um den Wald blühenden Wiesen verbunden, und trotz der Sehnsucht nach Zukunft das Gefühl, daß er da, zwischen Anemonen, Vergißmeinnicht, Orchideen, Enzian und dem herrlich grünbraunen Sauerampfer, tot liegen werde. Er streckte sich am Moose aus. <<Wie Dich hinübernehmen?>> fragte sich Homo (240).

> (He felt the hand of his loved one in his, her voice was in his ear, all parts of his body seemed to have been touched as if for the first time, he felt that his own self was like a form shaped by another body. But he had taken the power from his life. His heart had become humble and as poor as a beggar in the face of the loved one, he was close to the point where vows and tears would

stream from his soul.   Yet the decision stood that he would not
turn back and strangely, in his excitement, there was a link with
the meadows that bloomed all around the woods, and, in spite of
the longing for future the feeling that there, among anemones,
forget-me-nots, orchids, gentians and the magnificent green and
brown sorrel, he would lie dead.   He stretched himself out on the
moss.   <<How shall I take you over?>>   Homo asked himself.)

Homo's energy is no longer directed towards this world but towards the

next;   his desire is not for physical possession of his wife but for a

spiritual union in another dimension:

Da hatte er nun immer gemeint, in der Wirklichkeit zu leben, aber
war etwas unwirklicher, als daß ein Mensch für ihn etwas anderes
war als alle anderen Menschen?   Daß es unter den unzähligen
Körpern einen gab, von dem sein inneres Wesen fast ebenso abhing
wie von seinem eigenen Körper? (...).   Und es wurde ihm plötzlich
heiß von einer neuen Gewißheit.   Er war kein dem Glauben
zugeneigter Mensch, aber in diesem Augenblick war sein Inneres
erhellt.   Die Gedanken erleuchteten so wenig wie dunstige Kerzen
in dieser großen Helle seines Gefühls, es war nur ein herrliches,
von Jugend umflossenes Wort: Wiedervereinigung da.   Er nahm sie
in alle Ewigkeiten immer mit sich, und in dem Augenblick, wo er
sich diesem Gedanken hingab, waren die kleinen Entstellungen,
welche die Jahre der Geliebten zugefügt hatten, von ihr genommen,
es war ewiger erster Tag.   Jede weltläufige Betrachtung versank,
jede Möglichkeit des Überdrusses und der Untreue, denn niemand
wird die Ewigkeit für den Leichtsinn einer Viertelstunde opfern,
und er erfuhr zum erstenmal die Liebe ohne allen Zweifel als ein
himmlisches Sakrament.   Er erkannte die persönliche Vorsehung,
welche sein Leben in diese Einsamkeit gelenkt hatte, und fühlte
wie einen gar nicht mehr irdischen Schatz, sondern wie eine für
ihn bestimmte Zauberwelt den Boden mit Gold und Edelsteinen unter
seinen Füßen' (240-1).

(He had always thought he lived in reality but was there anything
more unreal than that, for him, one person was different from all
other people?   That among the countless other bodies there was
one on which his inner being depended almost as much as it did on
his own body? (...)   And suddenly he felt the warmth of a new
certainty.   He was not a man given to belief but at this moment
he felt a brightening within.   Thoughts, in this great brightness
of feeling, cast no more illumination than smoking candles, only
one magnificent word, around which flowed the waters of youth,
came to him: 'reuniting'.   He took her with him into all
eternities, and at the moment when he gave himself up to this idea

the minor disfigurements which the years had done to the loved one were taken from her, it was an eternal first day.   Every earthly observation ebbed away, every possibility of weariness and infidelity, for no one will sacrifice eternity for a frivolous quarter of an hour and, for the first time, he experienced love without any doubt whatsoever as a heavenly sacrament.   He recognised the personal providence which had directed his life into this loneliness and felt that the ground beneath his feet with its gold and precious stones was not an earthly treasure any longer but a world of magic made for him.)

This moment which seems at first unrelated to the rest of the 'Novelle' in fact prefigures Homo's death: it marks the disposition towards the transcendental without which Homo would neither have allowed himself to be trapped in the mine nor, once he was trapped, resign himself without a struggle to death. [29]

'Tonka' is to be understood in terms of the duality of this world and the next.   Tonka herself, despite the weight of evidence of her guilt has, as we have seen, an air of innocence and purity. Circumstantial evidence conspires to convict Tonka;   the young man's mother attempts to enforce society's condemnation of Tonka;   disease debilitates Tonka and pregnancy alters the shape and appearance of her body – there is even a hint of her death to come:

(...) alle Wandlungen des wunderbaren Vorgangs kamen, der, ohne zu zögern, den Mädchenkörper umformte zur Samenkapsel, alle Abmessungen veränderte, die Hüften breit machte und hinunterrückte, den Knien die scharfe Form nahm, den Hals kräftiger, die Brüste zum Euter machte, die Haut des Bauches mit feinen roten und blauen Adern durchzog, so daß man darüber erschrak, wie nah der Außenwelt das Blut kreiste, als ob das den Tod bedeuten könnte (301).

(Then came all the transformations of the strange process which, without hesitation, changed the body of the young girl into a seed

pod, altered all dimensions, made the hips broader and moved them
lower, took away the sharp contours of the knees, made the neck
more powerful, the breasts into an udder, drew fine red and blue
veins across the skin of the belly so that one was shocked at how
close to the outside world the blood was circulating as if that
might mean death.)

Neither the disapproval of the world at large, nor the tensions of

suspicion, nor the transformations of pregnancy, nor the dangers of

disease, nor all of these things together break the loyalty of the

young man to his mistress.   It seems here that the narrator is

demonstrating that all attempts to calculate human motivation are

subverted by an unquantifiable factor - the power of love.   Love

alone 'explains' the bond.   In an entry in the diary from the time of

his relationship with Herma Dietz, Musil makes the following

observation:

Das eigentümliche Wesen der Liebe zeigt sich deutlich im Traume.
Man träumt von der Geliebten.   Sie sieht ganz anders aus, ihre
Stimme hat einen anderen Klang und Fall.   Sie tut Dinge, welche
die Andere nie tun würde.   Dieser Nichtidentität bleibt man sich
fortwährend bewußt.   Dennoch ist man (...) gezwungen, das
Traumbild für sie zu halten.   Es ist gewissermaßen mit dem Namen
behaftet.   Und zwar in einer äußerst eindringlichen Weise, die
fremdeste Bewegung wird zu ihrer Bewegung, ja selbst ein Bauschen
weißer Unterröcke, wie (Herma) solche nie getragen, wurde einmal
dazu.   Und mit dem Namen ist die ganze wesenlose Zuneigung mit an
das zufällige Traumgebilde geknüpft (TbI,103-4).[30]

(The particular essence of love is clearly seen in a dream.   One
dreams of the loved one.   She looks quite different, her voice
has a different timbre and cadence.   She does things the other
would never do.   One is constantly aware of this non-identity.
Yet one is (...) forced to consider the dream image as her.   To
some extent this is attached to the name.   And, indeed, in an
extremely compelling fashion, the most alien movement becomes her
movement, and even fluffed-up white underskirts of the kind which
(Herma) never wore, once became part of this.   And with the name
the whole insubstantial sympathy is linked to the chance
dream-formation.)

This dream provides a key to understanding the experience of love in waking life: love is an emissary of the transcendental - the lover tries, with the desperation of a dreamer, to make love tally with the elements of actual experience. But he fails. It is only, as we saw above, after Tonka has died in hospital and the young man's frenetic will relaxes that the force of love fuses, in a moment of overwhelming power, with her image: 'Er fühlte sie von der Erde bis zum Kopf und ihr ganzes Leben' (306) ('He felt her and her whole life go right through him from head to foot'). The loss of wilfulness combines with the presence of death to give the young man a glimpse of the influence of the transcendental in this life.

Thus in the three 'Novellen' of Drei Frauen we find an underlying concern with love and with death as experiences which lead mankind beyond this world. Musil fills these works with a sense of significance out of all proportion with what we might call the 'natural' or 'real' weight of the events described.

Although there are underlying themes and concerns here there is no coherent pattern. The stories, despite their similarities, cannot be reduced to any general statement which might, for example, make the transcendental more accessible to readers. Objective experience, as Musil presents it to his readers, is inadequate to express the essence of love: love, this whole, is not the sum of the objective experiences on which it seems to focus - it is simply something different.

On 10 June 1915 Musil, reflecting on Martha Musil's much-loved,
but long-deceased, first husband, wrote in his diary : 'Einfall: Wer
hat im Jenseits das Vorrecht: Fritz oder ich?' (TbI,306) ('Suddenly
occurred to me: Who has priority in the realm of the transcendental:
Fritz or me?').   Such thoughts are typical of Musil, above all in
this period; indeed, as Drei Frauen amply demonstrates, Musil's
reflections on the theme of love, for all his concern with accurate
observation and fidelity to autobiographical fact, lead him into the
sphere of religion.   It is a theme that was to preoccupy him in his
major work, Der Mann ohne Eigenschaften.

EPILOGUE

When <u>Drei Frauen</u> appeared in 1924 Musil was only in his
mid-forties and had nearly two decades before him.   Sadly, with the
exception of the 1936 anthology of earlier writings, <u>Nachlaß zu
Lebzeiten</u> ('<u>Literary Estate of the Living Author</u>'), this was the last
complete work that Musil would publish.   By the mid-twenties, Musil
was already working hard on the novel that would later be entitled <u>Der
Mann ohne Eigenschaften</u>, the massive project which would take over the
rest of his life and remain unfinished at his death.

Most readers approach Musil through this major novel - perhaps
this is unfortunate, for the works we have examined in this study are
not only of outstanding merit in themselves but collectively form a
bridge to understanding <u>Der Mann ohne Eigenschaften</u>.   All the works
bear the stamp of Musil's perennial concerns and literary style,
refined with the passage of the years;   each gives particular
prominence to some skill or area of knowledge which would later be
available to Musil in his work on the major novel, into which it would
be integrated with characteristic subtlety.

<u>Die Verwirrungen des Zöglings Törleß</u> is the record of an
adolescence in which the fear of isolation and the dangers of
subjectivity are transformed into strikingly distinctive, and fiercely
independent, thoughts and observations.   It is, in its honesty and

self-confrontation, an uncompromising work. The personality of the
young engineer who writes the novel is still developing. He has
progressed beyond the stage described in the book, but this is still a
spiritual self-declaration - and perhaps a self-determining, too -
which is bound to offend both family sensibilities and the wider world
of public appearances which it criticises so strongly. Musil's
instinct for self-observation and his totally indiscreet willingness
to offer readers virtually uncensored access to what has taken place
in his mind, release the data on which much of Der Mann ohne
Eigenschaften is based. Ulrich, the hero of Der Mann ohne
Eigenschaften, is separated from Törleß by the wealth of knowledge and
experience which Musil has gathered in the intervening years and by
insights into creative writing that have been won in the unrelenting
struggles to complete the other works examined above; but, on the
other hand, the restless intellect, the fine-tuned perceptions, the
curious mix of scepticism and openness to all kinds of human emotions
bear witness to the closest of family resemblances. Both heroes
serve Musil as a focus for his personal attempts to find some kind of
intellectual and spiritual security in a puzzling, threatening world.
They offer, through the public medium of literature, a point of
reference for readers who share a similar predicament. It is
intriguing to see that the heroes of Musil's two novels, both born
like their author about 1880, belie their 'fin-de-siècle' origins and
seem so far ahead of their time that many a reader many decades their
junior not only feels, but positively identifies with, their problems.

In Vereinigungen, Musil breaks out of his subjective isolation
and opens up a new path for his creativity, a secret access through
empathy to the large cast of characters who will fill Der Mann ohne
Eigenschaften. The inner exploration of another mind (based on
experiments in vivid intuitions, which Musil pursued with a unique
blend of passion and scientific rigour) is expressed through an
astonishing vocabulary of specially-coined images.   This will, in
Der Mann ohne Eigenschaften, give Musil the opportunity to experiment
with two kinds of application for this skill.   First, there is the
relatively less-detailed sketch of a psychic personality which is
drawn - often with strong satirical overtones - from study of a
literary or philosophical work or from first-hand obervation (here I
am thinking of the full cast of relatively peripheral figures in Der
Mann ohne Eigenschaften, such as Feuermaul, the poet based on Franz
Werfel, or Meingast, the prophet based on Ludwig Klages);   second, and
far more important, there are the portraits of the figures who will be
central to Der Mann ohne Eigenschaften (and here I have in mind such
characters as Clarisse, Arnheim, Diotima and, of course, Moosbrugger
and Agathe).   If Musil had not had the experience of writing
Vereinigungen I doubt if those later figures could have been conceived
with the intimacy, the subtle penetration of mind and heart, that is
one of the major achievements of Der Mann ohne Eigenschaften (which I
examine in Robert Musil's 'Der Mann ohne Eigenschaften' - a critical
study, to be published in Cambridge in 1987-8).   In other words, a
work which appears self-indulgent and inward-looking to the point of
neurosis turns out in retrospect to have been a key which unlocked the

door of the outside world for its author.

Where Vereinigungen appeals privately to the reader through the
intimacy of a short story, Die Schwärmer is an attempt by Musil to
broadcast his Weltanschauung direct to the public.   Musil is as
uncompromising a dramatist as he is a writer of prose narrative and,
given the medium, all the more direct in his impact.   In Die Schwärmer
we sense a significant increase in self-confidence.   Musil makes his
points powerfully and unambiguously – he has left behind Törleß's
anguished self-doubts, he has shelved the moral ambiguities of
Vereinigungen and tackles head-on, with the forthrightness of some
committed platform-orator, the ills of contemporary civilisation:
'This, and this, and this, is what has to be changed,' he thunders
'life is precious – why do we squander it so thoughtlessly, why do we
shrink in such fear from our most powerful feelings?'   Of course,
the whole conception of the play is too ambitious, the dialogue too
demanding – no audience could sustain throughout the length of the
play the unrelenting emotional and intellectual effort demanded.   Had
he written further plays, Musil would no doubt have adapted his
expectations to the potential of the theatre and the audiences of his
day (so, unfortunately, this is a play that has to be read for it to
be appreciated).   But, in this work, we find the first powerful
expression of Musil's critical awareness of patterns of illusion in
the contemporary world, his denouncing of strategies of deception and
self-deception which have become almost invisible because they are
woven into the total pattern of everyday behaviour.   In Der Mann ohne

Eigenschaften Musil expresses the same criticism; it is more
comprehensive than in Die Schwärmer but it is so understated, so
modulated by subtle irony, that the play might almost be recommended
as an introductory commentary on views expounded at greater length,
and with greater subtlety, in Der Mann ohne Eigenschaften.

In Drei Frauen the mystical undercurrent of all Musil's other
works runs quietly along the surface of each separate narrative.
Readers of Der Mann ohne Eigenschaften are often puzzled by a radical
change of mood that takes place after Part II - the violence of
Moosbrugger, the murderer, the satire of society on the brink of
dissolution, the hectic thrust and parry of ideological conflict, the
complexities and romantic entanglements of the hero's life in
pre-World-War-I Vienna, give way, to a significant degree, to
contemplation in quiet places and to gentle dialogues in a garden.
But the dominant mood of Part III of the novel - with its sharp break
with the bustle of a city which stimulates the mind but starves the
soul - is one with which the reader of Drei Frauen is perfectly
familiar.   Here Musil selects three experiences in which he once
felt, with unmediated power, the force of the transcendental pulsing
in his own life - the death of a mistress, long separation from his
wife and the loss of self which came with a near-fatal illness.
Then, after intense reflection on the experiences themselves, he
experimented until he found linguistic means to convey to his readers
what they meant to him.   The resulting prose pieces are powerful
expressions by a secular author of fragments of religious experience.

Musil is now remembered, above all, for <u>Der Mann ohne</u>
<u>Eigenschaften</u>.   A later age, in which demands for formally perfect
and <u>finished</u> works are raised with greater urgency than they are
today, may look upon the books Musil published between 1906 and 1924
with much keener interest.   Even on their own, they might well be seen
as evidence to support a substantial literary reputation.

APPENDIX

Musil as a language tutor

    A letter from Musil to his step-daughter, Annina, written in
December 1930 from the midst of the most intense period of work on Der
Mann ohne Eigenschaften - a time when Musil's creative powers are at
their height - gives us a unique glimpse of Musil as a practical
critic of the use of language. Annina has written a short article on
negro sculpture and has sent it to her step-father for his comments.
Musil returns the article with suggestions for improvement. On the
following pages I have reproduced the first three paragraphs of
Annina's article, with the words and phrases which Musil criticises in
brackets and his proposed amendments underlined at the foot of the
page, together with notes with which he explains his amendments. (I
have numbered the amendments to help to identify the given position in
the text - the extract is taken from Briefe I,489-490 and 487-488.)

    This document can be read as evidence of the intensity and
precision of Musil's concern with language - it needs no commentary.

    (Many of the points would not survive translation so I have not
attempted to render the passage in English.)

Negerplastik

Bei der Versteigerung der Sammlung Hloucha (Intern. Kunst- und Auktionshaus, Berlin,) wurde zum ersten Mal in Deutschland eine (Kollektion) [1] von Bildwerken aus Afrika und Ozeanien mitversteigert.   In der Auktion selbst, die sehr angeregt verlief, zeigte es sich, daß in Fachkreisen die Kunst der Naturvölker sehr geschätzt wird (; bei) [2] der Vorbesichtigung aber ließ sich bemerken, daß ein großer Teil des Publikums (den) [3] Kunstwerken noch so verständnislos gegenübersteht wie vor 20 Jahren, (bevor) [4] die Kunstwissenschaft begann, sich mit (diesem) (bisher) [5] vernachlässigten Gebiet zu beschäftigen.

Die Schwierigkeiten, die (einem sofortigen) [6] Verständnis der primitiven Kunst (entgegenstehen), [7] liegen hauptsächlich in der fremdartigen und (daher oft) [8] [9] befremdenden Gestaltung des Menschen. Ein Teil dieser Wirkung ist (wohl allein dadurch schon) [10] zu erklären, daß eine uns fremde Rasse dargestellt ist, deren Gesichts- und Bewegungsausdruck (für) uns grotesk (erscheinen). [10a]   Abgesehen davon bestehen (tatsächliche Disproportionen) [11] in der Darstellung, z.B. ist oft der Kopf sehr groß im Verhältnis zu den Beinen oder irgendwelche Teile des Körpers, die dem Künstler gerade wesentlich erschienen, (wurden) [12] in besonderm Maßstab ausgeführt.

(Diese scheinbaren Unzulänglichkeiten) [13] [14] (bedingten eigentlich die allgemeine) [15] Mißachtung der Primitiven Kunst im 19. Jahrhundert.

Erst die Kunstwissenschaft der letzten 20 Jahre lehrte eine neue

Betrachtungsweise.   Sie (zeigte, daß sich) [15a] in den Bildwerken die

asthet. Gesetze nach: die Einheit des Raums wie auch die innere

Geschlossenheit (nachweisen lassen,) und - als eine (Eigengesätzlichkeit)
16 der primitiven Kunst - das Gesetz der Frontalität......

----

1 Auswahl:- Verdeutschung.

2 . Bei.

3 diesen:- Das Publikum steht doch nicht Kunstwerken i.a. verständnislos
gegenüber! Wenn Du <<den>> lassen wolltest, müßte es heißen:
<<gegenüberstand>>.

4 ehe: drückt das gemeinte Zeitverhältnis besser aus als bevor, auch
stünde sonst 2 X hintereinander - vor.

5 dem bis dahin: In Deinem ursprünglichen Text hängt diesem in der Luft
(...) (Das war) vor 20 Jahren! Da kann man nicht bisher sagen.

6 das unmittelbare (-) ein sofortiges! 1) ist nicht ein, sondern das
Verständnis gemeint! 2) ist <<sofortiges>> eine Kanzleiwortbildung.

7 hindern Schwierigkeiten stehen entgegen: Zeitgenössischer Schwulst!

8 darum und daher: Können für einander eintreten, aber dem genaueren
Gefühl entspricht hier darum, denn fremdartig und befremdend hängen hier
aus engste zusammen.

9 oft Die Schwierigkeiten liegen in der befremdeten Gestaltung und nicht
in der oft befremdenden.

10 schon dadurch (-) wohl allein dadurch schon: überflüssig! Wortwurst!

10a erscheint

11 aber auch wirkliche Mißverständnisse (-) Tatsächlich ist schon kein
besonderes Wort!   Es zu adjektivieren kein Anlass!

12 werden : vorher heißt es: ist .. der Kopf..

13 Dieses scheinbar Unzulängliche (-) scheinbar: adjektivischer Gebrauch
zu meiden, wo es geht.

14 Unzulänglichkeiten: modisch gewordener Gebrauch.

15 <u>war die Ursache der allgemeinen</u> (-) bedingten: Denkfehler! Sie waren keine Bedingung, sondern eine Ursache.

15a <u>wies</u>

16 <u>Besonderheit</u> (-) Eigengesetzlichkeit: Geschwollenes kunsthistorisches Jargonwort, wenn auch beliebt! (<u>Briefe</u> I,487-488).

Notes to Chapter 1 - Introduction

1. Elsewhere I examine the way in which Richard von Mises's idea that literary works are 'Gedankenexperimente' ('thought-experiments) contributes to an understanding of Musil's writing - see 'On reading "Der Mann ohne Eigenschaften"', in Sprachkunst, 9 (1978), 88-100; see also my book, Robert Musil's 'Der Mann ohne Eigenschaften' - a critical study, to be published by Cambridge University Press in 1987-8.

2. See David Luft, Robert Musil and the Crisis of European Culture, 1880-1942 (Berkeley/Los Angeles/London, 1980), pp.25-26.

3. See my work, Robert Musil's 'Der Mann ohne Eigenschaften' (...), particularly Chapter 2.

4. In a letter from Musil to his step-daughter he sends back to her a copy of an article she has written, together with his corrections. These give a unique insight into the way Musil reflected on language, and provide us with an impression of the care he took with the formulation of his own thoughts.   See the appendix to this book.

Notes to Chapter 2 - 'Törleß'

1. See Sibylle Mulot's fascinating work on Musil's early life: Der junge Musil.

2. See letter from Musil to Paul Wiegand - Briefe I,23-24.

3. See, for example, Adolf Frisé's notes on Musil's Tagebücher (TbII) in which countless statements like this one are traced to their sources.

4. Musil tends, for example, to use long strings of adjectives to identify features of some thing or idea as if he could achieve the desired effect by encircling the target with many shots rather than hitting the centre with one.

5. Is there, he asks, for example, 'etwas in uns (... worüber) wir so wenig Macht haben, daß wir nur ziellos tausend Samenkörner streuen können, bis aus einem plötzlich eine Saat wie eine dunkle Flamme schießt, die weit über uns hinauswächst?' (92) (my emphasis) ('something in us (over which) we have so little power that we can only go about aimlessly, sowing a thousand seeds until from one of them a shoot comes forth like a dark flame which grows up way over our heads?' (my emphasis)). As a mature author Musil would not have mixed his metaphors like this.

6. See 1938 letter to Viktor Zuckerkandl, Briefe I,879.

7. See Die Verwirrungen (...), p.7.

8. See Die Verwirrungen (...), p.78.

9. See Karl Corino, 'Törleß ignotus', Text + Kritik, Heft 21/22 ('Robert Musil'), second edition, 1972, 61-72.

10. Martin Swales, 'Narrator and Hero; Observations on Robert Musil's "Die Verwirrungen des Zöglings Törleß"', in Musil in Focus, edited by Lothar Huber and John J. White (London, 1982), pp.1-11, p.7.

11. Elisabeth C. Stopp, '"Die Verwirrungen des Zöglings Törleß" - Form and Content', Modern Language Review, Vol 63 (1968), 94-118, p.95.

12. See Briefe II,20.

13. Annie Reniers-Servrankx in the introduction to Robert Musil: Konstanz (...) argues that this was Musil's central concern; Sibylle Mulot suggests that Musil's new view of morality is explained by his training - he is an engineer who has turned his attention to society and become fascinated with social engineering. See Der junge Musil, p.24.

14. See Musil's own comment on this in a letter to Robert Lejeune in 1942 - Briefe I,1417; see also Harry Hatfield, 'An Unsentimental Education: Robert Musil's "Young Törleß"', in Crisis and Continuity in German Fiction (Ithaca/London, 1969), pp.35-48, pp.38-39, and Hans-Georg Pott, 'Das Traum des Leibes und der Rede im "Törleß"', in Robert Musil (Munich, 1984), pp.11-25.

15. See Thomas Mann, 'Betrachtungen eines Unpolitischen', in Werke (Frankfurt am Main, 1967/8).

16. See Die Verwirrungen (...), p.76.

17. See Die Verwirrungen (...), p.30. He fears the 'Heraustreten aus seiner bevorzugten Stellung unter die gemeinen Leute; unter sie, - tiefer als sie!' ('leaving his privileged position and moving down to the common people - indeed beneath them!').

18. See Törleß's condemnation of Basini: 'mag (Basini) sich draußen bessern, zu uns paßt er nicht mehr' (47) ('let (Basini) reform himself outside, he doesn't belong with us any more').

19. Musil points, for example, to Törleß's 'sinnliche (....) Veranlagung, welche verborgener, mächtiger und dunkler gefärbt war als die seiner Freunde' (17) ('sensual (...) predisposition which was better concealed, more powerful and of darker hue than that of his friends'); he also examines Törleß's sexual feelings as Törleß looks at Beineberg's hands (Die Verwirrungen (...), pp. 20-21).

20. Sigmund Freud, 'Über Psychoanalyse', Gesammelte Werke, 18 vols., edited by Anna Freud and others (London, 1945), VIII; though it is not clear whether Musil had actually read Freud by the time of the composition of Die Verwirrungen (...), in 1904 he certainly read Hermann Bahr, Dialog vom Tragischen (Berlin, 1904) - see excerpts in TbI,37-8. As Adolf Frisé points out - TbII, 29-30, Note 187 - Bahr here summarised aspects of the work of Freud and Josef Breuer.

21. Both Bozena and Törleß's mother have important roles in Die Verwirrungen (...): the novel starts with Törleß taking leave of his mother and ends with his leaving with her (as a more mature person who is more conscious, among other things, of both his and her sexuality - the final line of the work reads: 'Und er prüfte den leise parfümierten Geruch, der aus der Taille seiner Mutter aufstieg' (140) ('And he tested the delicately perfumed smell given off by his mother's body')). Bozena, who, as we saw is linked in Törleß's imagination to his mother, is a catalyst for a new, more objective view of how people in different parts of society actually behave. The peasants are proud of her because she knows the upper classes and how they behave in private (she has been a maid in Beineberg's aunt's household, she says), '(sie hat) der Welt so durch den Lack geguckt' (29) ('(she has) seen through the veneer of the world'); Törleß 'fühlte sich (....) ihren gemeinen Anspielungen fast wehrlos

preisgegeben' (32) ('felt (...) virtually defenceless in the face of
her base insinuations') - his 'method' is attacked by her sexual
innuendo directed against the upper classes.

22. Swales, 'Narrator and Hero (....)', p.3.

23. Uwe Baur, 'Zeit und Gesellschaftskritik in Robert Musils Roman
"Die Verwirrungen des Zöglings Törleß"', in Vom 'Törleß' zum 'Mann
ohne Eigenschaften', edited by Uwe Baur and Dietmar Goltschnigg
(München, Salzburg, 1973), pp.19-45, p.41.
    Musil insists that Törleß retains his integrity despite all that
is happening to him. See, for example, Törleß's own reaction to
having sex with Basini: 'Das bin nicht ich (....)! Morgen erst wieder
werde ich es sein!' (108) ('It isn't me (...) at all!   I'll only be
myself again tomorrow!') and the narrator's repeated assurances such
as: 'man darf auch wirklich nicht glauben, daß Basini in Törleß ein
richtiges (...) Begehren erregte' (109) ('one must not really imagine
that Basini gave rise to a genuine (...) desire on Torleß's part') and
'die ethische Widerstandskraft, (die Törleß) später so hoch schätzte,
fehlte damals noch' (114) ('the power of ethical resistance which
Törleß later valued so highly had not yet made its appearance at that
time'); see also the description of Törleß's agony of remorse after
the homosexual act: 'Er stieß seinen Fuß gegen die Erde und krümmte
seinen Leib zusammen, nur um sich dieser schmerzhaften Scham zu
entwinden' (110) ('He dashed his foot on the ground and bent double in
an attempt to get away from this painful sense of shame').

24. Musil gives this notion a characteristically intellectual twist in
his diary in 1902: 'Wir können eine großartige Erkenntnis nicht in uns
festhalten, sie welkt dahin, verknöchert und unversehens bleibt uns
nichts in Händen, als das armselige, logische Gerüste der Idee'
(TbI,17) ('We cannot hold on to any magnificent insight, it fades
away, becomes bone-hard and imperceptibly we are left with nothing but
the impoverished logical scaffolding of the idea').

25. Törleß distrusts words: 'Es kam wie eine Tollheit über Törleß,
Dinge, Vorgänge und Menschen als etwas Doppelsinniges zu empfinden.
Als etwas, das durch die Kraft irgendwelcher Erfinder an ein
harmloses, erklärendes Wort gefesselt war, und als etwas ganz Fremdes,
das jeden Augenblick sich davon loszureißen drohte' (64) ('Like a
madness there came over Törleß a sense that things, events and people
were something ambiguous.   That they were both something which, by
virtue of the power of some inventor was fettered to a harmless
explanatory word, and something quite alien which threatened to tear
itself loose from it at any moment'); when his father praised
Törless, as a child, for expressing pleasure with the words 'O es ist
schön' ('Oh, it is beautiful'), Törleß became embarrassed: 'Denn er
hätte ebenso gut sagen mögen: es ist schrecklich traurig. Es war ein
Versagen der Worte, das ihn da quälte, ein halbes Bewußtsein, daß die
Worte nur zufällige Ausflüchte für das Empfundene waren' (65) ('For he
might equally well have said: it is dreadfully sad.   It was a
failure of words which tortured him, a vague awareness that words were

only chance excuses for what had been perceived'). To the public
expression of aesthetic precocity is added private evidence of early
intellectual maturity!

26. The description of the school (Die Verwirrungen (...), p.8) and
the portrait of Bozena (Die Verwirrungen (...), pp.28–29) are
particularly clear examples of realist writing; the expressionist
level is found in the scene where the narrator is concerned with
Törleß's thoughts and feelings in bed one night – Die Verwirrungen
(...), pp.84–87 – and the scene where he tries to write, with Basini
sitting at a desk in the same room – Die Verwirrungen (...), pp.88–92.

27. See the section entitled 'The testing of the prince' in J.P.
Stern, On Realism (London, 1972), pp.5–19.

28. This may be compared with the description by Johannes von Allesch
of the way of thinking which Musil learnt at school 'die (...) durch
das Streben nach Natürlichkeit, Klarheit, Leichtfaßlichkeit und (...)
Vereinfachung (...) gekennzeichnet ist' ('which is characterised by a
striving for what is natural, for clarity, ease of comprehension and a
corresponding simplification (...)', in 'Robert Musil in der geistigen
Bewegung seiner Zeit', in Robert Musil: Leben, Werk, Wirkung, edited
by Karl Dinklage (Zurich/Leipzig/Vienna, 1960), pp.133–144.

29. By 'method' I am referring to René Descartes, 'Discours de la
Méthode pour bien conduire sa raison (...)', Oeuvres et Lettres,
edited by Alain Bridoux (Paris, 1953).

30. Törleß's reading at the time, we are told, had no influence 'auf
seinen Charakter' (13) ('on his character') – here the term
'Charakter' is simply an item from the uncritical idiom of the day.

31. Frederick G. Peters, Robert Musil – Master of the Hovering Life
(New York, 1978), p.30.

32. Sigmund Freud, who acknowledged the insights of many literary
figures into the unconscious, published his 'Drei Abhandlungen zur
Sexualtheorie' (see Werke, V), in which he refers to the Oedipus
complex, in 1905 (see pp.127–8).

33. On learning that Basini is the thief, Törleß senses an excitement
which is partly sexual; he feels a compulsion to imagine what
happened when Basini visited Bozena: 'Er mußte sich Basini bei Bozena
vorstellen' (46) (my emphasis) ('He had to imagine Basini with
Bozena').

34. Törleß wonders if the attraction which Basini exerts on him
consists simply in the fact 'daß er sich nicht in ihn hineindenken
konnte und ihn daher stets wie in unbestimmten Bildern empfand' (60)
('that he was not able to think his way into him and so was always
aware of him in terms of indefinite images').

Notes to Chapter 2 – 'Törleß'

35. When Törleß discusses this with Beineberg the latter demonstrates
an awareness suspiciously beyond his years in his explanation! His
words are: '(Die Akademiker) haben sich einen Weg in tausend
Schneckengängen durch ihr Gehirn gebohrt, und sie sehen bloß bis zur
nächsten Ecke zurück, ob der Faden noch hält, den sie hinter sich
herspinnen (....) Diese Erwachsenen und ganz Gescheiten haben sich
da vollständig in ein Netz eingesponnen, eine Masche stützt die
andere, so daß das Ganze Wunder wie natürlich aussieht; wo aber die
erste Masche steckt, durch die alles gehalten wird, weiß kein Mensch'
(82) ('(Academics have bored a way for themselves in a thousand
snail-paths through their brains, and they only look back as far as
the last corner to see if the thread which they are spinning behind
them is still holding (...) These adults, with their superior minds,
have spun their way completely into a net in which one knot supports
the next so that the whole thing looks amazingly natural; but where
the first knot is, on which all others depend, noone knows').

36. Musil, in 1902, made the following comment on his relationship
with Kant: 'Ich habe Kant nie zu Ende gelesen, aber ich lebe beruhigt
weiter und fürchte nicht vor Scham sterben zu müssen, daß ein Anderer
bereits die Welt restlos erfaßte' (TbI,12) ('I have never finished
reading Kant, but I go on living quite calmly and don't feel that I
ought to die of shame because someone else has already achieved total
understanding of the world').

37. Here, as so often, Nietzsche uses organic imagery. In the
introduction to 'Zur Genealogie der Moral' (in Werke, edited by
Giorgio Colli and Mazzino Montinari, Berlin, New York, 1967 onwards,
VI.$_2$, 'Vorrede', para. 2, pp.260-261) Nietzsche compares the act of
philosophising to a tree bearing fruit: 'mit der Notwendigkeit, mit
der ein Baum seine Früchte trägt, wachsen aus uns unsre Gedanken,
unsre Werte, unsre Jas und Neins und Wenns und Obs - verwandt und
bezüglich allesamt untereinander und Zeugnisse eines Willens, einer
Gesundheit, eines Erdreichs, einer Sonne. - Ob sie euch schmecken,
diese unsre Früchte? - Aber was geht das die Bäume an! Was geht das
uns an, uns Philosophen! ...' ('our thoughts, our values, our saying
yes and no, all grow out of us with the necessity with which a tree
bears its fruits - they are all interrelated and interconnected and
testify to one will, to one state of health, to one kingdom of earth,
to one sun - Do you like the taste of our fruits? - But what is that
to the trees! What is that to us, as philosophers!...')
    Törleß's development is similarly presented by Musil through the
image of the growth of a tree. Early in the work we are prepared for
the stimulus that the experiences he will face are to give to Törleß:
'in der Entwicklung einer jeden feinen moralischen Kraft gibt es einen
solchen frühen Punkt, wo sie die Seele schwächt, deren kühnste
Erfahrung sie einst vielleicht sein wird, - so als ob sich ihre
Wurzeln erst suchend senken und den Boden zerwühlen müßten, den sie
nachher zu stützen bestimmt sind' (25) ('at an early stage in the
development of each fine moral impulse there is just such a point
where it weakens the psyche (Seele) whose most daring experience it
will perhaps later become - as if its roots had first to feel their

way down and churn up the soil to which they will later give
support'); towards the end of the novel, after the experiences in
question have run their course, we read: 'Eine Entwicklung war
abgeschlossen, die Seele hatte einen neuen Jahresring angesetzt wie
ein junger Baum' (131) ('A development had run its course, the psyche
(Seele) had grown a new year-ring like a young tree').

38. Annie Reniers-Servrankx emphasises that Musil as a young man was
very aware 'eines wesentlichen Zusammenhangs zwischen seiner eigenen
Lebensproblematik und dem Problem der Gestaltung als dem eigentlichen
Problem der Dichtung und des Lebens' (Robert Musil, Konstanz (...),
p.265) ('of a fundamental connection between the problematic structure
of his own life and the problem of creativity as the essential problem
of fiction and of life'); in 1905 Musil made very lengthy excerpts
from Ellen Key's essay 'Die Entfaltung der Seele durch Lebenskunst'
(in Neue Rundschau, Heft 6, 1905, 641-686); among these is a
quotation in which Ellen Key expresses the special relationship
between art and life in this epoch: 'In der Kunst des Lebens ist es
ebenso wichtig wie in der bildenden Kunst den natürlichen Mittelpunkt
zu finden, auf den sich alles richten muß' (TbI,164) (my emphasis)
('In the art of living it is just as important as in the graphic arts
to find the natural centre towards which all things have to be
directed' (my emphasis)).

39. The reference has been established in the description of Törleß's
reaction to the peasants and their cottages (Die Verwirrungen (...),
p.17) and to Bozena and her room (Die Verwirrungen (...), p.33).

40. Light has a similar figurative role in a scene where Törleß,
under the influence of Basini who is sitting close to him, is seized
by the urge to write: 'Hastig, mit der Geschwindigkeit der Angst,
griff er nach der Feder und notierte sich einige Zeilen über seine
Entdeckung; noch einmal schien es in seinem Innern weithin wie ein
Licht zu sprühen, ... dann brach ein aschgrauer Regen über seine
Augen, und der bunte Glanz in seinem Geiste erlosch. .....' (92)
('Hastily, with the speed of fear, he reached for the pen and made a
few notes about his discovery; once again within him it seemed that a
light was sending out a wide spray of rays, ... then rain, as grey
as ashes, broke over his eyes and the bright radiance in his mind went
out.....')
    Törleß, in the speech to his masters which is incomprehensible
to them but not to the reader, touches upon his experience earlier of
the lamp and the dust in the scene we have examined (see Die
Verwirrungen des Zöglings Törleß, p.137).

41. See Geoffrey Leech, Semantics (Harmondsworth, 1974), particularly
Chapter Six, 'Components and Contrasts of Meaning', pp.95-125.

42. Uwe Baur comments as follows on the opening scene of the novel –
he is referring particularly to the station-master with his watch:
'Das Grundgesetz dieses Ausschnitts der Wirklichkeit erscheint im Bild
der Uhr, der Marionette, einem Topos der mechanistischen

Notes to Chapter 2 – 'Törleß'

Weltauffassung seit Descartes. Musil transponiert das Bild der
cartesianischen Deutung der Natur in den Bereich menschlicher
Verhaltensweisen und verdeutlicht so die Statik gewohnten Verhaltens,
den starren Gleichlauf normierten Daseins (...)' (in 'Zeit- und
Gesellschaftskritik (...)', p.24) ('The fundamental law of this
extract from reality appears in the image of the clock, of the
marionette, a topos of the mechanistic world-view since Descartes.
Musil transposes the image of the Cartesian interpretation of nature
into the realm of human ways of behaving and thus shows clearly that
statics is the law of routine behaviour, exemplifying the rigid
parallelism of existence running on in conformity with the norm
(...)').

43. See also, on this aspect of Musil's work, Annie
Reniers-Servrankx, Robert Musil, Konstanz (...), p.54 and p.62.

44. The constraints of the training to which Törleß and his
fellow-pupils are subjected are expressed in the image of the
institute building 'wo die jungen aufdrängenden Kräfte hinter grauen
Mauern festgehalten wurden (....)' ('where the young urgent powers are
penned in behind grey walls') (113).

45. Musil traverses the whole axis in two sentences towards the
beginning of the novel: 'Die hohe Anspannung, das Lauschen auf ein
ernstes Geheimnis und die Verantwortung, mitten in noch unbeschriebene
Beziehungen des Lebens zu blicken, hatte er nur für einen Augenblick
aushalten können. Dann war wieder jenes Gefühl des Allein- und
Verlassenseins über ihn gekommen, das stets dieser zu hohen
Anforderung folgte' (24) ('He had only been able to withstand for a
moment the high tension, the listening for some serious secret and the
responsibility for looking out on as yet unchartered relationships
with life. Then that feeling of being alone and deserted which
always followed this excessive exertion had come over him again').

46. Törleß expresses this himself as follows: 'In meinem Kopfe war
vordem alles so klar und deutlich geordnet; nun aber ist mir, als
seien meine Gedanken wie Wolken, und wenn ich an die bestimmten
Stellen komme, so ist es wie eine Lücke dazwischen, durch die man in
eine unendliche, unbestimmbare Weite sieht (...)' (81-82) ('Before,
everything in my head was so clearly and distinctly arranged; but now
it seems as if my thoughts are clouds, and when I arrive at specific
points it seems that there is a gap between them through which one has
a view into an endless, indeterminate distance (...)').

47. In an essay, 'Der deutsche Mensch als Symptom' (written in 1923),
Musil argues that such appearances are often deceptive: 'Der Mensch
ist (...) ein weitaus interessierterer Metaphysiker, als er gemeinhin
heute zugibt. Ein dumpfes Begleitgefühl seiner sonderbaren
kosmischen Situation verläßt ihn selten. Der Tod, die Winzigkeit der
ganzen Erde, das Fragliche der Ichillusion, die mit den Jahren
aufdringlicher werdende Sinnlosigkeit des Daseins: das sind Fragen,
die der gewöhnliche Mensch mit Spott abweist, und die er dennoch wie

die Wände eines schwarzen Raums sein ganzes Leben umschließen fühlt'
(GWII,1380) ('A man is (...) far more involved in metaphysics than he
will generally admit to today. He is seldom deserted by an
indistinct peripheral awareness of his strange cosmic situation.
Death, the microscopic dimensions of the earth as a whole, the
questionability of the illusion of the "I", the sense of the
meaninglessness of existence which becomes ever more insistent with
the passage of the years: these are questions which the normal person
rejects with scorn yet which he feels encircling his whole life like
the walls of a black room').

48. William Blake, Jerusalem, Chapter III, Plate 74.

49. See the full quotation, note 42 above.

50. Nietzsche, 'Die fröhliche Wissenschaft', Werke, V$_2$, pp.258-260;
the impression which this paragraph of Nietzsche's made on Musil can
be gauged from the beginning of the short sketch 'Ein Mensch ohne
Charakter' (from 'Nachlaß zu Lebzeiten', GWII,533-9) which opens as
follows: 'Man muß heute Charaktere wohl mit der Laterne suchen gehn;
und wahrscheinlich macht man sich noch dazu lächerlich, wenn man bei
Tag mit einem brennenden Licht umhergeht' (GWII,533) ('Today one
probably has to go searching for characters with a lantern; and one
will, in all likelihood, make oneself look ridiculous into the bargain
if one goes about by day with a light burning').

51. 'Die fröhliche Wissenschaft', para. 125; when Törleß looked into
the depths of the sky, we are told, he felt: 'wie ein kleines
lebendes Pünktchen unter dieser riesigen, durchsichtigen Leiche' (66)
('like a small living dot beneath this gigantic, transparent corpse')
- a curious and somehow, in the context, unlikely and unconvincing
image which presumably represents an illicit planting into Törleß's
youthful consciousness of the strong impression which Musil retained
from his reading of the Nietzsche paragraph in question.

52. 'Die fröhliche Wissenschaft', para. 125.

53. See the following dialogue between Törleß and Basini where Törleß
wants to know what effect the demeaning acts he is forced to perform
have on Basini: '(Törleß:) (...) ging da nicht durch dein ganzes
Wesen ein Riß? (...) als ob sich eben etwas Unsagbares in dir
vollzogen hätte? (Basini:) 'Gott, ich verstehe dich nicht; ich weiß
nicht, was du willst; ich kann dir nichts, gar nichts sagen' (103)
('(Törleß:) (...) didn't a split appear going right through your whole
being? (...) as if something for which no words could be found had run
its course in you? (Basini:) God, I don't understand you; I don't
know what you want; I can tell you nothing, nothing at all').

54. The fear is expressed in the following observation: 'Jede Nacht
bedeutete für ihn ein Nichts, ein Grab, ein Ausgelöschtwerden. Das
Vermögen, sich jeden Tag sterben zu legen, ohne sich darüber Gedanken
zu machen, hatte er noch nicht erlernt' (34) ('Every night meant, for

Notes to Chapter 2 - 'Törleß'

capacity to lie down to die every day without even giving it a
thought').

Notes to Chapter 2 - 'Törleß'

Notes to Chapter 3 - 'Vereinigungen'

1. See Osman Durrani, 'Die Vollendung der Liebe: Apocalypse or Utopia?', in Musil in Focus, pp.12-22, p.12.

2. See, on the actual relationships which provide the raw material for this text, the notes headed 'Rabe' ('Raven') (one of Musil's pet-names for Martha), TbII,958-962.

3. See David Luft, Robert Musil (...), p.75; it seems correct to assume that the kernel of the story of 'Die Vollendung der Liebe', sketched out from the man's point of view in the 'Profil eines Programms' (GWII,1319), represents Musil's own predicament.

4. Though the links between Musil's works and literary movements like realism, naturalism and expressionism have not been explored in detail, two articles are particularly helpful in analysing the narrative: see Rosmarie Zeller, '"Die Versuchung der stillen Veronika" - Eine Untersuchung ihres Bedeutungsaufbaus', in Dieter P.Farda and Ulrich Karthaus, editors, Sprachästhetische Sinnvermittlung - Robert Musil Symposium (Berlin, 1980), pp.135-153; Dieter Krusche, 'Robert Musil: "Vereinigungen"', in Kommunikation im Erzähltext, 2 vols (Munich, 1978), I, pp.137-153.

5. Michiko Mae examines the reception of Vereinigungen by Expressionist writers: Kurt Pinthus, the author of a well-known Expressionist anthology, compares Musil with a brain surgeon: 'Wie der Mediziner mit seinen Instrumenten säuberlich Schichten von Häuten und Muskeln abhebt und die Gehirnrinde bloßlegt, so enthüllt Musil mit der mühsamsten Sorgfalt die tiefsten Gefühle und Gedanken zweier sinnlicher Frauen' ('Just as a doctor uses his instruments to lift layers of skin and muscle and to neatly lay bare the surface of the brain so Musil reveals, with the most painstaking care, the deepest feelings and thoughts of two sensual women' (quoted in Mae, 'Robert Musils Novellenband <<Vereinigungen>> in der Kritik seiner Zeit', Doitsu Bungaku - Die deutsche Literatur, published by the Japanese Society for Germanistics, 65 (1980), 44-55, p.49); Musil's view of Expressionism, as Michiko Mae points out, was not so complimentary: 'der Naturalismus gab Wirklichkeit ohne Geist, der Expressionismus Geist ohne Wirklichkeit' (GWII,1059) ('Naturalism presented reality without spirit (Geist), Expressionism spirit (Geist) without reality').

6. See GWII,957.

7. Edmund Wilson gives a summary of the theory behind symbolist poetry which indicates how close Musil was to this movement: 'The assumptions which underlay Symbolism lead us to formulate some such doctrine as the following: every feeling or sensation we have, every moment of consciousness, is different from every other; and it is, in consequence, impossible to render our sensations as we actually

experience them through the conventional and universal language of ordinary literature.   Each poet has his unique personality;   each of his moments has its special tone, its special combination of elements.   And it is the poet's task to find, to invent, the special language which will alone be capable of expressing his personality and feelings.   Such a language must make use of symbols: what is so special, so fleeting and so vague cannot be conveyed by direct statement or description, but only by a succession of words, of images, which will serve to suggest it to the reader' (in Axel's Castle - A Study in the Imaginative Literature of 1870-1930), first published 1931, republished London, 1961, p.24).

8.   It is clear in a letter written in 1907 that, despite his agnosticism, Musil is marked by the Christian tradition;   he shows how the spirit is marooned in the body with all its imperfections and weaknesses (see Briefe I,35-36).

9.   Jürgen Schröder, 'Am Grenzwert der Sprache - zu Robert Musils Vereinigungen', Euphorion, 66 (1966), 311-334, p.333.

10. I have in mind poems such as the sonnet 'Une dentelle s'abolit' by Mallarmé.   The following verse illustrates how Mallarmé seeks to create a world which is close to being purely verbal:

Une dentelle s'abolit
Dans le doute du Jeu suprême
A n'entr'ouvrir comme un blasphème
Qu'absence éternelle de lit.

(Stephane Mallarmé, Poésies, Paris, 1945, p.147).

11. Roger Willemsen argues that Vereinigungen offers the clearest evidence of the influence of the philosopher Ernst Mach since here 'die Atomisierung des Ich in Bild- und Wahrnehmungskomplexe zum Kernvorgang des Geschehens wird' ('the atomising of the "I" in complexes of images and perceptions becomes the central process in what is happening') (in Das Existenzrecht der Dichtung, p.153);   Pott, however, suggests that in this story Musil is closer to Edmund Husserl.   Musil, he argues, portrays a process akin to Husserlian phenomenological reduction whereby, for example, the heroine, Claudine, dissociates her inner self from the actions in which she has been involved: 'Erlebnisinhalte, ebenso wie ihr empirisches Ich (auch ein Erlebnisinhalt) sind zu trennen von dem, was man das ihr selbst unbekannte, jedenfalls nicht begrifflich festzulegende innerste Gefühl nennen könnte' ('the substance of experiences, and her empirical self (also a substantial experience) are to be distinguished from what one might call her innermost feeling which is unfamiliar even to herself or which, at least, she cannot define in conceptual terms' (in Robert Musil, Munich, 1984), p.32.   Pott's argument seems to me to be more convincing.

12. See, for example, Musil's extraordinary account of a dream he has

had, in TbI,103-4.

13. See,, for example, Freud, 'Vorlesungen zur Einführung in die
Psychoanalyse', in Gesammelte Werke, XI, Lecture VII ('Manifester
Trauminhalt und latente Traumgedanken') ('Manifest Dream Content and
Latent Dream Thoughts'), pp.111-123

14. A draft letter to a woman in 1907 gives a glimpse into Musil's own
awareness of others: 'Ich fühle genau, was Du von mir willst und an
mir entbehrst. Du brauchst ein Gemüt, das Dich ganz in starke und
zärtliche Gefühle einhüllt. Wenn Du wüßtest, wie lebendig mir das
manchmal ist; so als ob ich Du wäre (...)' (Briefe I,29) (my
emphasis) ('I feel exactly what you want of me and what you find
lacking in me. You have need of a sensibility which wraps you up
completely in feelings which are both strong and tender. If only you
knew how strongly I am aware of this; as if I were you (...)').

15. In a letter in 1907 Musil indicates that he pursues studies of
deviance with unusual vigour: '(Ich) beschäftige (...) mich auch
wissenschaftlich mit Psychologie (...) und ich muß sagen, daß ich etwa
in den schönen Berichten der französischen Psychiater jede Abnormität
ebensogut nachempfinden kann, u. darstellen zu können glaube' (Briefe
I,24) ('(I) am involved (...) with psychology in a scientific capacity
as well (...) and I have to tell you that, for instance with respect
to the fine reports of the French psychiatrists, I believe I am able,
with equal intensity, to empathise with and give expression to, every
abnormality').

16. Jacqueline Magnou, '"Schicksale sind vom Zentralen aus gestaltet"
- "Die Vollendung der Liebe"', in Musil-Forum, 10 (1984), 69-76; see
also her article 'Grenzfall und Identitätsproblem (oder die Rolle der
Psychopathologie) in der literarischen Praxis und Theorie Musils
anhand der Novellen "Vereinigungen"', Beiträge zur Musil-Kritik,
edited by Gudrun Brokoph-Mauch, pp.129-147.

17. Jacqueline Magnou, '"Schicksale (...)"', p.69.

18. See, on Musil's theory of the 'Novelle' and its relevance for
Vereinigungen, Michiko Mae, 'Robert Musils Novellentheorie', Beiträge
zur Germanistik, 1(1980), 25-43.

19. Jürgen Schröder is particularly perceptive on this aspect of
Musil's text.   In his complex explanation based on an extract from
Vereinigungen he writes: 'Es geht um die Bestimmung des innersten
Selbst eines nur noch grammatikalisch auftretenden Subjekts (...), das
Ich wird durch das Gefühl bestimmt und nicht umgekehrt' ('It is a
question of the determining of the innermost self of a subject which
appears only in grammatical form (...), the "I" is determined by
feeling rather than the other way around') (in 'Am Grenzwert der
Sprache', p.330).

20. See Musil's own self-critical observation in a note on

Notes to Chapter 3 - 'Vereinigungen'

218

Vereinigungen written in 1935, in GWII,969.

21. In a letter in 1911 Musil tries to make Franz Blei look at the work in a new light; he indicates that such matters as the way individuals see things are not appropriate here: 'Sie schrieben: wer sieht hier zu? Der Autor? (...) Die handelnde Person? (...) Der point de vue liegt nicht im Autor u. nicht in der fertigen Person, er ist überhaupt kein point de vue, die Erzählungen haben keinen perspektivischen Zentralpunkt' (Briefe I,87-88) ('You wrote: who is it who is watching here? The author? The person involved in the action? (...) The 'point de vue' does not lie in the author (and) not in the finished person, indeed it is not a 'point de vue' at all, the stories have no central perspective').

22. See Durrani, 'Die Vollendung der Liebe', p.20.

23. See Briefe I,69.

24. See R.M.Rilke, Die Aufzeichnungen des Malte Laurids Brigge (Frankfurt am Main, 1963), p.45.

25. 'Rede zur Rilke-Feier in Berlin am 16. Januar 1927', GWII,1229-1242.

26. It has been suggested that the portrait of Johannes - such as it is - is based partly on Martha's first husband, but it is likely that Musil worked into it many elements drawn from first-hand experience.

27. See Briefe I,332.

28. See excerpts from Aristotle's Poetics in TbI,54-58.

29. See Sigmund Freud, 'Die Traumdeutung', Gesammelte Werke, II.

30. In this context, a statement by Dieter Krusche is of particular interest: 'Das Haus, in dem Veronika, Johannes und Demeter zusammengelebt haben, scheint zuweilen nichts anderes zu sein als das Seelengebäude der Veronika selbst' (my emphasis) ('The house in which Veronika, Johannes and Demeter have lived together seems on occasions to be none other than the edifice of Veronika's soul itself' (my emphasis)), 'Robert Musils "Vereinigungen"', p.138.

31. A. Schopenhauer, 'Die Welt als Wille und Vorstellung', in Sämtliche Werke, II and III, (Wiesbaden, 1961).

32. See Rosmarie Zeller's comments on this marriage of external and internal narrative levels in '"Die Versuchung der Stillen Veronika" - eine Untersuchung (...)', pp.146-147.

33. Musil, himself, would probably have added 'naturalism' here. While working on the final version of Vereinigungen Musil noted down

Notes to Chapter 3 - 'Vereinigungen'

fairly extensive reflections on naturalism in his diary, describing it
as 'ein niemals eingelöstes Versprechen' (TbI,217) ('a promise which
was never kept'); Musils virtually uncensored recording of intimate
details of private consciousness might indeed be seen to be taking
naturalism into hitherto unexplored territory.

Notes to Chapter 4 - 'Die Schwärmer'

1. Quoted in Robert Musil, 'Die Schwärmer', edited by Adolf Frisé, (Rowohlt Taschenbuch), Reinbek bei Hamburg, 1982, p.137.

2. See Paul Stefanek, 'Musils Posse "Vinzenz" und das Theater der Zwischenkriegszeit', Maske und Kothurn, 26 (1980), 249-270, pp.258-259.

3. Stefanek, 'Musils Posse (...)', p.251.

4. See the sensible commentary by Egon Naganowski, 'Robert Musils "Vinzenz", der Dadaismus und das Theater des Absurden', il teatro nella Mitteleuropa (Gorizia, 1980), 195-204.

5. Alfred Döblin wrote: 'Die Vorgänge (in "Vinzenz (...)") sind nichts. Das Geistige des Dialogs ist alles' ('The events (in "Vinzenz (...) " are nothing. The intellectual quality of the dialogue is everything' (quoted in Stefanek, 'Musils Posse (...)', p.267).

6. See a review of the action of the play by Wilhelm Braun, 'Musil's "Vinzenz und die Freundin bedeutender Männer"', Musil-Forum, 9 (1983), 173-178.

7. Robert Müller, in a review of the play, wrote: 'Der Dichter sagt so etwa: so theatralisch benehmen wir uns, weil wir es bei Shakespeare, Schiller und Wedekind gelernt haben (...) Das Publikum kommt sich sehr gescheit vor, wenn es diese Tragik lächerlich findet und vielleicht abgeschmackt. Aber wiederum ahnt es gar nicht, wie hier der Dichter längst vorher eine Satire schreiben wollte nämlich auf den tragischen Stil und zwar den tragischen Stil des Lebens selbst, das heute so ist, weil das Leben es so gelehrt hat' ('What the author is saying is roughly this: we behave in such a theatrical way because we have learnt to do so from Shakespeare, Schiller and Wedekind (...) The audience thinks it is very clever if it sees this tragic quality as ridiculous and perhaps inept. But then it has absolutely no inkling of the author's long-standing intention to write a satire about the tragic mode, and, specifically, about the tragic mode of life itself which is as it is because this was the way which life itself taught') (quoted in Stefanek, 'Musils Posse (...)', pp. 263-264).

8. See Robert Musil's own commentary on this: 'Der Schwärmerskandal' (GWII,1189-1193).

9. Quoted in Jörg Jesch, 'Robert Musil als Dramatiker', Text + Kritik, 21/22, second edition (1972), 49-60, p.49.

10. Matthias Matussek, 'Wort und Totschlag im Salon', in tip. Berlin West, , 1.1.82, quoted in Jan Berg, 'Theatrales Verstehen. Hans

Neuenfels' Berliner "Schwärmer" Inszenierung', Musil-Forum, 8 (1982), 151-162, p.158.

11. Friedrich Luft, 'Eine duftende Rosenmauer vor der Gartentür. Aus den Höllen der Innerlichkeit. Robert Musils "Schwärmer" im Berliner Schloßparktheater', in Die Welt, 17.12.81.

12. See reviews of the Neuenfels Berlin production of 'Die Schwärmer' by Marleen Stoessel, 'Mit Musil ins Theater der neuen Heftigkeit', in Theater heute, 2 (1982), 4-8, and Michael Merschmeier, 'Mit Neuenfels zu Musil: so wirklich wie möglich', in Theater heute, 2 (1982), 5-9; with reference to the Berlin production, Jan Berg analyses the often conflicting expectations and demands which theatre critics make of any production of Die Schwärmer in 'Theatrales Verstehen (...)'; see also Paul Stefanek and Monika Meister on Erwin Axer's Vienna production: '"Die Schwärmer" in Wien', Musil-Forum, 8 (1982), 137-150; Stefan Hardt is very critical of a 1984 Hamburg production by Niels-Peter Rudolph: 'Robert Musils "Schwärmer" in Hamburg', Musil-Forum, 9 (1983), 179-182.

13. Musil wrote: 'die Idee der Schwärmer, eine ganz gewöhnliche Handlung, aber unter bedeutenden Menschen spielen zu lassen, ist völlig illusionswidrig' (TbI,495) ('the idea in the Schwärmer of having a quite normal plot but one which is played out among important people is diametrically opposed to all illusion'); Martin Esslin gives a summary of the plot in 'Musil's Plays', in Musil in Focus, pp.23-40.

14. Musil read some of Schiller's essays while working on Die Schwärmer, making notes on 'Die Schaubühne als eine moralische Anstalt betrachtet' - see TbI,496-499.

15. GWII,1125.

16. Martin Esslin, had he been among those early directors who received a copy of the play, would probably have turned it down too! He writes: 'I have looked at (Musil's plays) in a purely practical way, with an eye to the possibility of actually producing them, albeit only as radio plays (...;) my view (of 'Die Schwärmer') was that it was unperformable, though in many ways brilliant and fascinating' (in 'Musil's Plays', p.23).

17. See, for example, the cryptic diary entry 'der sterile Idealismus (George)' (TbI,679) ('sterile idealism' (George)').

18. In fact, I believe that Musil, through the actions and reflections of Thomas, is trying to answer the question he asked in 'Der deutsche Mensch als Symptom': 'Wie (...) soll (...) die Anschauungsweise des wissenschaftlichen Denkens u. praktischen Lebens in die Sphäre der Lebensbetrachtung erhoben werden?' (GWII,1386) ('How (...) is the perspective of scientific thinking (and) practical living to be elevated to the realm of existential contemplation?').

Notes to Chapter 4 - 'Die Schwärmer'

19. Musil expresses a similar idea in 'Der deutsche Mensch als Symptom': 'Einem gläubigen Katholiken oder Juden, einem Offizier, einem Burschenschafter, einem ehrbaren Kaufmann, einem Mann von Rang ist in jeder Lebenslage eine viel geringere Zahl von Reaktionen möglich als einem freien Geist: Das erspart und sammelt Kraft. Grundsätze, Richtlinien, Vorbilder, Beschränktheiten sind Kraftakkumulatoren' (GWII,1380) ('In every situation in life there is a far more restricted range of possible reactions available to a practising Catholic or Jew, to an officer, a member of a student association, a respectable merchant, or a man of rank than to a 'free spirit': this both saves and collects energy. Principles, guidelines, patterns, restrictions are energy-accumulators').

20. See Thomas's penultimate line in the play where he says that 'Schwärmer' live in the 'Schöpfungszustand' ('state of creation').

21. See GWII,364.

22. See Sibylle Bauer's convincing interpretation of Maria in 'Ethik und Bewußtheit', in Sibylle Bauer and Ingrid Drevermann, Studien zu Robert Musil (Cologne, 1966), pp. 3–119, pp.18–22; the section of her study dealing with Die Schwärmer, ('Wahrhaftigkeitsproblematik (in den "Schwärmern")')- pp.7–44 – is particularly interesting.

23. In a letter to Thomas Mann, Musil points out how closely two of his own characters - and I assume he is referring to Anselm and Stader, the detective - resemble Felix Krull. (See Briefe I,335).

24. Neuenfels has considerably abridged the text, leaving often only the barest outline of the action. (This means that the film-goer misses many important, indeed some vital, reflections by the characters). Neuenfels's enthusiasm for Die Schwärmer itself borders on the ecstatic, and, since he has a clear perception of the high-points in the dialogue the film-script offers an interesting way to orientate oneself in the play. However, I imagine that watching the film - and, unfortunately, I have not had an opportunity to watch it - is the equivalent of reading an internally consistent, but necessarily narrow interpretation of the work, rather than seeing Musil's work as he himself conceived it (see Robert Musil, Die Schwärmer, edited, abridged and adapted by Hans Neuenfels, Reinbek bei Hamburg, 1985).

25. Michael Merschmeier, in his critique of Neuenfels's film, writes : 'Für Musils Stück (trifft) noch ausgeprägter als sonst die Erkenntnis zu (...), daß die beim Lesen rasch wandelbaren Phantasieräume und schillernden Vorstellungen auf der Bühne (mit den beschränkten technischen und visuellen Mitteln) nicht reproduzierbar sind. Der <<Möglichkeitssinn>>, beim Lesen immer und von diesem Stück besonders animiert, kann durch den <<Wirklichkeitssinn>> prinzipiell nicht befriedigt werden' ('Musil's play bears out with more than usual force the principle that the fast-changing spaces of imagination, the

Notes to Chapter 4 - 'Die Schwärmer'

quicksilver flow of fantasy, cannot be reproduced on the stage, given
its technological and visual restrictions. The <<sense of
possibility>>, which is always set in motion by reading and is
mobilised by this play in particular, cannot, of its very nature, be
satisfied by the <<sense of reality>>') ('Mit Neuenfels zu Musil
(...), p.9.).

26. Merschmeier confirms Esslin's view, as seen above,: 'Die wenigen
bisherigen Aufführungen der <<Schwärmer>> (...) scheinen (...) zu
belegen, daß Musils Theaterauffassung, die Dichtung und Sprache gegen
Effekt und Expressivität behauptet wissen wollte, in reiner Konsequenz
nicht durchsetzbar ist, weil sie der (...) auf Spannung und
Konfliktdarstellung gerichteten Erwartungshaltung der Zuschauer und
den Bedürfnissen der Theater-<<macher>> in wesentlichen Punkten
widerspricht' ('Mit Neuenfels zu Musil (...)', p.9.) ('The few
productions of the <<Schwärmer>> to date (...) seem (...) to prove
that Musil's conception of theatre, in which poetry and language are
brought to the fore at the expense of effect and expressiveness,
cannot be fully realised because it runs counter to the expectations
of the audience and the needs of those who <<make>> theatre which are
directed to the representation of tension and conflict'); see also
Stefanek's apt comment, '(Musil wirkte) abseits der Hauptströmung des
deutschen Theaters' ('(Musil was active) outside the main current of
the German theatre'), 'Musils Posse (...)', p.253.

224

1. See Adolf Frisé's note in GWII, 1746.

2. See Adolf Frisé's edition of the Tagebücher.

3. See TbII, 11-12.

4. See the moving account of the death of Herma in TbII, 879-880.

5. See, for example, the diary entry 'Die Sache mit dem Rufzeichen, diese lächerliche Sache, bringt die Katastrophe (..) (im Kalender)' (TbI,102) ('The question of the exclamation mark, this ridiculous affair, brings the catastrophe (..) (in the calendar)').

6. TbI,97.

7. The relationship with Herma with its alternating trust and suspicion, bears a strong resemblance to the relationship of Törleß and his mother in Die Verwirrungen (...).

8. Perhaps the primary relationship was intellectual - an imaginative exercise in which Robert Musil examined the way in which someone like himself would have responded to Nietzsche's philosophising if he had lived in a different environment and age and had thus been exposed to different challenges and tests.

9. Indeed, Martha Musil, with her black hair and dark complexion, was evidently the model for 'Die Portugiesin'.

10. See 'Die Portugiesin', GWII,263 and TbII,1055-1056, respectively.

11. TbII,1056-1057.

12. TbII,1060.

13. See diary, Heft I, (TbI,303-321).

14. See Pott, Robert Musil (Munich, 1984) pp.60-61 on Musil's use of the image of the scarab beetle. This insect was sacred to the Egyptians as a symbol of the cosmos. Musil's view of the union of earth and sun, represented by the hay, may also derive from Egyptian sources - see F.G.Peters, Robert Musil (...), p.116;

15. See, respectively, TbI,249,308,311,308,321.

16. Peters, Robert Musil (...), p.150.

17. This passage is taken, almost verbatim, from TbI,345-346.

18. See TbI,101.

19. See 'Tonka', GWII,306.

20. Kaiser and Wilkins pointed to mythological references in Drei
Frauen - they discussed, for example, the mythological origins of
Grigia: 'Die Bäuerin, deren wirklicher Name Maddalena Maria Lenzi ist,
wird von Homo Grigia genannt, 'Graue', nach ihrer eigenen Kuh.   Sie
ist eine symbolisch doppeldeutige Gestalt.   Als die Graue Kuh
entspricht sie der chthonischen Isis.   Musil war zu dieser Zeit mit
dem ägyptischen Mythos beschäftigt, besonders mit dem von Isis und
Osiris und dem damit verbundenen Thema von Opfertod und Auferstehung
('The peasant-woman, whose real name is Maddalena Maria Lenzi, is
called Grigia by Homo, 'The Grey One' after her own cow.   She is a
symbolically ambiguous figure.   As the grey cow she corresponds to
the chthontic Isis.   Musil was at this time interested in Egyptian
mythology, and particularly in the myth of Isis and Osiris and with
the related theme of sacrificial birth and resurrection') (Robert
Musil - eine Einführung (...), p.111); Ronald Paulson argues
convincingly that some of the apparently incoherent elements in the
'Novelle' in fact form a pattern of images derived from mythology:
according to him, a pig squealing in fear at his impending death is
Osiris anticipating dismemberment, the entombing of Homo in the
mountain is a return to the womb and thereby a symbol of
reincarnation, a frightened boy threatened with hanging is a
representation of the 'hanged god', Dionysos, indeed, even the pattern
on the wallpaper on which Homo's gaze alights suggests the vine,
sacred to Dionysos (in Robert Musil and the Ineffable.   Hieroglyph,
Myth, Fairy Tale and Sign, Stuttgart, 1982, pp.91ff).

21. See 'Die Portugiesin', (GWII,265).

22. See David Luft on Musil's analysis of the psychology of
capitalism, in Robert Musil and the Crisis (...), p.155.

23. Claudine Tissot, 'Tonka - Visions', in Sud - 'Robert Musil, 1982,
141-149, p.149.

24. See, for example, the strange story of the man who returns from
America and reclaims his 'wife', in 'Grigia', GWII,238.

25. See the analysis of this passage by Peter Henninger in 'Der Text
als Kompromiß', in Psychoanalytische und psychopathologische
Literaturinterpretation, edited by Bernd Urban (Darmstadt, 1981),
pp.398-420, pp.402-405.

26. c.f. Walter Sokel: '(The) dilemma (expressed in 'Tonka')
symbolises the conflict between religion (and Sokel has in mind such
aspects of Musil's work as the parallel which it offers to the miracle
of the Virgin Birth - PP) and the scepticism inherent in modern
rationalist thought' (in 'Kleist's Marquise of O., Kierkegaard's

Notes to Chapter 5 - 'Drei Frauen'

Abraham, and Musil's Tonka', in <u>Festschrift für Bernhard Blume,</u> (1967), pp.323-332, p.324).

27. See 'Tonka' GWII,281.

28. See TbII,1055.

29. The theme of <u>Vereinigungen</u> is continued here - physical infidelity is seen to be of little consequence given the bond of perfect trust between the two lovers.

30. This passage is clearly the source for a section in the 'Novelle' itself - see GWII,300.

SELECTED BIBLIOGRAPHY

Works by Musil

Gesammelte Werke, edited by Adolf Frisé, 2 vols (Reinbek bei Hamburg, 1978) (revised edition, 1981) (This edition is also available in paperback, in nine volumes, with identical pagination.)

Tagebücher, edited by Adolf Frisé, 2 vols (Reinbek bei Hamburg, 1976)

Briefe, edited by Adolf Frisé, 2 vols (Reinbek bei Hamburg, 1981)

'Beitrag zur Beurteilung der Lehren von Ernst Mach' (doctoral dissertation, Friedrich-Wilhelm-Universität, Berlin, 1908 (also available in book form, Reinbek bei Hamburg, 1980)

English translations of Musil's works by Ernst Kaiser and Eithne Wilkins:

'The Perfecting of a Love', in Botteghe Oscure, XVIII (Rome, 1956)

'The Temptation of Quiet Veronika', in Botteghe Oscure, XXV (Rome, 1960)

Tonka and Other Stories, (London, 1965)

Five Women (New York, 1966)

The Man without Qualities (London, 1953, 1954, 1960)

Other Translations into English

On Mach's Theories, translation of Musil's doctoral dissertation by G.H.von Wright (Munich/Vienna, 1982)

The Enthusiasts, translation of Die Schwärmer by Andrea Simon (New York, 1982)

'The German Personality as a Symptom', translation of 'Der deutsche Mensch als Symptom' by Ian David Hays, in Austrian Philosophy: Studies and Texts, ed. J.C.Nyiri (Munich, 1981), pp.173-200

(Two new editions of Musil's works in English are due to appear shortly: a volume in the German Library/Continuum series, containing The Confusions of Young Törleß and most of the 'Novellen' and short stories, and a volume with translations of Musil's essays by Burton Pike and David Luft. A date for the appearance of a new translation of The Man without Qualities, to be published by Knopf in New York and

Secker and Warburg in London, has not yet been fixed.)

Bibliographies

Thöming, Jürgen C., Robert-Musil-Bibliographie (Bad Homburg v.d.H., Berlin, Zürich, 1968)

Thöming, Jürgen C., 'Kommentierte Auswahlbibliographie zu Robert Musil', Text + Kritik, No. 21/22 ('Robert Musil'), second edition, 1972, 73-87

King, Lynda J., 'Robert Musil Bibliography 1976/1977', Musil-Forum, 4 (1978), 104-116

Mae, Michiko, Robert-Musil-Bibliographie 1977-1980, Musil-Forum, 6 (1980), 239-258

Mae, Michiko, Robert-Musil-Bibliographie 1980-1983, Musil-Forum, 9 (1983)

Arntzen Helmut, Musil-Kommentar sämtlicher zu Lebzeiten erschienener Schriften außer dem Roman "Der Mann ohne Eigenschaften", (Munich, 1980), pp.279-310

Secondary literature

Albertsen, Elisabeth, Ratio und Mystik im Werk Robert Musils (Munich, 1968)

Albertsen, Elisabeth, 'Ea oder die Freundin bedeutender Männer. Porträt einer Wiener Kaffeehaus-Muse', Musil-Forum, 5 (1979), 21-37 and 135-153

Allemann, Beda, Ironie und Dichtung, second edition (Pfullingen, 1969)

Arntzen, Helmut, Satirischer Stil (Bonn, 1960)

Arntzen, Helmut, Musil-Kommentar sämtlicher zu Lebzeiten erschienener Schriften außer dem Roman "Der Mann ohne Eigenschaften" (Munich, 1980)

Arntzen, Helmut, 'Symptomen-Theater. Robert Musil und das Theater seiner Zeit', Literatur und Kritik, No.149/150 (1980), 598-606

Aspetsberger, Friedbert, '"Der andere Zustand" in its contemporary context', in Musil in Focus (London, 1982), pp.54-73

Aue, Maximilian, 'Musil und die Romantik. Einige grundsätzliche Überlegungen', in Sprachästhetische Sinnvermittlung, ed. Farda and Karthaus, 125-134

Bauer, Sibylle, 'Ethik und Bewußtheit', in Sibylle Bauer and Ingrid Drevermann, Studien zu Robert Musil (Cologne, 1966)

Baur, Uwe, and Dietmar Goltschnigg, Vom "Törleß" zum "Mann ohne Eigenschaften" (Munich/Salzburg, 1973)

Baur, Uwe, 'Zeit und Gesellschaftskritik in Robert Musils Roman "Die Verwirrungen des Zöglings Törleß"', in Vom "Törleß" (...), ed. Baur and Goltschnigg, pp.19-45

Baur, Uwe and Elisabeth Castex, Robert Musil. Untersuchungen (Königstein, Taunus, 1980)

Baur, Uwe, 'Sport und subjektive Bewegungserfahrung bei Musil', in Robert Musil. Untersuchungen, ed. Baur and Castex, pp.99-112

Berg, Jan, 'Theatrales Verstehen. Hans Neuenfels' Berliner "Schwärmer" Inszenierung', Musil-Forum, 8 (1982), 151-162

Berghahn, Wilfried, Robert Musil - in Selbstzeugnissen und Bilddokumenten, (Reinbek bei Hamburg, 1963)

Braun, Wilhelm, 'Musil and the Pendulum of the Intellect', Monatshefte, 49 (1957), 109-119

Braun, Wilhelm, 'Musil's "Vinzenz und die Freundin bedeutender Männer"', Musil-Forum, 9 (1983), 173-178

Braun, Wilhelm, 'An Interpretation of Musil's Novelle "Tonka"', Monatshefte, 53 (1961), 73-85

Braun, Wilhelm, 'The Confusions of Törleß', Germanic Review, 40 (1965), 116-131

Brokoph-Mauch, Gudrun, editor, Beiträge zur Musil-Kritik (Bern/Frankfurt am Main, 1983)

Büren, Erhard von, Zur Bedeutung der Psychologie im Werk Robert Musils (Zurich/Freiburg i. Br., 1970)

Cohn, Dorrit, 'Psycho-Analogies: a Means for Rendering Consciousness', in Probleme des Erzählens, ed. Fritz Martini (Stuttgart, 1971)

Corino, Karl, 'Törleß ignotus', Text + Kritik, No.21/22 'Robert Musil', second edition, 1972, 61-72

Corino, Karl, '"Der Zaubervogel küßt die Füße". Zu Robert Musils Leben und Werk in den Jahren 1914-16', in Robert Musil - Literatur, Philosophie, Psychologie, ed. Strutz and Strutz (Munich/Salzburg, 1984), pp.143-172

230

Corino, Karl, Robert Musils "Vereinigungen" - Studien zu einer historisch-kritischen Ausgabe (Munich/Salzburg, 1974)

Corino, Karl, 'Zwischen Mystik und Theaterleidenschaft - Robert Musils Brünner Jahre (1898-1902)', in Robert Musil und die kulturellen Tendenzen seiner Zeit, ed. Strutz and Strutz, pp.11-28

Daigger, Annette, 'Tonka, une héroine de l'Homme sans qualités', in Sud 'Robert Musil' (Marseille, 1982), pp.133-137

Dinklage, Karl, editor, Robert Musil: Leben, Werk, Wirkung (Vienna and Reinbek bei Hamburg, 1960)

Dinklage, Karl, editor (with Elisabeth Albertsen and Karl Corino), Robert Musil - Studien zu seinem Werk (Reinbek bei Hamburg, 1970)

Durrani, Osman, 'Die Vollendung der Liebe: Apocalypse or Utopia?', in Musil in Focus, pp.12-22

Eibl, Karl, Robert Musil. Drei Frauen. Text, Materialien, Kommentar (München, Wien, 1978)

Esslin, Martin, 'Musil's Plays', in Musil in Focus, pp.23-40

Farda, Dieter P. and Ulrich Karthaus, editors, Sprachästhetische Sinnvermittlung. Robert Musil Symposium, Berlin, 1980 (Frankfurt am Main, 1982)

Fischer, Ernst, 'Das Werk Robert Musils: Versuch einer Würdigung', Sinn und Form, 9 (1957), 851-901

Frank, Manfred, 'Auf der Suche nach einem Grund - über den Umschlag von Erkenntniskritik in Mythologie bei Musil', in Mythos und Moderne, ed. Karl-Heinz Bohrer (Frankfurt am Main, 1983), pp.318-362

Franke, Hans-Peter, editor, Materialien zu Robert Musils "Die Verwirrungen des Zöglings Törleß" (Stuttgart, 1979)

Frisé, Adolf, Plädoyer für Robert Musil. Hinweise und Essays 1931 bis 1980 (Reinbek bei Hamburg, 1980)

Frisé, Adolf, 'Der Zeitgenosse Robert Musil', Literatur und Kritik, 16 (1981), 381-391

Frisé, Adolf, 'Erfahrungen mit Robert Musil', Musil-Forum, 8 (16-29)

Goltschnigg, Dietmar, Mystische Tradition im Roman Robert Musils - Martin Bubers "Ekstatische Konfessionen" im "Mann ohne Eigenschaften" (Heidelberg, 1974)

Gumtau, Helmut, Robert Musil (Berlin, 1967)

Hamburger, Michael, 'Explorers: Musil, Robert Walser, Kafka', in A Proliferation of Prophets (Manchester, 1983), pp.244-272

Hardt, Stefan, 'Robert Musils "Schwärmer" in Hamburg', Musil-Forum, 9 (1983), 179-182

Hatfield, Harry, 'An Unsentimental Education: Robert Musil's "Young Törleß"', in Crisis and Continuity in German Fiction (Ithaca/London, 1969), pp.35-48

Henninger, Peter, Der Buchstabe und der Geist (Frankfurt am Main, 1980)

Henninger, Peter, 'Der Text als Kompromiß. Versuch einer psychoanalytischen Textanalyse von Musils Erzählung "Tonka"', in Psychoanalytische und psychopathologische Literaturinterpretation, ed. Bernd Urban and Winfried Kudszus (Darmstadt, 1981)

Heydebrand, Renate von, editor, Robert Musil (Darmstadt, 1982)

Hickman, Hannah, '"Lebende Gedanken" und Emersons "Kreise"', in Robert Musil. Untersuchungen, ed. Baur and Castex, pp.139-151

Hickman, Hannah, 'Der junge Musil und R.W.Emerson', Musil-Forum, 6 (1980), 3-13

Hickman, Hannah, Robert Musil and the Culture of Vienna (London, Sydney, 1984)

Huber, Lothar and John J. White, editors, Musil in Focus - Papers from a Centenary Symposium (London, 1982)

Hüppauf, Bernd, 'Von Wien durch den Krieg nach Nirgendwo: Nation und utopisches Denken bei Musil und im Austromarxismus', Text + Kritik 'Robert Musil', Nos. 21/22, third edition, 1983, pp.1-28

Jesch, Jörg, 'Robert Musil als Dramatiker', in Text + Kritik, 21/22, second edition (1972), 49-60

Karthaus, Ulrich, 'Musil-Forschung und Musil-Deutung. Ein Literaturbericht', Deutsche Vierteljahrsschrift für Literaturwissenschaft und Geistesgeschichte, 39 (1965), 441-483

Kaiser, Ernst and Eithne Wilkins, Robert Musil: Eine Einführung in das Werk (Stuttgart, 1962)

Kermode, Frank, 'A Short View of Musil', in Puzzles and Epiphanies, second (revised) impression (London, 1963), pp.91-107

Krusche, Dieter, 'Robert Musil: "Vereinigungen"', in Kommunikation im Erzähltext, 2 vols (Munich, 1978), I, pp.137-153

Kühn, Dieter, 'Sätze und Ansätze (Musils Tagebücher)', Neue Rundschau, 88 (1977), 610-618

Luft, David S., Robert Musil and the Crisis of European Culture, 1880-1942 (Los Angeles, 1980)

Mae, Michiko, 'Robert Musils Novellentheorie', Beiträge zur Germanistik, edited by the Germanisten-Vereinigung at the University of Kanazawa, 1 (1980), 25-43

Mae, Michiko, 'Robert Musils Novellenband "Vereinigungen" in der Kritik seiner Zeit. Ein Beitrag zur historischen Rezeptionsanalyse', Doitsu Bungaku, edited by the Japanische Gesellschaft für Germanistik, 65 (1980), 44-55

Magnou, Jacqueline, 'Grenzfall und Identitätsproblem oder die Rolle der Psychopathologie in den literarischen Praxis und Theorie Musils anhand der Novellen: "Vereinigungen"', in Sprachästhetische Sinnvermittlung, ed. Farda and Karthaus, pp.103-116

Magnou, Jacqueline, '"Schicksale sind vom Zentralen aus gestaltet" - "Die Vollendung der Liebe"', Musil-Forum, 10 (1984), 69-76

Magnou, Jacqueline, 'Situation de Törleß, Sud 'Robert Musil' (Marseille, 1982) pp.112-128

Mayer, Hans, 'Erinnerung an Robert Musil', in Zur deutschen Literatur der Zeit (Reinbek bei Hamburg, 1967), pp.137-154

Meister, Monika and Paul Stefanek, 'Die Schwärmer in Wien', Musil-Forum, 8 (1982), 137-150

Merschmeier, Michael, 'Mit Neuenfels zu Musil: so wirklich wie möglich', Theater heute, 2/82, 5-9

Michel, Kurt Marcus, 'Die Utopie der Sprache', Akzente, 1 (1954), 23-35

Militzer, Gerti, 'Internationales Robert-Musil-Sommerseminar 1982 in Klagenfurt', Musil-Forum, 8 (1982), 163-167

Molino, Jean, 'Doubles - sur la logique de Musil', l'arc 'Robert Musil', No.74 (1978), pp.63-74

Moser, Walter, 'Musil à Paris', Critique, Nos.433-434, June/July 1983, pp.459-476

Müller, Götz, 'Isis und Osiris. Die Mythen in Robert Musils Roman "Der Mann ohne Eigenschaften"', Zeitschrift für deutsche Philologie, 102 (1983), 583-604

Mulot, Sibylle, Der junge Musil: Seine Beziehung zur Literatur und

233

Kunst der Jahrhundertwende, (Stuttgart, 1977)

Neuenfels, Hans, Robert Musil - "Die Schwärmer" (Reinbek bei Hamburg, 1985)

Nagonowski, Egon, 'Robert Musils "Vinzenz", der Dadaismus und das Theater des Absurden', Il teatro nella Mitteleuropa, (Gorizia, 1980), 195-204

Paulson, Ronald M, Robert Musil and the Ineffable: Hieroglyph, Myth, Fairy Tale and Sign (Stuttgart, 1982)

Paulson, Ronald M., 'Myth and Fairy-tale in Robert Musil's Grigia', in The Turn of the Century - German Literature and Art 1890-1915, ed. Gerald Chapple and Hans H. Schulte (Bonn, 1981), pp. 135-148

Payne Philip, 'Musil erforscht den Geist eines anderen Menschen - zum Porträt Moosbruggers im "Mann ohne Eigenschaften"', Literatur und Kritik, Nos.106-107 (1976), 389-404

Payne, Philip, 'Robert Musil, von innen gesehen. Betrachtungen zu den Tagebüchern', Musil-Forum, 6 (1980), 227-238

Payne, Philip, 'Robert Musil's Diaries', in Musil in Focus, ed. Huber and White, 131-143

Payne, Philip, 'Robert Musils Briefe an die Nachwelt', Neue Zürcher Zeitung, 26/27 June 1982, pp.67-68

Peters, Frederick G., 'Musil and Nietzsche: a Literary Study of a Philosophical Relationship' (PhD. dissertation, University of Cambridge, 1972)

Peters, Frederick G., Robert Musil - Master of the Hovering Life (New York, 1978)

Pike, Burton, Robert Musil: An Introduction to his Work (New York, 1961) (reissued in 1972)

Pott, Hans-Georg, Robert Musil (Munich, 1984)

Pütz, Heinz-Peter, 'Robert Musil', in Deutsche Dichter der Moderne, ed. Benno von Wiese (Berlin, 1965)

Reiss, Hans, 'Musil and the Writer's Task in the Age of Science and Technology', in Musil in Focus, ed. Huber and White, pp.41-53

Reniers-Servrankx, Annie, Robert Musil - Konstanz und Entwicklungen von Themen, Motiven und Strukturen in den Dichtungen (Bonn, 1972)

Requadt, Manfred, 'Robert Musil und das Dichten >>more geometrico<<', Text + Kritik 'Robert Musil', third edition, No. 21/22 (1983), pp.29-43

Roseberry, Robert L., Robert Musil: ein Forschungsbericht (Frankfurt am Main, 1974)

Roth, Marie-Louise, Robert Musil: Ethik und Ästhetik. Zum theoretischen Werk des Dichters (Munich, 1972)

Roth, Marie-Louise, 'Robert Musil-Forschung. Situation und Symptome', in Nachlaß- und Editionsprobleme bei modernen Schriftstellern, ed. Marie-Louise Roth, Renate Schröder-Werle and Hans Zeller (Berne, 1981), pp.23-29

Roth, Marie-Louise, 'Robert Musils Essayismus', Arbeitskreis Heinrich Mann special number, ed. Peter-Paul Schneider, (Lübeck, 1981), pp. 248-255

Roth, Marie-Louise, editor, L'Herne:'Robert Musil' (Paris, 1981)

Schaffnit, Hans Wolfgang, Mimesis als Problem: Studien zu einem ästhetischen Begriff der Dichtung aus Anlaß Robert Musils (Berlin, 1971)

Schelling, Ulrich, Identität und Wirklichkeit bei Robert Musil (Zürich, 1968)

Schneider, Rolf, Die problematisierte Wirklichkeit, - Leben und Werk Robert Musils - Versuch einer Interpretation (Berlin, 1975)

Schöne, Albrecht, 'Zum Gebrauch des Konjunktivs bei Robert Musil', Euphorion, 55 (1961), 196-220

Schramm, Ulf, Fiktion und Reflexionen: Überlegungen zu Musil und Beckett (Frankfurt, 1967)

Schröder, Jürgen, 'Am Grenzwert der Sprache. Zu Robert Musils "Vereinigungen"', Euphorion, 60 (1966), 173-187

Sokel, Walter H., 'Kleist's Marquise of O., Kierkegaard's Abraham, and Musil's Tonka: Three Stages of the Absurd as the Touchstone of Faith', Wisconsin Studies in Contemporary Literature, 8 (1967), 505-516

Stefanek, Paul, 'Musils Posse "Vinzenz" und das Theater der Zwischenkriegszeit', Maske und Kothurn. Vierteljahrsschrift für Theaterwissenschaft, 26 (1980), 249-270

Stefanek, Paul and Monika Meister, '"Die Schwärmer" in Wien', Musil-Forum, 8 (1982), 137-150

Stern, Joseph Peter, 'Viennese Kaleidoscope', The Listener, 1 November 1962, pp. 722-723

Stoessel, Marleen, 'Mit Musil ins Theater der neuen Heftigkeit', Theater heute, 2/82, 4-8

Stopp, Elisabeth, 'Musils "Törleß" - Content and Form', Modern Language Review, 63 (1968), 94-118

Strelka, Joseph, 'Robert Musil', in Kafka, Musil, Broch (Vienna, Hannover and Berne, 1959)

Strelka, Joseph, 'Claudine und Veronika - zur weiblichen Doppelfigur von Robert Musils "Vereinigungen"', in Probleme der Moderne: Studien zur deutschen Literatur von Nietzsche bis Brecht, ed. B. Bennett, A. Kaes, W.J.Lillyman (Tübingen, 1983)

Strutz Josef and Johann Strutz, editors, Robert Musil und die kulturellen Tendenzen seiner Zeit (Munich/Salzburg, 1983)

Strutz, Josef and Johann Strutz, Robert Musil - Literatur, Philosophie und Psychologie (Munich/Salzburg, 1984)

Swales, Martin, 'Narrator and hero - Observations on Robert Musil's "Törleß"', in Musil in Focus, ed. Huber and White, pp.1-11

Thöming, Jürgen C., 'Musil-Chronik', Text + Kritik: 'Robert Musil', Nos. 21/22 (1983), third edition, pp.149-152

Tissot, Christiane, 'Tonka - Visions', Sud: 'Robert Musil', special number (1982), pp.141-149

White, John J, '"Berühmt und unbekannt": Robert Musil's Collected Letters in Adolf Frisé's New Edition', German Life and Letters, 37 (1984), 232-249

Williams, Cedric E., 'Robert Musil', in The Broken Eagle - the Politics of Austrian Literature from Empire to Anschluß (London, 1974)

Willemsen, Roger, '"Man nimmt Franz Blei zu leicht!" - Robert Musil und "Das große Bestiarium der Literatur"', in Robert Musil und die kulturellen Tendenzen seiner Zeit, ed. Strutz and Strutz, pp.120-129

Willemsen, Roger, Das Existenzrecht der Dichtung. Zur Rekonstruktion einer systematischen Literaturtheorie im Werk Robert Musils (Munich, 1984)

Willemsen, Roger, Robert Musil - vom intellektuellen Eros (Munich/Zurich, 1985)

Zeller, Rosmarie, '"Die Versuchung der stillen Veronika" - eine Untersuchung ihres Bedeutungsaufbaus', in Sprachästhetische Sinnvermittlung (...), ed. Farda and Karthaus, pp.135-153

Zeller, Rosmarie, 'Zur Komposition von Musils "Drei Frauen"', in

Beiträge zur Musil-Kritik, ed. Gudrun Brokoph-Mauch (Berne/Frankfurt am Main, 1983), pp.25-48

Zeller, Rosmarie, 'Robert Musils Auseinandersetzung mit der realistischen Schreibweise', Musil-Forum, 6 (1980), 128-144

Zima, Pierre V., 'Musil', in L'ambivalence romanesque. Proust, Kafka, Musil (Paris, 1980), pp. 207-318